Victorville City Library
15011 Circle Dr
Victorville, CA 92395
760-245-4222

THE
COMPLETE
HOCKEY
DICTIONARY

THE COMPLETE HOCKEY DICTIONARY

Edited by **Andrew Podnieks**

Fenn Publishing Company Ltd.

Bolton, Ontario

Fenn Publishing Company Ltd.

THE COMPLETE HOCKEY DICTIONARY

A Fenn Publishing Book / First Published in 2007
All rights reserved
Copyright 2007 © Moydart Press / Fenn Publishing Company Ltd.

The content, opinion and subject matter contained herein is the written expression of the author and
does not reflect the opinion or ideology of the publisher, or that of the publisher's representatives.

Fenn Publishing Company Ltd.
Bolton, Ontario, Canada
www.hbfenn.com

The publisher gratefully acknowledges the support of the Canada Council for the Arts and the
Ontario Arts Council for its publishing program. We acknowledge the support of the Government of
Ontario through the Ontario Media Development Corporation's Ontario Book Initiative.

We acknowledge the financial support of the Government of Canada through the Book Publishing
Industry Development Program (BPIDP) for our publishing activities.

Care has been taken to trace ownership of copyright material in this book and to secure permissions.
The publishers will gladly receive any information that will enable them to rectify errors or omissions.

Text design: Kathryn Zante
Printed and bound in Canada

Library and Archives Canada Cataloguing in Publication

The complete hockey dictionary / Andrew Podnieks, general editor.

ISBN 978-1-55168-309-6

1. Hockey--Dictionaries. I. Podnieks, Andrew

GV847.C64 2007   796.96203   C2007-903068-8

Contents

Introduction

It took about 44 years for the Oxford English Dictionary to reach publication in 1928, over which time no fewer than half a dozen editors had passed away without their work towards a definitive celebration of the English language seeing the light of day. Given the monumental task of recording every word in the English language, this is not surprising.

One of the most prolific contributors to that first edition of the OED was William Chester Minor, a longtime resident of the Broadmoor Criminal Lunatic Asylum, Crowthorne, Berkshire (he was incarcerated there in 1872 after being acquitted of murder by reason of insanity). Given the extraordinary amount of painstaking research involved in tracking the first use of every word and its various uses, this also is not surprising.

Minor spent most of the rest of his life reading books, compiling lists of words and their meanings, and becoming friends with the first editor of the OED, James Murray.

Happily, I have lived to see this hockey dictionary come to light, and I have done so without having required a stay in a mental-health facility (barely). Hopefully, however, this book will be held to a similar standard to that of the OED, albeit in a far, far humbler sphere, of course. It has taken me many years of

research to finally deliver a volume I can begin to think of as comprehensive, and the process to get from the first word to the last was always the same: scraps of paper, napkins, anything I could write on when a word came into my head. I gathered these entries through a variety of means.

At the start, I had only to sit on my couch and brainstorm. I watched hockey game after hockey game with pen and paper in hand; I went through hundreds of scrapbooks at the Hockey Hall of Fame, all of which were chock full of newspaper clippings from the 1800s through to the present day. I took care to examine these pages thoroughly, day by day, year by year, to record the ever-changing language.

What amazed me was how many words—common words—were taken by people in the hockey world and applied to specific aspects of the sport. A word such as "doorstep" goes from being that part of the house where the milkman places the weekly order to the front of the goal. "Hot," which refers to either spicy food or a high temperature, is transmogrified into a goalie who can't be beaten, a player who scores with regularity, or a shot that is hard to handle (also "sizzling").

Some other observations about this dictionary are in order. First, it is not an encyclopaedia, so you will not be given lengthy essays on entries such as "Summit Series" or "National Hockey League." Second, I have tried to keep proper names to a minimum; so, major teams and arenas are listed, but not every team and every arena I could unearth. Third, since the book needs a reference point, I have used as the focal points Canada (the birthplace of hockey) and the NHL (the world's most important league). Of course, there are hundreds of words and phrases in use outside the NHL, but this simply is a strong and sensible reference point for phrases such as "farm team" or "the Show." Fourth, I have added a healthy "foreign" component to represent European and international hockey usage—without turning this into a polyglot dictionary. Finally, I have used words that were or are part of the lexicon, rather than obscure words that have never had a life of their own. In other words, just because someone's uncle called a puck a "black pie" doesn't mean it should be contained in this volume. Similarly, phrases such as "great play" or "big game," which are not specific to hockey, are not to be found here.

Lord knows a few words or phrases may have slipped through the cracks; there are also, most certainly, regional terms of which I'm not aware—and I'd love to hear from rational souls who can provide proof of their contributions—but by and large I think this volume goes a long way towards documenting and compiling a thorough accounting of the history of the game through its words and phrases. I can only hope you agree.

Andrew Podnieks
Toronto 2007

Aa

A 1. designation for a level of play in the GTHL, A being the lowest of three (AA, AAA) 2. short for assist in points standings or statistics column 3. letter worn on a player's sweater denoting assistant or alternate captain

AA designation for a level of play in the GTHL, AA being the middle of three (pronounced "double A")

AAA designation for a level of play in the GTHL, AAA being the highest of the three (pronounced "triple A")

AC joint acromioclavicular joint; part of the shoulder most susceptible to separation

ACHA *American Collegiate Hockey Association*

ACL anterior cruciate ligament; a ligament in the centre of the knee frequently injured in hockey through knee-on-knee contact, severe twisting, or excessive stretching of the surrounding area

A.E.M.A. Athletic Equipment Managers' Association; governing body of the profession

AHAUS Amateur Hockey Association of the United States; governing body of all amateur and international activities involving the United States (now known as USA Hockey)

AHL American Hockey League

AND official IIHF abbreviation for Andorra

ARG official IIHF abbreviation for Argentina

ARM official IIHF abbreviation for Armenia

A.T.C. athletic trainer certificate (earned after passing a test given by the National Athletic Trainers' Association)

AUS official IIHF abbreviation for Australia

AUT official IIHF abbreviation for Austria

avg. abbreviation for *goals-against average*

AZE official IIHF abbreviation for Azerbaijan

A Pool designation used by the IIHF until 2000 to denote the top group of teams in international hockey (followed by B, C, and D Pools)

a lot great deal of power, on a hard and perfect shot ("he got a lot on that shot")

abandoned stick broken stick that is discarded on ice during play

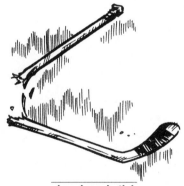

abandoned stick

Abby Hoffman Cup trophy awarded to women's senior hockey champion of Canada

abdominal apron prohibited piece of goalie equipment that provides extra coverage for a goalie

abduction movement of a bone away from the core of the body

abrasion injury which causes skin to rub off

abscess infection causing pus

absence 1. state of being out of the lineup, usu. because of injury 2. period of time a player is out of lineup

absent not in the lineup

absorption padding material along the inside base of the net to ensure the puck stays in once it enters

abuse 1. physical punishment, generally absorbed in front of the opposing goal 2. ~ **of officials** verbal or physical attack on an official

abusive language foul language directed toward an official which, in hockey's early days, resulted in a fine

acceleration initial skating strides building to maximum speed

accent on youth team-building strategy that favours young players rather than older ones

accept 1. receive a pass 2. ~ **terms** agree to a contract

accidental high stick a high-stick judged to be without malice, resulting in a two- or four-minute penalty rather than the major penalty or game misconduct assessed for an intentional high-stick

account 1. showing or performance in a game 2. reporter's story of a game 3. ~ **for** make a contribution in scoring, shots, or any statistical area

accountable culpability on the part of a player for an error

accurate of a shot: perfectly directed to its target

ace 1. top player 2. common nickname for a star player

Ace Bailey Benefit Game played February 14, 1934, at Maple Leaf Gardens in Toronto for the player whose career was ended by injury; regarded as the forerunner to the NHL's All-Star Game

Achilles 1. ~ **heel** any weakness of a

player or team 2. ~ **tendon** tendon at back of foot, susceptible to being cut by skate blades

acquire bring a new player to a team via trade or other means

acquisition player who is new to a team

acrobat goalie who achieves success by displaying great flexibility, mobility, and quickness

acrobatic of a goalie: given to flopping and diving in his crease to make saves

acrobatic

action 1. play in progress 2. **return to** ~ play in a game after an absence, usu. due to injury

Action Magazine Edmonton Oilers' game-night program

actions negative conduct

active 1. of a player: still playing (not retired) 2. of a period of time: marked by plenty of trades, usu. immediately before trading deadlines

Adams Division one of four NHL divisions, 1974-1993

Adams, Jack, Award see ***Jack Adams Award***

Adams Trophy short for Jack Adams Trophy, awarded annually in the NHL to the coach of the year

add 1. score again ("they added a fifth goal in the third") 2. ~ **to the lead** score a goal while already ahead in the game 3. ~ **muscle** add a player, who plays with a physical emphasis, to the roster or game

addition 1. new player to a team 2. **nice ~** new player to a team who makes a particularly impressive contribution right away

address the media conduct a formal news conference after an important event; usu. held by coach, general manager, or players

adduction movement of a bone toward the core of the body

adhesion scar tissue that forms around a scar and restricts flexibility or movement of the area around the scar

admire a pass stand still, watching the puck, after making a pass instead of keeping one's head up on the play, leaving oneself vulnerable to a body-check

admirers fans

admirers

area any specific part of the ice

admit defeat lose game

Adult Goal 1. model of hockey stick made by the Monarch Hockey Stick Company of New Hamburg, Ontario 2. model of hockey stick made by the McVean's Stick Company of Dresden, Ontario

advance 1. move puck towards enemy goal 2. win a round of playoffs to move on to another round 3. **~ scouting** act of assessing the talent

and tendencies of opponents that a team will be playing in the near future

advertised reputed to be; promoted as ("he's advertised as the next big thing")

aerobic form of exercise characterized by lengthy periods of high intensity and an increased heart rate

affair 1. game 2. brawl

A-form contract, prior to the era of the Amateur Draft, which invited a player to an NHL team's training camp, without any commitment from either the team or the player beyond the invitation

after the whistle occurring after play has been stopped (usu. pushing and shoving)

afterburners top speed, which is usu. much faster than the average player ("once he got the puck, he turned on the afterburners and no one was going to catch him")

aftermath period of time following (and in consequence of) a brawl, bad loss, or negative occurrence

afternoon game game played during the day rather than at night

agent person (often a lawyer) who represents a player in contract negotiations with a team or other organization

aggravate make worse, usu. an injury

aggregate team

aggressive 1. style of play which emphasizes hitting or forechecking 2. **~ forechecking** extra effort to create a turnover in the opponent's end 3. **~ penalty kill** situation in which a short-handed team repeatedly tries to force a turnover

agile able to move speedily and quickly, exhibiting stretching ability and quick reflexes (usu. applies to a goalie)

agitate frustrate an opponent

agitator player whose words or play frustrate an opponent into playing poorly or taking retaliatory penalties, or throw him off his game in some way

agree 1. (19th C.) come to terms on a referee for a challenge match 2. ~ **to a contract** of a player and team: come to terms on a deal

ahead 1. of the puck: forward to a teammate closer to the offensive zone 2. ~ **of play** of a player: skating offside or causing some other disadvantageous play while that player's team is on offence

ailing describes a player feeling less than 100 per cent, whether because of injury or illness

ailment injury

aim 1. direct the puck accurately when shooting 2. long-term goal of a team

Air Canada Centre home arena for the Toronto Maple Leafs since February 20, 1999

Air Canada Cup former name (1979-2003) of Canadian midget hockey championship (renamed the Telus Cup, 2004-present)

air hockey table hockey game in which a plastic disc is propelled across a small rink, supported by a cushion of air

AirKnit lightweight synthetic mesh fabric commonly used in modern hockey sweaters

airplane dive (archaic) last-ditch defensive effort to thwart a breakaway or good scoring chance by diving, stick extended, to poke the puck away from an opponent

Albert slang for lousy hockey player

Alberta Oilers original name of Edmonton Oilers during first WHA season (1972-73)

Alexandra Studios business operated by photographers Lou and Nat Turofsky of Toronto; most famous hockey studio in the world from the late 1920s to the late 1950s

alchamadijik Mi'kmaq for hurley, precursor to hockey

alibi excuse, usu. for a goal or bad play

all 1. describes one team dominating play ("it's all Team Sweden in this period") 2. a tie score (i.e., "four-all" means the score is 4-4) 3. ~ **alone** player who is not being checked 4. ~ **evening** describes a tendency that remains consistent throughout a game ("they've been strong on the puck all evening") 5. ~-**important game** contest of particular significance in the standings or between two rivals 6. ~-**important faceoff** faceoff of particular significance, usu. inside a blueline or late in a game 7. ~-**out** desperate or relentless 8. ~ **over** a. game that has ended ("and it's all over") b. domination by one team for a period of time ("the Leafs are all over the Flyers this period") c. check carefully 9. ~ **the way** a. rush in which a player skates with the puck from one end of the ice to the other b. call by a linesman on a deliberate offside, indicating that the faceoff will take place not outside the blueline but in the offending team's end of the ice

Allan Cup trophy, first awarded at the end of the 1907-08 season, emblematic of the senior amateur championship of Canada

alley 1. area along the boards, notably in the corners 2. metaphoric place where, according to Conn Smythe, players must be able to win in order to win on the scoreboard ("if you can't beat 'em in the alley, you can't beat 'em on the ice")

All-Montreal major pro team in Canadian Hockey Association (CHA), 1909-10

allow 1. give up a goal (by a team) 2. permit a controversial goal to stand ("the referee is going to allow that one")

all-rookie team all-star team selected at the end of a season, comprising only first-year or rookie-eligible players

all-round player player gifted in many facets of the game (i.e., scoring, defence, hitting, faceoffs, etc.)

all-star 1. elite player in any league or on any team 2. ~ **team** a. end-of-season selection of the best players in a league at all positions (goal, defence, forward) b. team selected by IIHF at the conclusion of international tournament 3. ~ **voting** selection by fans or media for the best players of a team, league, or tournament, the cumulative number of which determines the members of an all-star team

All-Star 1. short for the All-Star Game weekend or any part thereof 2. model of hockey stick made by the Monarch Hockey Stick Company of New Hamburg, Ontario 3. model of hockey stick made by the Ingersoll Hockey Stick Factory

All-Star Game

All-Star Game 1. special game featuring the most skilled players in any league, usu. held once a year, midway through the season 2. ~ **ballot** system of choosing the team for an All-Star Game that allows fans to choose players who will participate in the All-Star Game 3. ~ **Dinner** formal dinner usu. held immediately after an All-Star Game, honouring the best players in a league for a particular year

alone 1. of a player: with a clear break in on goal 2. of a player: unchecked by any opponent 3. of a puck carrier: surrounded by opponents with no one to pass to

alongside 1. on a line with ("Smith is playing alongside Taylor and Johnson") 2. of a defence pair: playing together

Alpenliga league including teams from only Austria, Italy, and Slovenia (1994-99)

also-rans teams effectively eliminated from playoff contention even though there are games remaining in the regular season

altercation physical confrontation between two or more players—usu. opponents, but sometimes teammates or coach and player

altered uniform sweater that has been tampered with in such a way that it contravenes league rules

alternate 1. ~ **captain** player who wears an "A" on his sweater and acts as a captain while the captain is not on the ice 2. ~ **governor** team executive who has the power to represent and vote on behalf of a governor at league meetings

aluminum shaft shaft of a stick made of or encased in aluminum so as to produce a harder shot

alyutalugit (19th C.) game, similar to hockey, played by Alaskan Inuit

amateur 1. player who is not paid for playing over and above basic living expenses 2. ~ **card** official document certifying one's status as an unpaid player and entitling him to play in amateur competitions 3. ~ **star** important player in the amateur leagues who is usu. desired by professional teams 4. ~ **status** official standing of a player, conferred by a governing body, that forbids him to accept money to play or to sign a contract for pay unless he officially becomes a professional 5. ~ **tryout** trial with a professional team that allows an amateur player to participate in a very limited number of games in a pro league (usu. three or five) without harming his amateur status, thus affording the pro team to assess his talents

Amateur Draft system under which NHL teams claimed the exclusive right to sign players from junior levels of hockey, from 1963 to 1979 (replaced by Entry Draft)

Amateur Hockey Association of the United States see *AHAUS*

Amateur Practise brand of hockey stick made by Doolittles of Ayr, Ontario

Amazing Amerks alternative nickname for New York Americans

ambassador player who represents his team, league, or country with the utmost distinction on and off the ice

American 1. at first, a pejorative to describe a player who was born in the USA and thus not talented; later used simply to describe a player by his place of birth (USA) 2. ~ **college** U.S. university where hockey is offered on a scholarship basis, allowing a player to develop his hockey skills and get an education of sorts at the same time 3. ~ **high school** highest level of high-school hockey and an important place for NHL scouts to begin to evaluate talented, young, often American-born players

American Airlines Center Dallas Stars' home rink (2001-present)

American Collegiate Hockey Association governing body for U.S. university hockey programs that are not affiliated with NCAA (founded 1991)

American Division one of two divisions in the NHL (with the Canadian Division) from 1926 to 1938

American Hockey League minor league founded in 1940; NHL's primary professional development league

Americans 1. nickname of one of New York's NHL teams (1925-42) 2. nickname of Rochester's AHL team (1956-present)

American Soo team in the IHL, hockey's first pro league, based in Sault St. Marie, Michigan, 1904-07

America West Arena Phoenix Coyotes' home rink (1996-2003)

Amerks alternate nickname for New York or Rochester Americans

amigo term used by Hockey Hall of Fame to describe an escort for its newest inductees during induction weekend

anabolic steroid drug that encourages tissue growth, designed to enhance muscularity (and illegal for international competition)

anaerobic form of exercise characterized by short periods of high intensity, primarily intended to build strength

Anaheim Arena alternate name for the Honda Center, home of the NHL's Anaheim Ducks

analysis any study of or commentary on plays and games aimed at offering a better understanding of the results

ancient 1. ~ **history** rivalry between players or teams that is long past but by no means entirely forgotten 2. ~ **rivals** competitive relationship between players and teams that has a long and strong history

Ancient Capital (archaic) newspaper jargon for Quebec City ("Montreal travels to the Ancient Capital for a game tonight")

Andorra IIHF member nation since 1995

anemic weak, usu. in reference to poor offence, particularly on the power play

angle 1. position of the shooter relative to the goalie or net which allows for better or worse opportunity to score 2. a kind of shoot-in in which the puck hits the corner of the rink and ricochets to a point in front of the net 3. **play the** ⁓ of a goalie: position oneself to block as much net as possible from the shooter's line of vision

angry words heated on-ice discussion between two or more players

animal goon; talentless player

animated discussion conversation between players, or players and officials, during the course of a game

ankle guard

ankle 1. joint that connects the leg to the foot and which is most commonly injured when blocking shots 2. ⁓ **cam** camera position cut out of a section of the base of the boards which allows for low-angle, dramatic photographs 3. ⁓ **cutter** U.S. term for a hard shot about four inches off the ice (i.e., ankle-high) 4. ⁓ **guard** protec-

tive gear for the ankles which is put on over the skate, making blocking of shots less painful and preventing Achilles heel injuries (usu. worn by defencemen) 5. ⁓ **protector** type of ankle guard 6. ⁓ **skater** poor skater who cannot skate upright because of weak ankles

announce 1. broadcast play-by-play account of a game 2. ⁓ **the lineup** make known to officials, fans, or journalists the players who will appear in any particular game

announcement any public statement to the media, most often to formalize a trade or retirement of a player

answer 1. score a goal after the other team has scored 2. ⁓ **the bell** fight when the situation calls for fistic support or proof of a team's resilience

anthem singer

anthem 1. national song, played before the start of games in North America or after games in international hockey 2. ⁓ **singer** person who performs the national anthem(s) before the start of a game

anti-defence rule (archaic) rule which allowed no more than three defenders to stand in their own zone before the offence carried the puck over the blueline

anti-inflammatory any product (such as medication or ointment) that relieves an inflamed muscle

anticipate envision what will happen on the ice before it does

anticipation ability to read the play well

anxious moments those flurries in a game during which the defending team is in danger of giving up a critical goal

appeal 1. qualities of a player that make him desirable for a team to acquire 2. protest an official's call

appear play in a game or practice

appearance official credit, in the statistics, for playing in a game; usu. applied to a goalie ("he's made five appearances this year")

applause cheering by fans

applesauce (1940s) newspaper jargon for applause

application effort to join a team or league

apply pressure forecheck intensely, or control the puck for an extended period

apprenticeship time early in a career when a player learns how to play at an elite level

arb(s) slang for *arbitration*

arbiter slang for *referee*

arbitration summertime process by which a team and player resolve a contract dispute, usu. over salary, through a third party

ardent fan sarcastic for reporter

arena building where ice is maintained for the express purpose of playing hockey

Arena brand of hockey stick made by Doolittles of St. Marys, Ontario

Arena Cup trophy presented by the Arena Corporation of Montreal to the champions of the Eastern Canada Amateur Hockey Association, 1905-08

Arena Gardens more commonly called Mutual Street Arena, home of the Toronto Arenas (1917-19), Toronto St. Pats (1919-27), and Toronto Maple Leafs (1927-31)

Arena Riga principal arena in Riga, Latvia

Arenas nickname of the Toronto team in the NHL, 1917-19

Argentina IIHF member nation since 1998

argue 1. dispute a call by an official 2. exchange heated words with an opposing player(s)

argument game

arm comes up means by which a referee signals that he is about to call a penalty

arm pads worn by goalies to prevent injury

arm pads

armband 1. orange strip of cloth worn by the referee around his right arm to distinguish himself from linesmen 2. (archaic) black strip of cloth worn by players during a game to acknowledge the death of an important player or other person

Armenia IIHF member nation since 2004

arrive at the rink get to the dressing room to prepare for a game

arrived of a player: matured and become a star

Arrowhead Pond former name for the Honda Center, home rink of the Anaheim Ducks

artful dodger (early 20th C.) after Charles Dickens character; player who dekes and feints well, avoiding checks

arthroscopy surgical procedure using an arthroscope during which a joint can be more fully examined or repaired

artificial ice ice made through a process of refrigeration

artist skilled player

artistry skill displayed by a superior player

Art Ross 1. ~ **net** goal net devised by Art Ross featuring W-shaped base to ensure pucks are trapped in the net rather than exiting quickly 2. ~ **shot** shot so slow you can read the name on the puck 3. ~ **Trophy** awarded annually to NHL player with the most scoring points (goals and assists combined) 4. ~-**Tyer Puck** puck designed by Art Ross featuring consistent size and weight through process of manufacture; official puck of the NHL in the 1930s

A's short for New York Americans

Asia-Oceania Junior Championship under-18 tournament started in 1984 and featuring teams from the Far East

Asian Cup tournament (1990 to 1996) featuring Kazakhstan, Japan, China, and Korea

ask waivers make a player available to others in the league for a specified selling price

Asociacion Argentina de Hockey Sobre Hielo en Linea governing body of ice and inline hockey in Argentina

aspen kind of wood used in the making of hockey sticks, notably for the shaft

assault 1. determined rush by a team on opposing goal 2. vicious attack by one player on another

assess 1. usu. in the case of a general manager or scout: make a determination of a team or player's level of talent and ability 2. ~ **a penalty** of a referree: penalize a player

asset player with particular value either for the team or for a possible trade

assignment 1. player's specific job for a game (i.e., "Sampson's assignment tonight is to check Jackson") 2. of officials: task of handling a particular game

assist 1. pass that leads directly to a goal; a maximum of two of which are awarded for each goal scored 2. come to the aid of a teammate 3. help out in a managerial capacity

assistant 1. ~ **captain** player who wears an "A" on his sweater and is the captain designate on the ice when the captain is on the bench or not playing 2. ~ **coach** person who helps the coach, either during a game or practice 3. ~ **equipment manager** person who helps the equipment manager handle players' equipment during the season 4. ~ **general manager** person who helps the general manager with contract negotiations, trades, or any other aspect of that job 5. ~ **trainer** person who helps the trainer maintain the physical health of players during the season and through the summer 6. ~ **referee** second referee

astray inaccurate (as a pass)

at a loss unable to explain, usu. a bad play or defeat

at the helm of a coach: in command of a team

at the mercy of

at the mercy of badly out of position, as a goalie when an opponent has the puck in excellent scoring position

athletic therapist person who works year-round with players to ensure their physical well-being through exercise, diet, and training

Atlanta Flames NHL member team, 1972-80 (moved to Calgary)

Atlanta Thrashers NHL member team, 1999-present

Atlantic Division one of two divisions in the Eastern Conference, 1993-98, and one of three in the Eastern Conference, 1998-present

Atlantic Hockey NCAA Division I hockey league, established 2003, primarily comprising teams in northeastern U.S.

Atlantic League established in 1995, featuring six teams from France, Denmark, and the Netherlands

atom level of hockey for players age 9-10

Atomic Balm heating ointment used to treat muscle pains

atrophy of a muscle: diminish in strength from lack of use

attack 1. move aggressively into the offensive zone 2. vicious assault on an opponent, usu. with stick 3. team on offence 4. **go on the ~** make the transition from defence to offence 5.

~ **the puck** forecheck; try to force the puck carrier to make a turnover 6. ~ **the puck carrier** force a turnover

attacker player with the puck

attacking 1. ~ **team** team in possession of the puck and trying to score 2. ~ **zone** area beyond opponent's blueline, where scoring is most possible

attempt 1. try 2. ~ **a shot** try to get the puck on goal 3. ~ **to injure** a deliberate and vicious attack on another player, punishable by five-minute major and game misconduct

attend to of the trainer: step onto the ice to treat an injured player

attendance number of spectators attending a particular game or series of games

attention 1. medical treatment 2. shadowing of an opponent

attract 1. ~ **a crowd** create a situation which causes many players to gather 2. ~ **attention** what a great prospect or player who is desired by many teams or who is shadowed closely on ice during a game does

attraction player who draws crowds to his team's games ("he's the star attraction")

Aud nickname for Buffalo's Memorial Auditorium ("the Sabres are playing at the Aud tonight")

Australia IIHF member nation since 1950

Australian Ice Hockey Federation governing body of hockey in Australia

Austria IIHF member nation since 1912

authority play with ⁓ play with confidence and success

autograph 1. souvenir signature from a player 2. slang for signature by a player on a contract with his team 3. ⁓ **collector** person who aquires many player autographs as a hobby or to sell to others as a business venture

autograph collector

automatic 1. ⁓ **fine** monetary punishment of a player by a league for actions that violate that league's rules, constitutions, or by-laws 2. ⁓ **penalty** punishment of a player by a league for actions that violate that league's rules, constitutions, or by-laws 3. ⁓ **pinch** offensive-zone situation in which the puck comes around to the weak side (i.e., where no opponents are positioned) and the defenceman stays at the attacking blueline to keep the puck in 4. ⁓ **suspension** barring of a player from game action as a result of breaking the league's rules, generally as a result of on-ice violence

Automobile City nickname for Detroit

Automobile D type of skate with a thin blade attached to the boot

automobile skates so-called because they were made by CCM, in 1901; they featured aluminum soles and heel plates, and were attached to street shoes with straps and clamps

auxiliary forward (archaic) utility forward or extra forward

available 1. of a player: ready to play 2. of a player: in the open and waiting for a pass 3. describes a player whom a general manager is willing to trade 4. ⁓ **list** list of names, compiled by teams prior to a draft, of players that other teams are free to select

Avalanche nickname of Colorado team in the NHL, 1995-present

Avco Cup championship trophy of the World Hockey Association for the full term of its existence (1972-79)

average 1. describes a player of middling calibre, in terms of speed, shot, or other skills 2. short for goals-against average, a goaltending statistic

Avs alternative nickname for Colorado Avalanche

awarded goal goal that is credited to a player by a referee, even though the puck did not enter the net (i.e., a goal that is prevented from going into an open net by a defensive player throwing his stick to stop the puck)

Awards Night that night in June every year when the NHL hands out its trophies to the league's elite players

away 1. of a team: travelling or playing at an arena other than its home rink 2. ⁓ **from the play** at a point on the ice that is not where the puck is being played 3. ⁓ **game** road game 4. ⁓ **he goes** expression to describe a player as he begins an end-to-end rush

axe fire

Azerbaijan IIHF member nation since 1992

Bb

BCJHL *British Columbia Junior Hockey League*

BEL official IIHF abbreviation for Belgium

BLR official IIHF abbreviation for Belarus

BRA official IIHF abbreviation for Brazil

BUL official IIHF abbreviation for Bulgaria

B pool designation used by the IIHF until 2000 to denote the second-best group of teams in international hockey (after A pool)

Babe Pratt Trophy annual award for the best defenceman on the Vancouver Canucks

Babe Siebert Memorial Game game played in Montreal in 1939 to raise funds for the family of the late Babe Siebert

baby young player

Baby Bulls 18-year-old players who joined the WHA at a time when the NHL restricted players younger than 20 from playing in its league

Baby Leafs alternative nickname for the St. John's Maple Leafs, Toronto's former AHL farm team

back 1. direction of a pass to the point from a player the corner 2. call by a player for a drop pass 3. of a player: having returned to lineup or game 4. of a player: having returned to ice after serving a penalty 5. early term for the defence position before point

and cover point were introduced to the game 6. ~-**breaker** goal that ensures defeat 7. ~ **door** area of the crease which is to the rear of the goalie (i.e., the open side) 8. ~ **in action** of a player: having returned to the lineup 9. ~ **of the net** a. score ("that shot found the back of the net") b. area behind the end red line and directly behind the goal net 10. ~ **on the beam** of a player: having returned to top form after an injury or a slump 11. ~ **pass** pass made whereby a player looks forward but passes to a player behind him 12. ~ **referee** referee farthest from where the puck is being played 13. ~-**to-back** consecutive 14. **get** ~ **to basics** play simple hockey, usu. after a series of losses or poor play 15. ~ **up** support a teammate

backbone 1. player who is most important to a team's success 2. willingness to absorb punishment or deal with adversity

backcheck of a forward: skate deep into his own end, after being in the offensive end, to cover an opponent in the hopes of preventing a good scoring chance

Backchecker official magazine of the Minneapolis Millers Booster Club

backer 1. someone who bets on a team 2. part owner of a team 3. supporter; fan

backfire to have an unintended, negative result because of a misplay

backhand type of shot or pass using the back side of the blade to the one the player usually uses

backhander a backhand shot

backline blueline

backliner defenceman

backload to structure a contract so that most of the benefits (salaries, incentives, bonuses) are paid later in its term

backpedal 1. skate backward 2. backcheck quickly

backup team's second goalie who primarily sits on the bench with the team and plays only occasionally

backward skating skating which takes a player in the opposite direction than he is facing

backyard rink natural-ice rink made outdoors on the lawn of a private residence during winter months

bad 1. ~ **angle** a position from which it would be very difficult to score a goal 2. ~**-angle shot** shot taken from an angle which is unlikely to result in a goal 3. ~ **blood** animosity between opposing players or teams 4. ~ **bounce** unexpected roll of the puck which has fortuitous consequences for the opposition 5. ~ **break** unlucky event or circumstance 6. ~ **feelings** var. of *bad blood* 7. ~ **goal** goal which, from the perspective of the defending team, should not have been allowed 8. ~ **habit** tendency of a player or team to make errors that frequently result in turnovers or scoring chances 9. ~ **man** (archaic) player with a reputation as a fighter or one vilified by opponents and their fans 10. ~**-man honours** (archaic) penalty minutes leader 11. ~**-man title** a. var. of *bad-man honours* b. status conferred on a player deemed to be the toughest or most intimidating fighter 12. ~ **pass** poor attempt to move puck to a teammate, which results in a turnover 13. ~ **penalty** infraction caused by laziness or being out of position rather than aggressive play

baffle play (archaic) fast deke

bag score (a goal)

bag skate extremely intense practice (i.e., one in which the players skate until they're "bagged")

baggataway Indian name for early version of lacrosse; precursor to hockey

Bailey, Ace, Benefit Game see *Ace Bailey Benefit Game*

Bailey-Shore incident violent attack during the game of December 12, 1933, in Boston when Eddie Shore of the Bruins ended the career of Toronto's Ace Bailey with a vicious attack that almost killed Bailey; see also *Ace Bailey Benefit Game*

balance 1. remainder of, usu. the season 2. perfect fit of players on a team 3. that which is obtained by skating properly without any wobble or uncertainty

balanced attack team with offensive ability on all four lines

balcony (U.S. term) upper seats of an arena

Balkan League tournament annual series of games played between teams from Bulgaria, Yugoslavia, and Romania

ball 1. object used to score in hockey's early days on outdoor rinks and frozen ponds 2. term used to describe puck in early days of its introduction to the game 3. ~ **hockey** hockey played using a ball instead of a puck, usu. on the street or in a gymnasium

ball hockey

Baltica Cup successor (in name) to the *Izvestia tournament*, 1997-2002, after which it was renamed Moscow International Tournament

ban suspension

banana blade (1960s) severely hooked blade, long since made illegal by the NHL

banana blade

bandy early form of European hockey played outdoors on a rink closer in size to a soccer field, with a ball and hooked sticks

bang 1. ~-and-crash style of hockey marked by hitting and physical play 2. ~ away try to shoot after picking up a rebound directly in front of the net 3. ~-bang play play that happens very quickly 4. ~ home score a goal from in close 5. ~ in var. of *bang home*

banged up suffering from several minor injuries, none of which is enough to keep the player out of the lineup

banished sent away as punishment, usu. to minors, penalty box, or press box

bank 1. ~ in score by shooting the puck off an opponent and into the goal 2. ~ off pass or shoot the puck off the body of a player who can't get out of the way to avoid being hit by the puck 3. ~ pass pass off the boards to a teammate

Bank Atlantic Center home arena of Florida Panthers (formerly known as Office Depot Center)

banner 1. flag or pennant raised to the rafters after a team wins a division, conference, or league title 2. ~ season excellent year 3. ~ year var. of *banner season*

banquet celebration, usu. for Stanley Cup or World Championship victors

bantam level of youth hockey for players age 13-14

bar 1. short for crossbar or goalpost 2. disallow (e.g., bar reporters from dressing room)

bar mask type of goalie mask designed in the mid-1960s by Roy Weatherbee, made of fibreglass and resin, custom fitted for each goalie

bargain 1. newly or recently acquired player whose performance greatly exceeds the price the team paid to get him 2. negotiate a trade

barge 1. ~ in on goal use of physical strength rather than finesse to go to the net, usu. with the puck 2. ~ through skate past opponents using physical strength rather than finesse

barn old arena

barnburner exciting hockey game

Barney & Berry (late 19th C.) makers of round-bladed skates for fancy skating

barnstorming tour series of exhibition games played after the season by NHL teams, usu. in small towns across Canada

Barons nickname of Cleveland team in the NHL, 1976-78

barrage sustained attack in the offensive zone

Barrie Flyers Allan Cup champions in 1974 and Memorial Cup champions in 1951 and 1953

Barton Street Arena home rink of NHL Hamilton Tigers, 1920-25

base 1. lowest part of goalpost 2. ~ plate lowest part of iron net 3. ~

salary salary before bonuses or extras

basement 1. last place 2. ~ **dweller** team in last place

bash hit hard

basics 1. elemental parts of a game 2. **get back to** ~ play simple hockey, usu. after a series of losses or poor play

basket goal, usu. used in tandem with *biscuit* for puck ("he put the biscuit in the basket")

Bastien, Baz, Memorial Award see *Baz Bastien Memorial Award*

bat hit puck out of mid-air

baton Quebeçois for hockey stick

baton

battered beaten up

battered silverware Stanley Cup, in reference to its long history and many bumps and bruises

battle 1. fierce game 2. confrontation between two players during a game 3. ~ **along the boards** struggle between two or more players along boards for possession of puck or position 4. ~ **for position** a. struggle for superior placement in the standings b. compete with opponents for territory in front of goal 5. ~ **for possession** any struggle between two or more players for possession of the puck 6. ~ **for the puck** var. of *battle for possession* 7. **playoff** ~ struggle between two or more teams for placement in the standings that will qualify them for the playoffs

Battle of Alberta name for the Edmonton Oilers-Calgary Flames rivalry

Battle of Ontario name for the Toronto Maple Leafs-Ottawa Senators rivalry

Battle of Quebec name for the Montreal Canadiens-Quebec Nordiques rivalry of the 1980s

battler tenacious player who won't give up

Battleship model of hockey stick

Bauer premier equipment manufacturer in Canada

Baz Bastien Memorial Award good-guy award presented to a member of the Pittsburgh Hornets (AHL) who was most co-operative with media and fans during the year

beach hockey kind of hockey introduced by ESPN featuring a portable in-line rink meant to be installed on a beach

beachball item a goalie can't stop when he's not playing well

beak slang for nose

Beanpot tournament annual competition between the four Boston-area universities—Harvard, Northeastern, Boston University, and Boston College—the winner receiving a trophy in the shape of a beanpot

Beantown Boston

Beantowners Boston Bruins

beat 1. defeat 2. ~ **cleanly** a. score without the goalie touching the puck b. deke an opponent without him making even incidental contact c. win a faceoff uncontested 3. ~ **man to the puck** acquire possession of the puck prior to an opponent 4. ~ **out** defeat or eliminate 5. ~ **the man** deke opponent or perform in any way superior to an opponent

beaten down and out ("they're a beaten team after losing the first three games of this series")

Beatrice Aeros premier women's hockey team in National Women's Hockey League, 1999-2003

beauty great goal or play

beaver tailing act of a goalie slamming his stick on the ice to warn his teammates that a penalty to the opposition is about to expire

beef 1. complaint 2. muscle 3. ~ **up** add fighters to a lineup

Bee Hive Golden Corn Syrup product sold most successfully in the 1940s and '50s; manufacturer offered fans photos of NHL players in exchange for a number of labels

beer league night-time recreational league made up of working men looking for regular exercise

beg off excuse oneself, usu. from practice

behave 1. show discipline under duress 2. **get puck to** ~ control bouncing puck with stick so that it lies flat on the ice and is easy to skate with, shoot, or pass ("she couldn't get a clean shot away because the puck wouldn't behave for her")

behind 1. trailing ("they're behind two goals with five minutes to play") 2. travelling in the opposite direction to the one intended (as an inaccurate pass) 3. ~ **the play** occurrence at the opposite end of the ice to where the play is currently taking place ("he took a slash well behind the play") 4. ~ **the net** area of the ice between the end boards and the end red line

Belarus IIHF member nation since 1992

Belgium IIHF member nation since 1908

bell 1. device sounded to announce end of each period and game (sometimes a horn or buzzer) 2. ~ **rung** suffer a head injury, usu. euphemism for concussion

Bell Centre see *Centre Bell*

Bellerive Champion model of hockey stick

Belleville McFarlands Allan Cup winners in 1958

belong 1. be property of 2. demonstrate worthiness to play in the NHL ("he proves he belongs in this league")

belt hit an opponent hard

belt

Beltcamp Icemaker pioneering method of icemaking developed by Beltz Engineering Laboratories and founder Chuck Beltz of Michigan

bench 1. area where players sit during a game when they're not on the ice 2. of a coach: decide not to use a player who is dressed and on the bench, usu. because of poor play 3. ~ **boss** coach 4. ~ **jockey** coach 5. ~ **minor** two-minute penalty assessed as the result of an infraction that occurs on the bench—usu., too many men on the ice or foul language directed by the coach towards an on-ice official 6. ~ **minor penalty** var. of *bench minor* 7. ~ **warmer** player who sees little ice time during a game 9. ~ **warming** penalty

benched 1. given a penalty 2. status of a player whose ice time is curtailed drastically by the coach, usu. as punishment for poor play

benedict (archaic) married hockey player (as opposed to bachelor)

benefit game any game not part of a regular schedule, the receipts from which are earmarked for some charitable cause

Bergvall system playoff system used at 1920 Olympics to determine champion

Berlin southern Ontario team that challenged for the Stanley Cup in March 1910 and March 1911

Berchtesgaden nickname for front row of green seats at Maple Leaf Gardens, where Conn Smythe used to watch games and phone down to the bench to give instructions to the coach

Berne Arena principal arena in Bern, Switzerland (boasts the best attendance in European leagues)

berth 1. place, usu. on a team   2. **playoff** ~ place in the playoffs ("with the win, they've clinched a playoff berth for the first time in three years")

best behaviour deportment of player who does nothing overly physical or violent to aggravate opponent—or league office

best-dressed coach unofficial title given to that coach who wears flashy but tasteful clothing behind the bench

Best Defenceman award presented by IIHF at the conclusion of an international tournament to the best defenceman as adjudged by the IIHF directorate

Best Forward award presented by IIHF at the conclusion of an international tournament to the best forward as adjudged by the IIHF directorate

Best Goalie award presented by IIHF at the conclusion of an international tournament to the best goalie as adjudged by the IIHF directorate

best-of- 1. ~**two** (archaic) playoff format in which the team with the greater number of aggregate goals after two games wins the series 2. ~**of-three** playoff format in which the first team that wins two games wins the series 3. ~**-of-five** playoff format in which the first team that wins three games wins the series 4. ~**-of-seven** playoff format in which the first team that wins four games wins the series 5. ~**-of-nine** (archaic) playoff format in which the first team that wins five games wins the series

Best Player award presented by IIHF game at the conclusion of an international game to the top player from each team

bet stake a sum of money on the predicted outcome of a game

betting practice of trying to make money by predicting the winner of a game

bettor person who places bets

between 1. ~ **periods** interval separating the end of one period from the beginning of the next (also *intermission*) 2. ~ **the legs** of a shot: between the pads of the goalie, usu. into the net 3. ~ **the pipes** playing goal ("Sami Jo Small is between the pipes tonight")

Between the Lines Washington Capitals' game-night program

B-form contract, prior to the era of the Amateur Draft, which gave an NHL team the option to sign a young player in return for a small fee, usually paid toward the schooling of the player and guaranteeing that team right of first refusal on his NHL playing rights

Bickell Cup Toronto Maple Leafs team trophy presented to an individual for "a tremendous feat, one season of spectacular play, or remarkable service over a number of years"

bid 1. make a pitch for 2. try to make a team 3. attempt to win 4. **shutout ~** attempt by a goalie to record a shutout, usu. used only late in a game

big 1. **~ club** a. NHL team ("he's joining the big club tomorrow night") b. team whose players are mostly larger than average size 2. **come up ~** make a major contribution, usu. under pressure ("he came up big by making a save at the crucial moment of the game") 3. **~ crowd** group of players in a small area 4. **~ dance** slang for the Stanley Cup finals 5. **~ fellow** (archaic) strong player 6. **~ goal** important score 7. **~ gun** top scorer 8. **~ gunner** prolific scorer 9. **~ ice** colloquial Canadian term for European-size ice surface 10. **~ league** NHL 11. **~-league debut** first NHL game 12. **~-league play** some small feat that exhibits a high degree of proficiency 13. **~ leaguer** NHL player 14. **~ line** team's top forward unit 15. **~ noise** (archaic) star ("he was the big noise of the game") 16. **~ play** significant play, esp. one that determines the outcome of a game 17. **~ save** important save by a goaltender 18. **~ show** NHL 19. **~ tent** NHL 20. **~ time** a. NHL b. in a significant way

Big Bad Bruins alternate nickname of Boston Bruins of late 1960s and early '70s, known for both explosive offence and physical play

bill promote ("Lecavalier was billed as the Michael Jordan of hockey")

Bill Masterton Memorial Trophy annual NHL award for "perseverance, sportsmanship, and dedication to hockey"

billet family that boards a young player from another city or country for a tournament or (especially in junior hockey) a season

bingo description of a sound made by perfect shot or hard hit

birch kind of wood used in the making of hockey sticks, primarily for the shaft

bird dog scout, usu. of amateur talent, usu. found in small towns and cold arenas

bird dog

birthday skates gift of skates or anything else to a player on his birthday as enticement to get him to play for a particular team without, technically, paying the player or luring him out of a contract with another team (usu. at minor-league level)

biscuit slang for puck

bite dirty tactic during fight or scrum

bitterly fought describes an unusually competitive game or series

Black Aces small group of players on any team who take part in practices but rarely play

black eye 1. bruising around the eye, as the result of a blow 2. violent on-ice incident that hurts hockey's reputation

Black Hawks nickname of Chicago team in the NHL (spelling commonly used 1926-85)

black tape adhesive tape of that colour used to protect blade of a stick and enable players to cushion the puck more easily on it

black trousers pants worn by on-ice officials (referees and linesmen)

Blackhawks nickname of Chicago team in the NHL (official spelling since 1985)

blade 1. sharpened metal runner of a skate; the part that comes in contact with ice 2. broad, often hooked part of stick used for shooting and passing 3. ~ **artist** star player 4. ~**d hero** star player 5. ~ **holder** plastic attachment to boot of skate that holds blade in place

blades slang for skates ("bring your blades to the arena")

blades

Blades name of Boston Bruins' mascot

Blake's Tavern bar owned and operated by Toe Blake in Montreal, most famous for celebrations after Stanley Cup parades in that city

blank shut out (the opposing team)

blanket 1. to shut out 2. strong defensive play

blast 1. shoot the puck hard 2. a hard shot 3. complain vociferously ("blast the referee!")

Blaze Calgary Flames' game-night program

blaze shoot hard

blazing 1. great speed 2. ~ **shot** hard

shot 3. ~ **speed** characteristic of an extremely fast skater

bleachers uppermost seats in an arena

Bleu, Blanc, et Rouge alternative nickname for Montreal Canadiens

blind pass pass made without looking at the intended target

blinding speed var. of *blazing speed*

blindside deliver an unexpected, dirty hit from somewhere outside the opponent's field of vision

blistering shot var. of *blazing shot*

blitz all-out attack

block 1. inhibit an opponent's progress 2. (archaic) piece of wood used to make puck 3. ~ **a pass** prevent a pass from being completed 4. ~ **a rush** prevent a rush from occurring 5. ~ **a shot** prevent a shot from reaching the goal 6. ~ **skates** see *stock skates* 7. ~ **the path** get in the way of

block a shot

blockbuster major, usu. trade

blocked shot 1. successful prevention of the puck from reaching the defending goal by obstructing its path with the body 2. ~**s** statistic kept by the NHL

blocker glove worn on the hand with which the goalie holds the stick, used to deflect pucks out of harm's way

blocking 1. ~**arm** arm on which a goalie wears a blocker 2. ~**-arm save**

stop made by a goalie, using the blocker or that arm 3. ~ **glove** var. of *blocker* 4. ~ **save** var. of *blocking-arm save*

blood 1. vital fluid that flows freely when a player is cut, and whose presence dictates that a major penalty be called rather than a minor penalty ("the referee sees blood, so he has no choice but to give Simpson five") 2. vengeance ("he's looking for blood after that high stick")

bloodletting violent game

blooper long, high shot that challenges (and often fools) goalies

blossom develop (of a young player: "she's blossoming into a genuine star with the national team")

blow 1. bungle an excellent chance 2. ~ **a game** lose a game that the team should have won 3. ~ **a lead** lose a lead that seemed insurmountable 4. ~ **a tire** fall inexplicably 5. ~ **by** skate quickly past an opponent 6. ~ **his cool** fail to maintain composure 7. ~ **it by** score a goal with a fast shot the goalie is unable to stop 8. ~ **the play dead** of an official: whistle for a stoppage in play 8. ~ **the puck by the goalie** score a goal on a very hard shot

Blue and White 1. alternative nickname for Toronto Maple Leafs 2. ~ **game** intrasquad game played near the end of Leafs' training camp, in which one side wears blue sweaters and the other wears white

Blue Bombers alternative nickname for New York Rangers

Blue Book New York Rangers' game-night program

blue ice goal crease (so called because that section of ice is painted blue)

Blue Jackets nickname of Columbus's NHL team, 2000-present

blue puck that colour of puck used in WHA

blueline one of two blue lines on the ice that separate the offensive zones from the centre-ice area

blueliner defenceman

bluenote musical symbol that comprises the logo of the St. Louis Blues

Blues 1. colour of seats at Maple Leaf Gardens and later Air Canada Centre in Toronto 2. nickname of St. Louis team in NHL, 1967-present 3. alternative nickname for New York Rangers

Blueshirt New York Rangers' team guidebook

Blueshirts alternative nickname for New York Rangers

board 1. short for scoreboard 2. check illegally 3. ~ **advertising** advertisements that are affixed to the boards for display during a game 4. ~ **check** check along the boards 5. ~ **checking** term—used primarily in Europe and archaic in Canada—for a dangerous hit along boards 6. ~ **meeting** conference of team executives to discuss trades, payroll, or other team concerns

Board of Directors highest executives within a team who oversee all matters pertaining to its operation

Board of Governors body made up of one representative from every team, which meets to oversee all matters pertaining to the league's operation

boarding illegal check along the boards, resulting in two-minute or five-minute penalty

boards 1. structures, made of wood or other materials, that enclose the playing surface (ice) 2. call by a teammate to play the puck off the boards 3. **hard** ~ boards from which the puck caroms quickly 4. **soft** ~ boards from which the puck caroms very little

boast 1. have on team ("they boast three forwards over six feet tall")

2. own, usu. a record ("he can boast three 100-point seasons with the Flames")

bob skates children's skates with double blades designed to facilitate learning to skate

Bob Johnson Memorial Award Pittsburgh Penguins team dedication award

Bob Nystrom Award leadership award given by the New York Islanders in honour of one of their former stars

bobtailed hockey (archaic) pejorative term, used in the early days of six-man hockey in eastern Canada, by proponents of the seven-man game which preceded it

bodies are flying situation in a game marked by numerous hard checks

body 1. short for bodycheck 2. ~ **an opponent off the puck** check the puck carrier and recover the puck 3. ~ **fat percentage** ratio of body fat to a person's weight; scientific measurement of a player's level of fitness 4. ~ **position** situation of the body relative to the play 5. ~ **slam** var. of *bodycheck* 6. **use the** ~ play physically

bodycheck hit a player

bodycheck

Bodycheck Ottawa Senators' game-night program

bodychecker player who executes a bodycheck

bodychecking in women's hockey, a penalty for unnecessary or excessive physical contact

bolster 1. ~ **the defence** strengthen the defence corps by adding a new player (or having an injured player return) 2. ~ **the lineup** strengthen the team's roster with the addition of a new player (or return of an injured player)

bolt 1. block of wood from which a one-piece hockey stick is crafted 2. leave a game or team suddenly

Bolts alternative nickname for Tampa Bay Lightning

bomb 1. beat badly 2. hard punch in a fight

bombard attack relentlessly

bonding close relationships developed among players, usu. on road trips when players room with each other

bone-crushing check hard check

bone scan medical test used to determine the extent of injuries to bones

bone skates skates with blades made from shank bones of, usu., horses, oxen, and sheep

bonehead play bad play; error

boner bad play

bonus additional money paid to a player—over and above salary—for achieving certain statistical milestones during a season (e.g., 20 goals scored, 40 assists, 60 games played)

boo disapproving sounds made by hostile fans

boobirds those fans who boo

boom 1. shoot hard 2. **lower the** ~ deliver a fierce check

boomer player with a hard shot (notably Bernie "Boom Boom" Geoffrion)

boomerang stunning turn of events, esp. when a team incurs a penalty, then scores a goal short-handed

booming 1. ~ **drive** hard shot 2. ~ **shot** var. of *booming drive*

boost 1. lift, usu. one's spirits 2. increase, usu. the score

booster fan

boot 1. botch the play or commit an error 2. part of the skate into which a player inserts his foot 3. **hard** ~ skate boot which offers little flexibility or range of motion 4. ~ **hockey** var. of street or road hockey (i.e., played in winter boots instead of skates) 5. **soft** ~ skate boot which offers flexibility and range of motion

booth short for broadcast booth

bootheel slang for *puck*

Border Cities Arena arena in Windsor, Ontario which was home rink of the Detroit Cougars (1926-29)

Border City Detroit

borrow 1. (archaic) acquire a player from another team on a temporary basis 2. use a teammate's stick, when one's own has broken while play continues, until a replacement may be obtained from the bench

Boston Arena original home arena of Boston Bruins, 1924-28; known since 1979 as Matthews Arena, home of Northeastern University hockey teams

Boston Bruins NHL member team since 1924

Boston Flu apocryphal ailment, said to affect visiting players intimidated by playing the Boston Bruins of the late 1960s and early 1970s (see *Big Bad Bruins*) when Boston was the best— and toughest—team in the NHL (see also *Philadelphia Flu*)

Boston Garden home arena of Boston Bruins, 1928-95

Boston Tea Party (archaic, circa 1930s) big brawl

both ends where a player who is adept at both of offence and defence excels ("he's terrific at both ends of the ice")

bother check an opponent efficiently without getting a penalty

bother

bothered by 1. irritated by, usu. an injury ("he's been bothered by a sore elbow for two weeks now") 2. **being ~** being checked closely by an opponent

bottle popper high, hard shot that knocks the goalie's water bottle off the top of the net after going in

bottle popper

bottle up clog, usu. the middle of the ice

bounce 1. unpredictable skip or hop of a puck 2. **~ around** a. play for several different teams, esp. in minor leagues   b. hit frequently during a game or shift 3. **~ back** recover from bad start to game or season 4. **lucky ~** fortuitous carom of the puck 5. **~ off** absorb a hit well

bouncing puck puck that is difficult to control

bounder bouncing puck

bouquets (archaic) words of praise

bout fight

bow 1. lose to 2. make one's debut with team or in league 3. **~ out** be eliminated from playoffs or tournament 4. **~ to** go down to defeat

bowl over check; knock down

bow-legged awkward style of skating

box 1. defensive formation adopted while a team is playing short-handed (also *box formation*) 2. short for *penalty box* 3. **~es** short for *box*

seats ("we sat in the boxes last night and had a great view of the bench") 4. **~ net** first goal nets for hockey with full frame and mesh, designed in Halifax in 1899 5. **~ office** area of arena where tickets are sold 6. **~ seats** excellent seat closest to ice 7. **~ seater** fan who sits in the boxes 8. **~ toe** hard, durable toe of skate designed to absorb force of contact with the foot

boy young player

boys 1. diminutive of men 2. players ("okay, boys, let's go out there and play our best")

Boys model of hockey stick made by Doolittles of St. Marys, Ontario

Boy's Expert brand of Hilborn hockey stick made by the Salyerds company of Preston, Ontario

Boy's Red brand of Hilborn hockey stick made by the Salyerds company of Preston, Ontario

brain trust GM or other person or people who control the team

brainy smart

brake 1. stop suddenly 2. **put on the ~s** stop suddenly

brand style, usu. of hockey ("they play a dull brand of hockey once they get the lead")

Brandon Wheat Kings Manitoba team that challenged for the Stanley Cup in March 1904

Brantford Alexanders Allan Cup champions in 1977

Brantford Motts Clamatos Allan Cup champions in 1987

brass GMs or executives in charge of a team

"Brass Bonanza" piece of music played by Hartford Whalers at the beginning of every period and after each Hartford goal

brawl extended fight involving several players on ice, or even players from the bench who have stepped onto the ice to fight

brawling fighting

brawny physically imposing

Brazil IIHF member nation since 1984

Bread Line (1930s to 1940s) New York Rangers' threesome of Mac Colville, Neil Colville, and Alex Shibicky, so named for their importance to the team

break 1. time out of any sort during a game 2. lapse in the schedule that permits players some time off 3. play that has an impact on the game's result 4. fortuitous opportunity 5. ⁓ **away** make a surprise offensive thrust 6. ⁓ **camp** conclude team's training camp on eve of regular season 7. ⁓ **a contract** refuse to honour a contract, instead of sitting out and demanding to be traded or to have the contract renegotiated 8. ⁓ **in** a. ⁓ **new equipment** soften new equipment to make it pliable and comfortable b. of a goalie: prepare pads to make them malleable c. ⁓ **on goal** find a path to a clear scoring chance 9. ⁓ **into the NHL** play well enough to earn a regular spot in the lineup with an NHL team 10. ⁓ **out of a slump** score or play well after a number of games without a goal or marked by poor play 11. ⁓**-shins** early colloquial reference for hockey (to "play break-shins") 12. ⁓ **a stick** render a stick unusable 13. ⁓ **a sweat** make an effort—usu. used in the negative ("he barely broke a sweat in his 12 minutes of ice time") 14. ⁓ **a tie** score a goal that puts the team ahead by one goal 15. ⁓ **training** violate curfew or rules intended to ensure that players lead a healthy lifestyle 16. ⁓ **up** a. change players on a forward line b. stymie an opposition rush

breakaway play in which the puck carrier eludes all defenders and has only the goalie to beat

breakaway

Breakaway Florida Panthers' game-night program

breakout 1. set play designed to move puck out of defensive end 2. ⁓ **pass** pass by a defenceman to a forward to begin an attack

breather respite, usu. on bench

breed kind of player ("goalies are a special breed of athlete")

breezers hockey pants (term used exclusively in northwestern United States, so called because hockey pants are loose at the bottom, allowing air to circulate easily)

Bregent Expert brand of hockey stick

Brendan Byrne Arena former name of New Jersey Devils' home arena (1982-96; renamed Continental Airlines Arena)

brick wall goalie playing very well

brief 1. ⁓ **absence** short time away from a team, usu. during a game, because of slight injury or equipment trouble 2. ⁓ **fling** short-lived success 3. ⁓ **power-play** situation in which a team has man advantage for much less than the full two minutes because the team incurred a minor penalty shortly after the short-handed team did

brimming full (of confidence)

brine solution fed through pipes beneath the floor of an artificial rink to make ice

bring 1. carry puck 2. ⁓ **down (an opponent)** trip or interfere with a player so that he falls to the ice

brisk 1. fast, energetic 2. ⁓ **pace** good speed and flow by both teams in a game 3. ⁓ **workout** high-tempo practice

Broad Street shuffle term for the brawling of the Philadelphia Flyers of 1970s ("the benches have cleared and every player on the ice is doing the Broad Street shuffle")

Broadway Blue New York Rangers' game-night program

Broadway Blueshirts alternative nickname for New York Rangers

broadcast 1. TV or radio presentation of a game 2. ⁓ **booth** area high above the ice where members of broadcast media watch and describe the game 3. ⁓ **media** radio and television reporters

broadcast booth

British Columbia Junior Hockey League provincial Junior A league for that province

Broad Street Bullies alternative nickname for Philadelphia Flyers in 1970s when the team used fighting and intimidation as means to achieve victory

broken 1. ⁓ **nose** fracture of the proboscis 2. ⁓ **play** a. attempted combination passing rendered ineffectual by the defence b. any good scoring chance that comes after a scramble for the puck 3. ⁓ **skate** (archaic) common problem of the blade itself breaking, forcing

players to retire during a game   4. ~
stick stick rendered unusable because it
has split into two or more pieces

bronze medal award for placing third
in international competition

Brooklyn Americans NHL member
team, 1941-42; formerly the New
York Americans

broom give them the ~ win a playoff
series without losing a single game
(i.e., sweep the series)

brother act two or more brothers
playing for the same team

brouhaha melee or physical confrontation

Brown equipment manufacturer

Bruins nickname of Boston NHL team

bruise hit hard

bruiser heavy hitter ("he's a real
bruiser")

bruising known as a tough player ("he's
a bruising defenceman")

B's short for Boston Bruins

B-style goal net net with a B-frame at
its base to hold netting

B-style goal net

buck slang for 100 ("he weighs a buck
seventy" means he weighs 170
pounds)

bucket 1. helmet   2. ~ **fighting** see
locker boxing

Buds alternative nickname for Toronto
Maple Leafs

Buffalo Sabres NHL member team,
1970-present

bug screen visor

bugle nose

bugler slang for referee

build 1. ~ **a lead** score two or more
goals consecutively to take control of
a game   2. ~ **a team** draft, trade, and
sign players to make a second-rate
team into a contender

Builder in the Hockey Hall of Fame,
category of Honoured Member that
recognizes men who have contributed
to the game in a non-playing capacity

Bulgaria IIHF member nation since
1963

bulge 1. ~ **the net** score   2. ~ **the twine**
var. of *bulge the net*

Bulldogs nickname of Quebec's professional team, 1908-20

bullet hard shot

bulletins updates of scores from radio in
early days

bull ring gambling areas inside Maple
Leaf Gardens (1930s to 1950s)

bully 1. (archaic) faceoff   2. goon

bump 1. check   2. ~ **and grind** boring
style of hockey featuring checking
and few scoring chances   3. ~ **into** hit
accidentally   4. ~ **player off the puck**
make physical contact with the puck
carrier so that he loses possession of it

bumps and bruises minor injuries a
player or team suffers, esp. during a
playoff series

bunch crowd around net

Bundesliga Austrian league

bunker private booth behind one
section of gold seats at Maple Leaf
Gardens from which owner Harold
Ballard watched games

bunting decorations hung up around
arena for important games or events

such as Stanley Cup finals, attendance of a dignitary, etc.

burst of speed quick and unexpected acceleration which catches the defence off guard

bury 1. score 2. hit an opponent hard 3. send a player to the minors for a long period of time

bus league minor pro or amateur league where teams travel by bus rather than by plane

bush league 1. low-level minor league 2. pejorative term for poorly run league or organization

busher player from a bush league; amateur with less than professional-quality skills

bust 1. player, esp. a new arrival, who fails to live up to expectations 2. bad trade 2. ~ **one's butt off** skate hard

bustle hustle

busy 1. describes a goalie who faces many shots 2. ~ **night** night when many games are scheduled

butcher player who uses his stick with excessive violence

butchery act perpetrated by a butcher

butt end of a stick where knob or tape is affixed for safety

butt-end dirty use of butt to hit an opponent in the face or stomach

butt-ending act of using butt with intent to injure

butterfly style of goaltending in which the goalie stands with his knees together and feet wide apart, allowing him to drop to his knees and get back up quickly

buy 1. acquire though cash purchase 2. ~ **into** accept a philosophy, usu., a coaching system

buzz 1. intense skating 2. frenetic action around opponent's goal 3. great excitement surrounding a game

buzzer sound signalling the beginning and end of all periods

bystander fan

Cc

C 1. abbreviation for centre 2. letter worn on a player's sweater denoting captain

CAHA *Canadian Amateur Hockey Association*

CAN official IIHF abbreviation for Canada

CATA Canadian Athletic Therapist Association

CBA collective bargaining agreement

CCCP abbreviation for Soviet Union, worn on that country's sweaters

CCCP sweater

CCHA *Central Collegiate Hockey Association*

CCM Canada Cycle & Motor Co. Ltd., which began manufacturing hockey equipment in 1905 (now owned by Reebok)

CH letters which comprise the Montreal Canadiens' logo, standing for Club de Hockey

CHA Canadian Hockey Association (renamed *Hockey Canada* in 2003)

CHL 1. *Canadian Hockey League* 2. *Central Hockey League*

CHN official IIHF abbreviation for China

CIAU *Canadian Interuniversity Athletic Union*

CIS 1. *Commonwealth of Independent States* 2. *Canadian Interuniversity Sport*

CKFH Toronto radio station operated by Foster Hewitt (CK plus his initials) as the flagship for his Maple Leafs radio broadcasts

CPHL *Central Professional Hockey League*

CRO official IIHF abbreviation for Croatia

C.S.C.S. Certified Strength and Conditioning Specialist, a person who has passed an exam given by the National Strength and Conditioning Association

CSR official IIHF abbreviation for the former Czechoslovakia (replaced by CZE for Czech Republic in 1993 and SVK for Slovakia in 1994)

CSSR abbreviation for Czechoslovakia, worn on that country's sweaters

CZE official IIHF abbreviation for Czech Republic

C pool designation used by IIHF until 2000 to denote third level (after A and B pools) of teams in international hockey

cage 1. goal net 2. penalty box 3. illegal webbing from thumb to finger on goalie glove 4. ~ **cop** goalie 5. ~ **custodian** goalie 6. ~ **guardian** goalie

Calder circuit nickname for NHL during the presidency of Frank Calder (1917-43)

Calder Cup AHL championship trophy

Calder loop nickname for NHL during the presidency of Frank Calder (1917-43)

Calder Memorial Trophy NHL trophy awarded annually to the best rookie

calendar season or league schedule

calf protector piece of equipment used by goalies to protect the lower leg

Calgary Canadians Memorial Cup champions in 1926

Calgary Corral home arena of the Calgary Flames, 1980-83 (also known as Stampede Corral)

Calgary Cup pre-1988 Olympic tournament featuring teams from Canada, USA, Czechoslovakia, and the Soviet Union

Calgary Flames NHL member team, 1980-present (formerly Atlanta Flames)

Calgary Stampeders Allan Cup champions in 1946

calibre quality, usu. of play

California (Golden) Seals NHL member team, 1967-76 (also known as Oakland Seals; moved to Cleveland)

calisthenics stretching and warmup exercises performed before a game or practice

call 1. any decision by an on-ice official which results in a stoppage of play 2. announce a game 3. ~ **back** nullify a play, usu. a goal 4. ~ **for the puck** in the case of a player, alert a teammate to pass the puck 5. ~ **it quits** retire 6. ~ **on** usu. in the case of a coach, to ask a player to perform a special assignment ("coach Green has called on Avery to stop Ottawa's big line tonight") 7. ~ **on the carpet** in the case of league officials, to summon a player to discuss violent or inappropriate action on ice 8. ~ **a penalty** in the case of a referee, decide to stop play and assess a penalty 9. ~ **the play dead** blow the whistle to stop play 10. ~ **up** promote a player from the minors or junior hockey to play for the major-league team 11. ~-**up** player who is promoted from a lesser team to a superior team for a short time 12. **be ~ed upon** respond to a challenging situation with a superior effort, usu. a goalie who is "called upon" to make big saves

call for the puck

Cambridge Hornets Allan Cup champions in 1983

cameo (archaic) league debut

camp 1. short for training camp 2. establish position beside the goalie to accept a cross-crease pass or scoop in a rebound ("Botterill is camped to the side of the net")

campaign season

campaigner player

campaigning playing over the course of a season

can opener illegal check that involves putting one's stick between an opponent's legs and pushing, thus knocking him down or off balance (coined by Toronto defenceman Bryan McCabe)

Can-Pro short for Canadian Professional Hockey League

Canada IIHF member nation since 1920

Canada Calling radio program hosted by Foster Hewitt; a weekly NHL roundup of play produced for Canada's military troops worldwide

Canada Cup six- or eight-team "open" international tournament (i.e., no restrictions on the use of professionals) contested in 1976, 1981, 1984, 1987, and 1991 (replaced by World Cup in 1996)

Canadian 1. model of hockey stick made by Monarch Hockey Stick Company of New Hamburg, Ontario 2. slang for a player in a European league who does not have three years' experience overseas and as a result is not considered a native but instead one of a designated number of "import" players allowed on each roster

Canadian Airlines Saddledome name of home arena of the Calgary Flames between 1996 and 2000 (previously known as Olympic Saddledome; later known as Pengrowth Saddledome)

Canadian Amateur Hockey Association governing body of amateur hockey in Canada, 1914-94 (renamed *Canadian Hockey Association*)

Canadian Assistance Program NHL program (1999-2005) that provided monies to Canadian teams in the NHL, based on season's ticket sales, to offset the effects of the exchange rate between Canadian and U.S. dollars (most players, even in Canada, are paid in U.S. dollars)

Canadian Division one of two divisions in the NHL (with the American Division), 1926-38

Canadian hockey style of play typical of Canada, namely a more physical game with more emotional intensity than what is usually displayed in Europe

Canadian Hockey former name for *Hockey Canada*, the nation's governing body for the sport

Canadian Hockey Association 1. professional league, successor to Eastern Canada Amateur Hockey Association, which folded early in its only season (1909-10) 2. former name for *Hockey Canada*

Canadian Hockey League umbrella organization that oversees the operation of the country's three major junior leagues — the OHL, QMJHL, and WHL

Canadian Husky brand of hockey stick made by EL-WIG in Durham, Ontario, its signature models being Junior Pro, Mustang, Wildcat Senior, Pro, and Pro Goal

Canadian Interuniversity Athletic Union (CIAU) former name for Canadian Interuniversity Sport

Canadian Interuniversity Sport (CIS) governing body for university athletics in Canada

Canadian National Team inaugurated by Father David Bauer in 1961 and continuing in one form or another until the late 1990s, playing exhibition games worldwide and preparing players for important international competitions, usu. the Olympics and World Championships

Canadian Pro model of hockey stick produced by National in Durham, Ontario

Canadian Professional Hockey League minor pro league centred in Ontario, 1926-30

Canadian Soo member team of the International Hockey League, 1904-07, the only Canadian entry in the first all-professional league

Canadien brand of hockey stick

Canadiens nickname for Montreal pro team, 1909-present

Canadiens sont là! "Canadiens are there," a common slogan to promote the team on the road in the 1920s and used sporadically even in modern times

Canadiens Sports Magazine Montreal Canadiens' game-night program in 1940s and '50s

candidate newly discovered player who has a chance of making a team ("he is a candidate to play right wing with the big club this season")

cane material used in the production of early shin pads because of its strength and durability

'Canes alternative nickname of Carolina Hurricanes

canned fired

cannon hard shot

cannon

cannonading blast expression coined by Montreal Canadiens play-by-play announcer Danny Gallivan to describe a hard shot

canny clever

canter period

Canucks 1. nickname of Vancouver team in NHL, 1970-present, and minor-league teams in Vancouver, 1945-70 2. slang for Canadians, usu. in international competition

cap 1. short for captain 2. short for salary cap ("we'll never play under a cap") 3. ~ **a comeback** score a goal that gives a team a tie or lead after trailing by at least two goals 4. ~ **a performance by** add a final display of skill to an excellent night (in the case of a team or individual) 5. ~ **space** amount of money a team may spend on salaries before reaching the salary cap limit

capacity 1. full house 2. ~ **crowd** full house

Capital Center home arena of Washington Capitals, in Landover, Maryland, 1974-97 (known briefly as U.S. Airways Arena)

Capital Club (early 20th C.) name used for Ottawa Silver Seven

capitalize 1. convert a scoring chance into a goal 2. **fail to** ~ fail to score or take advantage of an opportune situation

Capitals nickname of Washington team in NHL, 1974-present

capable in the case of a referee: able or experienced

Caps alternative nickname for Washington Capitals

captain leader of a hockey team and the only man allowed, under rules, to confront on-ice officials over controversial calls

Captain Video nickname given to Roger Neilson while coaching Toronto in the late 1970s when he was at the forefront of using videotape to analyze team and player performance

capture 1. score a goal 2. win possession (esp. the puck or championship trophy) 3. sign a player "**car!**" warning road-hockey players give each other on the impending arrival of a vehicle through their makeshift arena

carbon copy same result or performance as seen in a previous game

carborundum stone small rectangle of stone used to sharpen skates

carbs short for carbohydrates; important part of a player's diet before a game

card short for trading card, depicting a player in uniform, sets of which are released each year and are collected, traded, and sold

card

card show exposition at which retailers and dealers buy and sell memorabilia and merchandise, primarily trading cards

careening 1. caroming, as a wayward puck 2. lurching motion of a player who has been knocked off-balance

career 1. time spent playing hockey 2. ~-**ending** short for *career-ending injury* ("that hit could have been career-ending right there") 3. ~-**ending injury** a serious injury that prevents a player from continuing his career 4. ~-**high** statistical feat by a

player that is his best to date 5. ~ **minor leaguer** player whose career is rooted in the minors and who can expect only a brief call-up to the NHL 6. ~-**threatening injury** serious injury that imperils a player's ability to play 7. ~ **year** excellent season, a statistical blip rather than a true indication of future greatness

careless 1. action taken without thought 2. ~ **pass** errant pass that results in a turnover or excellent scoring chance by the opponent 3. ~ **use of stick** dangerous play with the stick, often resulting in injury and a penalty

Carena arena near Viking, Alberta, where the six Sutter brothers played youth hockey (so named because a car was raffled off to raise money for its construction in the 1950s)

Carlton Street Cashbox nickname for Maple Leaf Gardens, coined in the 1970s by sportswriter Dick Beddoes because, under Harold Ballard, the Leafs were profitable despite inconsistent on-ice performances

Carlton the Bear Toronto Maple Leafs mascot

carom 1. ricochet (of a shot) off the boards 2. ~ **play** (19th C.) bank pass off the boards from one man to another

carry 1. dominate play ("Vancouver has been carrying the play all night") 2. list a given number of players on a team's roster ("the Canucks are carrying 23 players") 3. ~ **an extra player** travel with more players than needed to play a game 4. ~ **into the boards** direct an opponent, usu. puck carrier, into the boards and out of harm's way 5. ~ **the puck** skate with the puck 6. ~ **one's stick high** skate with stick raised above shoulders 7. ⁓ **the team** be the player whose success is essential to the team's ("Brodeur has carried the team all year long")

cartilage smooth tissue that covers bones and prevents any two bones from rubbing together directly

carve deliver a vicious high stick ("he carved him right above the eye")

cash 1. method of transferring a player from one team to another ("they sold him to Quebec for cash") 2. ⁓ **customers** fans 3. ⁓ **in** score, usu. on the power play

cast adrift release a player outright

castoff former player of a team

casual describes a player who has what seems to be a sure goal but who takes the opportunity too lightly and misses ("Rooth was a little too casual on the play")

casualty injured player

cat ball, made of wood or cork, used in early bandy

cat-like reflexes attribute of a skilful goalie, usu. featuring quick legs or a quick glove

CAT scan computerized axial tomography; computer-assisted image of an injured body part

catch 1. grab puck, usu. by a goalie with glove 2. meet player in race to puck or race to net ("he caught up with his man") 3. hit corner of net with a shot, scoring a goal ("he caught the far side with that shot") 4. of a referee: notice an infraction ("Smith caught Leger hooking Davidson near centre ice") 5. ⁓ **napping** make a deft move that catches a goalie or defender off-guard 6. ⁓ **on a line change** of a team: make quick moves to create an advantageous situation while the opponent is changing players during play 7. ⁓ **player in**

scoring race earn a number of goals and assists to tie or surpass a leading scorer 8. ⁓ **team in standings** win a number of games in succession to earn enough points to tie or surpass another team, usu. in a playoff race

catch

catcher goalie's glove

catching glove var. of *catcher*

catching hand hand on which the goalie wears his catcher

cause fits frustrate an opponent by applying consistent offensive pressure ("the Johnson line has been causing fits for Caron in goal")

cause trouble 1. look to start a fight 2. of a puck carrier: cause particular concern for a goalie because of his moves or shot

cause trouble

cavort 1. play with (i.e., a successful line) 2. skate

cellar 1. last place in the standings 2. ~ **dweller** team that sits in last place in the standings

cement hands possess little scoring ability or touch around the goal

cement head player whose prime function is to fight

Center Ice New Jersey Devils' game-night program

Center Ice brand name on NHL players' practice sweaters when they were manufactured by CCM/Koho

Central Collegiate Hockey Association twelve-team conference in Division I of NCAA

Central Division division of the NHL, created in 1993; one of two divisions in the Western Conference, 1993-98, and one of three in the Western Conference, 1998-present

Central Hockey League name of a series of U.S.-based minor leagues (1931-35, 1968-84, 1992-present) with teams primarily located in Midwest and Midsouth

Central Professional Hockey League minor league (1963-68) renamed the *Central Hockey League*

Central Registry NHL's repository of data regarding player contracts, transactions, draft eligibility, and other operations

Central Scouting service provided by NHL to its teams which offers detailed reports on all draft-eligible players worldwide

centre 1. middle forward, and the player who traditionally takes face-offs 2. move the puck into the slot (area in front of the net—"he centres it to Albright, who lets go a terrific shot") 3. ~ **of attention** star player who is generally shadowed in an

effort to prevent him from scoring or dominating a game 4. ~ **ice** area in the middle of the rink between the bluelines 5. ~-**ice area** more generally, area between the bluelines 6. ~ **ice circle** faceoff area in the middle of rink where the puck is dropped to start all periods and to start play after a goal or an incorrect icing call 7. ~-**ice faceoff** faceoff held at the middle of the rink 8. ~-**ice faceoff spot** small dot at the centre of the faceoff circle at centre ice 9. ~ **line** red line that divides the rink into two equal halves 10. ~ **red line** var. of *centre line*

Centre Bell home arena of Montreal Canadiens

Centre Molson former name of Montreal Canadiens' home arena (renamed Centre Bell)

centring pass pass made from the side of the ice towards the goal to create a scoring chance

ceremonial faceoff unofficial puck drop conducted at centre ice between two team captains, prior to a game; the puck is dropped by a special guest or dignitary

ceremony any formal on-ice presentation staged before, during, or after a game

certain goal shot that should have gone into the net but, for whatever incredible reason (bad miss, great save), does not

Ceska Pojistovna Cup annual tournament (1998-present) staged in the Czech Republic and featuring Europe's top national teams (known as Pragobanka Cup, 1994-97)

C-form (archaic) standard contract used into the 1960s, signed by a player who had reached his 16th birthday, guaranteeing his rights to that team for as long as he played (and usu. calling for a signing bonus of $100)

chain 1. organization ("he's playing in the Winnipeg chain") 2. ~ **system** a team's developmental system, from the NHL team to the minors to junior, all the way down to regional club teams

chairman (usu. international) person who presides over a committee established within the IIHF

Championship model of Hilborn hockey stick made by Salyerds of Preston, Ontario

champion team that wins a tournament or league playoff

championship 1. tournament contested by the best teams in a league (or between several countries) to determine an overall winner 2. prize given to top team after a year's play or at the end of a tournament 3. ~ **form** describes a team playing as well as it can or in a manner that indicates it is capable of winning a league or tournament title

chalk up record, usu. a victory or a shutout

challenge 1. issue a request to play the reigning champion for the Stanley Cup (from 1893 to early 1910s, when league systems and playoffs replaced challenges) 2. ~ **the man** attack the puck carrier to force a turnover or stymie a rush 3. ~ **the shooter** of a goalie: to come out of the net to cut down a shooter's angle and, therefore, reduce the likelihood of a goal

Challenge Cup 1. the official and first name of what quickly became known as the Stanley Cup; so called because any champion team in Canada could ask to play the defending champions to claim the Cup 2. best-of-three series between NHL All-Stars and

Team USSR in February 1979 to replace NHL All-Star game

Challenge trophy var. of *Stanley Cup*

challengers team that requested the right to play the holders of the Stanley Cup

champs short for champions

chance scoring opportunity

change 1. amend roster 2. ~ **direction** deflect puck to alter its presumed course 3. ~ **ends** at a prescribed interval, defend a different end of the ice; teams change ends after each period; in international hockey (until the early 1970s), teams also changed at 10:00 of the third period 4. ~ **in personnel** trade or other move made to a team's lineup by a general manager 5. ~ **lines** substitute one trio of forwards for another 6. ~ **of heart** reversal of a decision, usu. by a player to sign with a team 7. ~ **of pace** alteration of course that runs contrary to the way a team has been run, during a season or within a game 8. ~ **of players** line change 9. ~ **of scenery** move from one team to another 10. ~ **on the fly** a method of substituting players while play proceeds 11. ~ **on the go** var. of *change on the fly*

change lines

Channel One Cup successor (in name) to the *Rosno Cup* (formerly the *Izvestia tournament*), 2005-present

chaps (archaic) players ("the chaps are in fighting trim for the game tonight")

chapter (archaic, usu. western Canadian) period of play

character player player who exhibits some skill but also determination, physical abilities, and an unbending will to win

charge 1. skate hard at a player with the intention of injuring him, usu. subject to a two-minute, and sometimes five-minute, penalty 2. young player taken under the wing of a coach or team 3. late surge or rally in a game or season

charged penalized

charges team or players

charging two-minute penalty for hitting a player after taking at least two strides without gliding before contact

charity pejorative for bad play resulting in good chance for opposition ("that pass was an act of charity")

charley horse injury to quadriceps muscle

Charlie Conacher Team Trophy award (inaugurated in the late 1960s and presented only for a few years) to the winner of the season series between Toronto and Montreal

Charlottetown Islanders Allan Cup champions in 1991

Charlton Standard reference book that aids in determining value and quality of hockey cards

chart 1. method of scouting and tracking a player's development or a team's tendencies over a period of time 2. **depth** ~ list of a team's players, usu. broken down by position, ranked in order of importance ("he's ranked seventh among defencemen on the team's depth chart")

charter special plane at team's disposal to ensure smooth and convenient travel any time of day

chase 1. skate hard in pursuit of an opponent or puck 2. call a penalty ("the referee chased Fontinato for a violent hit on Ezinicki") 3. ~ **after a man** skate hard to catch up to an opponent 4. ~ **a jinx** defeat an opponent for the first time in a long time 5. ~ **a loose puck** compete with an opponent to get to a free puck first 6. ~ **the puck** skate hard to get the puck

chase

Chatham Maroons Allan Cup champions in 1960

chattel 1. young prospect 2. property

cheap 1. ~ **call** any inconsequential infraction of the rules which is whistled down by the referee 2. ~ **penalty** relatively unimportant infraction punished by the referee ("that was a cheap penalty—he didn't need to call that.") 3. ~ **shot** dirty hit 4. ~**-shot artist** player notorious for dirty hits

cheat gain advantage, usu. by a player on a faceoff or by a goalie who uses oversize equipment

cheating 1. small infraction (i.e., on a faceoff) 2. any illegal tactic

cheer(s) roars from the crowd

check 1. hit an opponent, eliminate him from play, or strip him of the puck 2. opponent who should be marked ("he's your check out there tonight") 3. **~ from behind** hit a player in the back (i.e., while he is not looking), generally along the boards, the most dangerous kind of hit in hockey and punishable by game misconduct if serious enough

checker 1. any player who checks an opponent 2. a player whose greatest asset is his defensive ability ("he may be the best checker in the league these days")

Checkerdome alternative name of St. Louis Arena when Ralston-Purina owned the Blues, 1977-83

checking 1. overall physical play in a game ("the checking has been tight all night long") 2. **~ back** (archaic) backchecking 3. **~ game** style of play that relies on defence ("the Flames play a checking game") 4. **~ line** three-man forward unit whose primary task is to cover the other team's best players, focusing on preventing goals rather than scoring them ("coach Quinn is going to send his checking line out every time Lemieux's line is out there") 5. **~ to the head** in international hockey, a foul punishable by a two-minute minor plus automatic ten-minute misconduct

cheese cutters (archaic) children's double-bladed skates

chemistry 1. intangible ability of players to play particularly well with each other when they might not play as well with different linemates 2. **team ~** the gelling of a team into a cohesive unit of 20 players

cherry-picker usu. in shinny, any player who stands near the opposition blueline waiting for a breakaway pass and refuses to play defensively

chest pads (archaic) piece of goalie

equipment that protects the the body from the neck to t

chest protector successor to the ... pad, worn by a goalie to cover the top front portion of his body

Chicago Blackhawks NHL member team since 1926

Chicago Coliseum home arena of the Chicago Blackhawks, 1926-29, 1932

Chicago Hawks short for Chicago Blackhawks

Chicago Stadium home arena of the Chicago Blackhawks, 1929-94

Chicago Stadium Review Chicago Black Hawks' game-night program

Chicago Stand-Bys Black Hawks fan club during the 1940s

Chicagos journalistic slang for Chicago Blackhawks

chicken player who is afraid of physical contact

Chiclets slang for teeth ("I lost two Chiclets in the last game")

Chiclets

chief rival most notable opponent

chief scout most important member of a team's scouting department

Chihawks alternative nickname for Chicago Blackhawks

China IIHF member nation since 1963

Chinese Taipei IIHF member nation since 1987

chin strap piece of equipment that fastens the helmet closely to the head to ensure it remains in place during play

chin strap

chip 1. ~ **in** contribute 2. ~ **it in** score 3. ~ **it off the glass** use the Plexiglas, in a defensive manoeuvre, to bank the puck outside one's own blueline without incurring an icing call 4. ~ **it out** smack the puck beyond one's own blueline in whatever manner is possible; a defensive manoeuvre 5. ~ **it over** move the puck beyond the opposition blueline by whatever means possible 6. ~ **on one's shoulder** play in a wild, physical fashion as a result of some external motivation ("he's been playing with a chip on his shoulder ever since that hit in the first period") 7. ~ **shot** golf-like shot that involves raising the puck quickly, whether to get the puck into the opponent's end of the ice or to score from near the goal

chippy of play: dirty or illegal, usu. involving an excess of hooking, slashing, and other stick-related offences that slow a game down and prevent skill from prevailing

chirp complain, usu. to referees

Chocolatetown nickname for Hershey, Pennsylvania, home of AHL's Hershey Bears

choice of end prerogative enjoyed by home team when hockey was played outdoors and the direction of the sun and quality of ice were significant factors

Chomedy Laval Warriors Allan Cup champions in 1990

chop 1. hack at the puck 2. slash an opponent 3. ~ **down** bring down an opponent with violent use of the stick

choppy describes game that lacks flow or exhibition of skill

chops teeth

chores goaltending duties ("Puputti has the chores in goal tonight")

Christian foremost hockey stick manufacturer in the United States

chronic injury injury that recurs throughout a player's career

chukker polo term for period, often used by journalists from the 19th century to 1960s

chunk period of time

church hockey system of youth hockey which operated primarily in the 1920s and '30s

cinch sure thing

Cinderella team team that enjoys unexpected success—notably, the Chicago Blackhawks of 1937-38, which won a Stanley Cup despite a losing record in the regular season

circle 1. faceoff dot inside the two bluelines 2. move in a rounding motion, either a player or as a team

circuit league

citadel goal net ("Chabot is minding the citadel with great effectiveness tonight")

Civic Arena former name of the Pittsburgh Penguins' home arena (now known as Mellon Arena)

claim 1. (archaic) score a goal 2. ~ **off waivers** acquire a player whom another team has offered in exchange only for a sum of money

clamour excitement

clamp down referee a game while paying strict attention to the rules

clamp-on type of skate blade originated in Canada circa 1888

clan team (e.g., "the Gorman clan are in town tonight," referring to the Chicago Blackhawks, the team Tommy Gorman coached)

Clancy, King, Memorial Trophy see *King Clancy Memorial Trophy*

clang sound of a shot that rings off the post

clap 1. applaud 2. impose a fine

Clarence Campbell Conference one of two conferences in NHL, 1974-93, the other being the Prince of Wales Conference

Clarence S. Campbell Bowl trophy presented, from 1967-74, to the regular-season champion of the NHL's West Division; from 1974-81, to the regular-season champion of the Clarence Campbell Conference; from 1981-93, to the playoff champion of the Campbell Conference; and, since 1993, to the playoff champion of the Western Conference

claret blood ("he's left a fair bit of claret on the ice as he heads to the medical room")

Clarks brand of stick made in Breslau, Ontario, its most notable models being Junior, Northern, and Professional

Clarkson Cup trophy for women's hockey in Canada donated by Adrienne Clarkson in 2006 during her time as governor-general

clash 1. any game, esp. between close rivals ("Toronto and Montreal clash tonight at the Air Canada Centre") 2.

fight 3. heavy hit 4. off-ice disagreement between teammates, or player and coach, or any members of a team

class 1. division of hockey, usu. used in lower levels ("this is not the same class of hockey as you'll find in the NHL") 2. player who carries himself with dignity on and off ice 3. ~ **of hockey** calibre of play

clavicle collarbone

clean 1. resurface ice prior to a game or period 2. ~ **check** forceful but legal hit 3. ~ **draw** a. faceoff in which the puck is dropped fairly b. faceoff in which one player wins the draw uncontested 4. ~ **hit** var. of *clean check* 5. ~ **ice** resurfaced ice 6. ~ **play** feature of a game in which few, if any, penalties are called

clean draw

clear 1. ~ **away** move a man or puck out of harm's way 2. ~ **break** breakaway or rush where no opponent stands between the puck carrier and the goalie 3. ~ **breakaway** var. of *clear break* 4. ~-**cut breakaway** var. of *clear break* 5. **in the** ~ a. open, unmarked, and in good position to receive a pass for a good scoring chance b. in alone on the goalie, on a breakaway 6. ~ **out** move the puck to the centre-ice area 7. ~ **a player from in front of the net** use great force to remove an opponent from the area directly in front of the goalie (slot), to prevent the goalie from being screened or the opponent from being in a position to deflect a shot or get a rebound 8. ~ **the puck** shoot puck out of the defensive end and over the blueline to stem offensive pressure 9. ~ **the rubber** var. of *clear the puck* 10. ~ **the slot** use physical force to get an opponent out of the goalie's line of vision 11. ~ **the zone** a. get the puck out of the defensive zone b. vacate the offensive end (necessary if the defensive team has succeeded in clearing the puck across the blueline, but it has been shot back in; all attackers must leave the offensive end to avoid an offside call—see *tag-up rule*)

clearing 1. in the case of a goalie: shooting the puck out of his own end 2. ~ **attempt** any effort to get the puck away from the goal 3. ~ **pass** any movement of the puck from one man to another which eliminates the possibility of a scoring chance by the opposition

Cleveland Barons 1. NHL member team, 1976-78 (formerly California Golden Seals) 2. AHL member team, 1940-72 and 2001-06 3. IAHL member team, 1937-40

clever 1. smart or effective (of a play or player) 2. ~ **passing** intelligent or effective movement of the puck by a team or player 3. ~ **play** skilled play

click 1. work well together 2. score

climb 1. in the case of a team: move up in the standings 2. in the case of a player: move up in the scoring race

cling 1. hold on to a tenuous lead 2. grab an opponent to hold him up or prevent him from moving into a superior position

clinch 1. win game 2. win title or championship of any sort ("Montreal clinched first place" or "Anderson clinched the scoring title") 3. bear hug

clincher goal that secures victory

clinic 1. hockey camp where skills are taught 2. room near playing surface where players go to receive immediate treatment for an injury sustained during play, usu. a cut needing stitches 3. **put on a** ~ display remarkable set of skill repeatedly during a game

clip 1. knee an opponent 2. cut with a high stick 3. pace of a game 4. defeat ("Halifax clipped Brandon 4-2")

clipping football-style tackle, illegal in hockey, punishable by two-minute penalty

clock 1. short for scoreclock 2. hit extremely hard ("he absolutely clocked Jarvis crossing the blueline")

clock

clog jam the middle of the ice with defenders to prevent flow and bog down attack

close 1. ~ **call** near-miss on goal or narrow avoidance of an injury or collision 2. ~**-checking game** game dominated by defensive play 3. ~ **game** any game in which the score or play is nearly equal 4. ~ **in** near the goalie 5. ~ **quarters** near the goalie or in a group of players 6. ~ **range** near the goalie, usu. in reference to a shot or scoring chance

close the door 1. tend goal effectively 2. of a team: co-operate effectively to secure victory

closing the hand on the puck protecting the puck with the glove to prevent an opponent from gaining possession, punishable by two-minute penalty

club 1. hockey team 2. hit opponent viciously with stick 3. ~ **doctor** qualified physician who works for a team 4. ~ **president** director who oversees operation of a team and who in turn answers to the board of directors

Club de Hockey French name for Montreal Canadiens, as displayed in the CH of the team logo

Club de Hockey Canadien corporate name of the Montreal Canadiens

clutch 1. grab and hold up; prevent an opponent from skating freely 2. ~-and-grab style of hockey that is used by slow teams to defend against faster, more skilled teams 3. ~ **performer** player who excels in important games or at important times during a game

coach 1. leader of a team who stands behind the bench during games, directs practices, and develops a team strategy 2. to guide a team or player

Coach's Corner first-intermission segment on *Hockey Night in Canada*, featuring host Ron MacLean and former Boston Bruins coach Don Cherry

coach's decision 1. any order given by the coach, usu. used in newsworthy or controversial circumstances 2. any move made by a coach re: the game lineup, playing strategy, or anything else to do with on-ice management of the team

Coaching Association of Canada national body that accredits, instructs, and certifies all coaches in Canada

coaching reins the job of coaching ("Neilson is taking over the coaching reins of a team in last place")

coaching staff staff members who help the head coach run a team, usu. consisting of assistant coaches, video coach, and goaltending coach

coast 1. play to easy victory 2. ~ **game** (early 20th C.) a. game played by teams in the Pacific Coast Hockey Association b. style of hockey played in PCHA 3. ~ **rules** seven-man hockey (same as *Western rules*) as opposed to Eastern hockey which permitted only six players on ice 4. ~ **to coast** a. national broadcast b. end-to-end rush

coax out lure a defenceman out of position

cob slang for shutout ("we won the game six-cob")

cobwebs fuzzy-headedness; euphemism for a concussion, usu. resulting from a hard hit or collision

cobwebs

Cocktail League slang for ECHL—or, more generally, any league in which the game is not taken seriously

coccyx tail bone

code 1. rules of the game 2. unwritten rules of conduct (i.e., don't make a hot dog move when scoring into an empty net; don't shoot the puck into the opponent's empty net at the end of the pre-game warmup)

cog important part of a team

coincident 1. of penalties: assessed simultaneously to equal number of players on both teams, of equal duration, resulting in no odd-man advantage 2. ~ **major penalties** five-minute penalties or misconducts given simultaneously to an equal number of players on both teams 3. ~ **minor penalties** two-minute penalties given simultaneously to an equal number of players on both teams

coincidental majors var. of *coincident major penalties*

coincidental minors var. of *coincident minor penalties*

coincidental penalties var. of *coincident penalties*

cold attribute of air in most small arenas

ColHL abbreviation for *Colonial Hockey League*

collapse 1. defensive strategy or unintentional habit in which players skate back in towards their goalie 2. fall unconscious 3. blow a big lead (in a game or the standings)

collapsed lung medical problem that prevents lung from inflating properly

collar 1. (archaic) stop a man, usu. by holding him 2. padded upper rear part of the inside of a skate boot 3. penalize

collaring (19th C.) type of penalty now known as holding

collect 1. earn 2. record 3. ~ **oneself** regroup or recover from a bad hit or bad patch of play

collectible any item associated with the game that can be sold, traded, or auctioned to and by memorabilia collectors

collection of stars All-Star Game or other event in which many top players can be seen at the same time

collective bargaining agreement (CBA) contract between league and players specifying terms and conditions under which league may operate

College Hockey America conference in Division I of NCAA, with a five-team men's division and a five-team women's division

collide 1. run into, hit accidentally 2. play ("Calgary and Edmonton collide Saturday night")

collision any hard hit between two players in which at least one is unsuspecting of the harshness of the contact

Colonial Hockey League low minor league, 1991-97 (renamed United Hockey League)

Colorado Avalanche NHL member team since 1995 (formerly Quebec Nordiques)

Colorado Rockies NHL member team, 1976-82 (previously the Kansas City Scouts; later the New Jersey Devils)

colour commentator partner to play-by-play man who generally speaks during stoppages in play, explaining in greater detail the happenings on ice

coloured band feature found on the shaft of hockey sticks to identify various brands and models, usually using a combination of red, blue, black, and green stripes

Coloured Hockey League hockey league that flourished briefly in the Maritimes around 1900

colourful 1. flashy, skilled player 2. ~ **character** skilled player also known for outrageous clothing or comments over and above his playing abilities

Columbia brand of hockey stick

comb high-stick an opponent

combat 1. game action 2. fight 3. counter

combatants two or more fighters

combination 1. (archaic) forward line playing well as a unit ("they played well in combination"), as opposed to today, when three forwards "play as a line" 2. good passing 3. ~ **game** style of play in which the primary means of attack is good, crisp passing among the three forwards

combined movement 1. combination play, used in the early 20th century when team play started to take over from individual play

come 1. ~ **away** a. with the puck: emerge from among a group of players trying to gain possession b. emerge from a game ("the Marlies came away with a big win this afternoon") 2. ~ **back** a. backcheck b. return to action 3. ~ **back to haunt** of a play: having the potential to have dire consequences, not immediately but later in the game or season ("that goal could come back to haunt the Americans") 4. ~ **from behind** rally to tie or win a game 5. ~ **off the bench** a. play in the game b. join a fight 6. ~ **onto the ice** a. players, to start a game b. fan, coach, or anyone who doesn't rightly belong on the ice 7. ~ **out** of a goalie: leave the crease to cut down an angle, play the puck, go to the bench, or for any other reason 8. ~ **out of own end** switch from defence to offence, carrying the puck out of the defensive end 9. ~ **to blows** fight 10. ~ **to terms** reach agreement on a contract 11. ~ **up** a. skate toward the opposition goal b. rush the puck c. join the rush 12. ~ **up big** make a great play or save 13. ~ **up large** var. of *come up big* 14. ~ **up with the puck** gain possession of the puck after a multi-player scramble

comeback 1. overcoming of a deficit in a game to tie or win 2. resume playing after retiring or after missing a significant amount of time because of a serious injury

comer short for up-and-comer; prospect

coming and going alternating constantly between offence and defence

coming-out party tournament or series of games in which a player matures into a star, reaching new levels of skill and demonstrating previously unseen ability

commanding lead significant lead (i.e., three or more goals)

commemorative patch patch worn on players' sweaters to commemorate an important event or person to that team or league

commercial time-out designated stoppages in play during a game to allow for commercials

Commish short for NHL Commissioner Gary Bettman

commissioner person hired by the board of governors to oversee league operations

commit a foul perpetrate an infraction

committee any group of players that represents a larger group

Commonwealth of Independent States (CIS) name under which athletes from the newly independent nations of the former Soviet Union competed at the 1992 Olympics

Compaq Center former name (2001-02) of San Jose Sharks' home rink (renamed HP Pavillion)

compensation 1. word used by NHLPA to mean salary 2. **equal** ~ policy in the NHL in 1970s and '80s whereby a team that lost a player to another team via free agency received a player of equal value in return 3. **fair** ~ an equitable and agreed-upon exchange of players or cash

compensatory draft pick draft choice awarded to a team by the league to compensate for outstanding circumstances during a trade or other occurrence related to that team

complain make opinions known to the referee regarding an unpopular call

complain

complete 1. finalize a transaction 2. ~ **player** a player who can do everything well (play defence, score, check, skate, shoot hard, etc.) 3. ~ **scorer** player who can score under any circumstances 4. ~ **season** full schedule 5. ~ **stick** unbroken stick fit for play 6. ~ **the scoring** score game's final goal ("and Manley's goal into the empty net completes the scoring here tonight")

composite stick stick made of an aggregate of different materials, such as graphite and Kevlar

Conacher, Charlie, Team Trophy see *Charlie Conacher Team Trophy*

concession stands areas behind the seats where fans may purchase various comestibles during the game, esp. at intermission

concessions those foods sold at concession stands or by designated purveyors in the seating areas themselves

conclusion end of game

concussion head injury, graded I, II, or III based on the severity of the brain damage suffered

conditioning 1. training; also, the level of fitness resulting from that training 2. ~ **stint** period of time, usu. brief, during which a bona fide NHLer plays at a lower level after recuperating from an injury

conference 1. one of two or more large groupings of teams within a league, usu. geographically, which are subdivided into divisions 2. ~ **call** phone call with multiple participants, for the purpose of a player being made available for an interview by many people from around the world 2. ~ **champion** team that finishes first in a particular conference at the end of the regular season or playoffs 3. ~ **finals** playoff series between the top two teams in the conference to determine which will proceed to the league championship series

conflict game

Conn Smythe Sports Celebrity Dinner annual charity event held in Toronto to raise money for the Easter Seal

44

Society, which assists young people with physical disabilities (established 1952)

Conn Smythe Trophy trophy presented annually to the best player in the Stanley Cup playoffs

connect 1. score 2. play well together

conquest defeat

consistent of steadily high calibre (describes a player's or team's performance)

consolation game in an international tournament, game during the consolation round

consolation round in international play, round of games between teams that do not qualify for the medal round, usu. to determine which team(s) is demoted for play the following year

contact 1. marked by physical play ("hockey is a contact sport") 2. league in which body-checking is permitted ("is this league contact or non-contact?")

contain 1. hold a star player off the scoresheet or permit him to have only minimal impact on the outcome ("the key is for the Jets to contain Gretzky") 2. play a restrictive, defensive style, even at the expense of scoring

contender team with a real chance to win the championship

contest game

contestants fighters

Continental Airlines Arena name (since 1996) of home arena of the New Jersey Devils (formerly known as Brendan Byrne Arena)

Continental Cup annual tournament featuring club champions from all European leagues (one per country) that do not qualify for the more prestigious European Champions Cup

contract 1. binding agreement between team and player for a fixed number of years at a particular salary 2. ~ **dispute** any disagreement between player and team regarding salary, length of contract, bonuses, etc., which prevents or threatens to prevent the player from playing for that team 3. ~ **hassle** var. of *contract dispute* 4. ~ **extension** agreement between player and team to lengthen the term of a player's current contract 5. ~ **negotiations** discussions between a team and, usu., a player's agent or representative with the goal of agreeing to terms on a contract

control 1. dictate the pace of a game ("the Senators are in control of this game") 2. **complete** ~ emphatic var. of *control* to describe a team's almost certain victory ("the Senators are in complete control of this game") 3. ~ **one's emotions** play energetic hockey while avoiding taking retaliatory or silly penalties 4. ~ **one's own destiny** of a team: be in a position where victory will allow it to move closer to its goals while defeat will leave its destiny at the mercy of the performance of other teams 5. ~ **the play** maintain puck possession for long periods and play with superior effort to the opponent 6. ~ **the puck** maintain possession of the puck frequently or for long stretches

controlled emotion perform with great intensity and maximum efficiency without taking retaliatory or silly penalties

contusion injury caused by a blow from a dull object

convert 1. score 2. change from playing as a forward to playing as a defenceman, or vice versa ("Clark converted from defence to forward when he moved up to the NHL") 3. ~ **a pass** successfully make a pass

convincing argument calibre of play at a tryout or at training camp which exceeds the coach's expectations and suggests the possibility of the player making the team ("based on his play since camp opened, Smith is making a convincing argument that he belongs in the league")

cook try to make a trade ("he's got something cooking with Ottawa")

cookie shelf top of the net where the flashy players shoot the puck ("he blasted it cookie shelf and the goalie didn't have a chance")

cookie shelf

cool 1. calm under pressure 2. ⁓ **his heels** go to the penalty box ("Darwin will cool his heels for two minutes after tripping Haakinen") 3. ⁓ **off** a. recompose oneself, usu. by sitting on the bench b. serve a penalty ("and he'll have two minutes to cool off after hauling down his man on the play")

Cool Shots television program produced by the NHLPA to profile and promote NHL players and their lives off ice

cooler 1. penalty box 2. ⁓ **heads** those which prevail in tough situations (i.e., through calm, rational actions)

Cooper Canadian maker of hockey equipment

Cooperall style of long hockey pants introduced in early 1980s which provided protection for the entire lower body; widely used in junior hockey but adapted only by Hartford and Philadelphia in NHL

co-ordination ability to move hands, eyes, and all body parts in proper sequence at great speed

cop 1. goon 2. referee

copy ticket, used primarily during Original Six days ("he's hoping to find a copy for tonight's sold-out game")

Cornwall Royals Memorial Cup champions in 1972, 1980, and 1981

cord cottage goal net

cords net

Core States Center former name of Philadelphia Flyers' home arena, 1996-1998 (renamed First Union Center)

Corel Centre name of Ottawa Senators' home arena, 1996-2006 (renamed Scotiabank Place)

cork hit someone hard

corker 1. hard hit 2. very exciting or entertaining player ("he's a real corker when he has the puck")

corking first-rate

corkscrew rush end-to-end rush with plenty of dekes and feints, not in a straight line

corner check an opponent in such a way that he has nowhere to skate with the puck and no way to pass it to a teammate

Corner Brook Royals Allan Cup champions in 1986

corner man player who is particularly adept at going into the corners to get the puck and come away with it

corners curved parts of the rink where the end boards and side boards join

corporate box private box which offers amenities such as bar service, quality food, and excellent sightlines of the ice

corral 1. hold, rein in, or check a man 2. gain control of a loose puck

Cortina d'Ampezzo Italian city which hosted the 1956 Olympic Winter Games

cortisone anti-inflammatory medication, usu. injected

cost certainty abilities of teams to predict relative revenues and expenditures from season to season

costly error bad mistake resulting in a penalty, good scoring opportunity, or, usu. a goal by the opposition

costly penalty penalty that allows the opponent to score on a power play or which negates great pressure and control by the team being penalized

cough up give up, usu. puck

Council group of elected officials within the IIHF that decides all matters pertaining to an international hockey event—rules of play, disciplinary matters, etc.

count 1. to score ("Vancouver counted twice in that third period") 2. score of game ("Toronto wins by a 3-2 count")

counter 1. (archaic) a goal 2. offset

cover 1. guard or shadow a player 2. back up a teammate ("Smith covered for Johnson, who was caught flat-

cover

footed on the play") 3. ~ **a lot of the net** of a goalie: play well positionally or wear an abundance of equipment 4. ~**-point** (archaic) position now known as defence 5. ~ **up** freeze puck (usu. done by goalie)

covered rink any indoor arena; term used primarily until 1930s, when many games were still played outdoors

coveted 1. much-sought-after player 2. epithet often used to describe the Stanley Cup

cowbell signaling device used in early days of the game (before whistles)

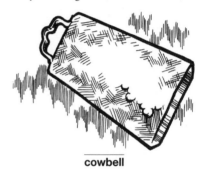

cowbell

cowling white plastic protector for the toes of goalie skates

Cow Palace San Francisco arena, home of San Jose Sharks, 1991-93

cowpie slang for puck, originating in rural areas where cow manure often substituted for a puck when kids played outdoors

Coyotes nickname of Phoenix's team in NHL

crack 1. excellent, top-flight 2. slash 3. ~ **the armour** score; penetrate deep into the opponent's end 4. ~ **the defence** get through the defence on a rush 5. ~ **down** be extra vigilant, usu. in reference to referees paying closer attention to obstruction 6. ~ **in the ice** any area of the ice which displays fissures which can either be dangerous or depreciate the quality of the playing surface 7. ~ **the lineup** make the team

cradle 1. control the puck 2. ~ **hockey** kid's hockey

Cranbrook Royals Allan Cup champions in 1982

crash 1. smack hard into 2. **~-and-bang** style of play defined by heavy forechecking, taking the man, and playing physical hockey to create turnovers and scoring chances 3. ~ **ice** come out with determination 4. ~ **the net** skate hard to the goal, colliding with the goalie—or the net, knocking it off its moorings

crazy bounce an odd bounce of the puck that gives the puck carrier or player receiving a pass a tougher time of handling it than expected

cream hit hard

Creamery Town nickname for Renfrew, Ontario

crease 1. area around the goal net designated for the goalie alone to move in 2. ~ **rule** any rule over the years which keeps the goalie protected in his crease and punishes opposing players who violate this area; punishments range from a stoppage of play, to a penalty (if the player makes illegal contact with a goalie), to the nullification of a goal if the referee rules a goalie was interfered with in his crease while the puck entered the net

create 1. ~ **havoc** disrupt the goalie's concentration, usu. by crowding the slot and blocking goalie's vision 2. ~ **scoring chances** efforts made by one team to generate offence ("they've created most of their scoring chances off the rush") 3. ~ **traffic** var. of *create havoc*

creative quality of playmaker who makes exceptional passes

credit determine which player scored and assisted on a goal, esp. if puck

was tipped into the net or play was unclear ("when we see the goal on the replay, it looks like Anderson will get credit for the goal")

crest 1. emblem or logo worn on the front of team sweater 2. **~ing** act of sewing a crest or logo onto a sweater

crew 1. team 2. any group, usu. ice crew in charge of maintaining the ice

crewcuts (archaic) young players, notably 1956-57 Toronto Maple Leafs under coach Howie Meeker

criminal charges accusations of a criminal offence, legal charges brought against a player for reprehensible on-ice conduct that legal authorities deem punishable as a civic, not sporting, matter

cringer cowardly player who won't go into the corners

cripple injure a player badly

crippled team that is badly undermanned or suffering from maladies like the flu ("they have been crippled by injuries so far this season")

crisp of a pass: sharp, accurate

criss-cross pattern of skating whereby the player on the left wing ends up on the right and vice versa

critics fans of or media covering a particular team

Croatia IIHF member nation since 1992

crook lower part of stick where shaft meets blade

crop 1. group of new players, usu. those selected in Entry Draft ("there is a great crop of 18-year-olds at this year's draft") 2. ~ **up** arise unexpectedly (e.g., a bad habit)

crossbar top of the goal net which connects one post to the other

cross 1. **~-crease pass** pass that goes through the goal crease 2. **~-ice pass** pass that goes from one side of the ice to the other 3. ~ **sticks** a. play ("these two teams cross sticks again next week") b. engage in violent behaviour using sticks   4. ~ **the line** a. commit a foul beyond what is accepted as ordinary rough play b. of the puck: enter the net (i.e., cross the goal line) 5. ~-**training** training for hockey by developing skills in other sports such as golf, running, basketball, etc.

cross-check illegal hit with the stick while holding it in both hands

cross-over 1. var. of *criss-cross* 2. the act of taking one skate and stepping over the other to generate speed and motion from a standing position, often in a sideways motion 3. ~ **step** any step with the skate that helps to execute a cross-over stride

crouch 1. pant leg 2. stance in which the goaltender readies himself, esp. when there is a flurry of activity around the crease

crouch

crow 1. boast about a win, brag 2. **eat ~** admit to being wrong, usu. reluctantly ("he guaranteed his team

would win tonight, but we made him eat crow")

crowd 1. fans in attendance 2. group of players in a small area on ice 3. check closely ("Anderson has crowded Lemieux all night") 4. ~ **the crease** two or more players on the attacking team go to the net to look for a rebound or distract the goalie 5. ~ **gathers** group of players push and shove after a whistle 6. ~ **in the penalty box** one or both teams have at least four players in the penalty box ("there's quite a crowd in the penalty box after that skirmish") 7. ~-**pleaser** player who is admired by fans for his ability and his personality 8. ~**ed standings** logjam in the standings, usu. at the top

Crown brand of hockey stick, its most notable model being The King

crown jewels private parts

Crumb Bum Award award given by the New York Rangers to the player whose service to youngsters is particularly admirable

crunching check hard hit

crush 1. check vigorously along the boards 2. demoralize opponent with a goal

crushing blow goal that more or less seals defeat for a team, usu. in the third period

cryotherapy use of cold to treat injuries

crystal ball metaphoric object used to predict a team's future performance

Cuban heels style of early skates

cudgel (archaic) hockey stick

cue stick

cup short for protective cup

Cup 1. (usu. capitalized) short for Stanley Cup 2. ~ **celebrations** victory party in the dressing room after a team wins the Stanley Cup 3. ~ **holders** current Stanley Cup champions 4. ~ **parade** civic reception to honour the hometown team's Stanley Cup victory 5. **~-clinching goal** game-winning goal in the deciding game of the Stanley Cup finals 6. **~-deciding goal** var. of *Cup-clinching goal* 7. **~-winning goal** var. of *Cup-clinching goal*

cup of coffee brief appearance (usu. with an NHL or higher-level team)

Cup of the Low Countries annual tournament since 1995, now with 12 participating teams, initially from Belgium and Holland

curfew time by which players on road trips must be in bed

curl turn

Curse of Muldoon purported hex put on the Chicago Blackhawks in 1927 after team owner Major Frederic McLaughlin fired coach Pete Muldoon despite a good season, prompting the coach to vow that the team would never finish in first place

curtain raiser first game of the season or first home game of the season

Curtis curve warp in the shaft of a specially made goalie stick to make most of it lie flat on the ice (illegal in pro leagues)

curvature the bend in the blade of a stick

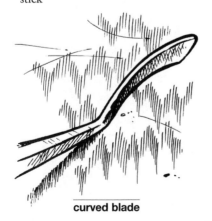

curved blade

curve short for *curvature*

curved 1. ~ **blade** stick blade with a bend in it, as opposed to a straight blade 2. ~ **shot** method of shooting the puck so that there is warp in its movement, first practised by Harry Cameron and Gordon Roberts 3. ~ **stick** stick with a curved blade

cushion comfortable lead, in a game in the standings, or, in the case of a player, the scoring race ("the Finns have a three-goal cushion after that goal")

custodian goaltender

custody possession of the Stanley Cup

Custom Pro model of hockey stick made by Monarch Hockey Stick Company of New Hamburg, Ontario

customers fans

cut

cut 1. gash or wound, usually requiring stitches 2. turn sharply while skating 3. release a player from a team 4. ~ **across the middle** make a sudden turn from the wing to the centre of the ice, usu. on a rush crossing the blueline 5. ~ **down** chop violently with stick 6. ~ **down the angle** of a goalie: move out of the crease to reduce a puck carrier's view of the net

7. ~ **in on goal** make a sharp turn from the wing to the slot 8. ~ **loose** release (a player) 9. ~ **off a pass** intercept a pass by anticipating the play 10. ~ **up the ice** a. make ice full of holes and gashes after, for instance, an intense practice b. move towards opposition goal

Cuts Heal slogan reflective of tough, Canadian hockey mentality

cute prone to great displays of skill with the puck, but with few results ("he's being too cute with the puck")

cycle 1. pass the puck repeatedly along the boards in the corners and behind the net in the offensive end 2. ~ **down low** var. of *cycle*, specifically in the offensive end ("down low")

Cyclone Taylor Trophy Vancouver Canucks team MVP award named after the great star of the early days of the game who played most of his career in British Columbia

Czechoslovakia IIHF member nation until 1993, when the country split into the Czech Republic and Slovakia

Czech Republic IIHF member nation since 1993 (previously part of Czechoslovakia)

Dd

d 1. short for defence (pronounced "dee": "our d. came up big for us tonight") 2. **d.-to-d. pass** pass made by one defenceman to his playing partner 3. **~-man** short for defenceman

D abbreviation for defence

DEN official IIHF abbreviation for Denmark

DL disabled list

DNP abbreviation for "did not play"

DNQ abbreviation for "did not qualify" (for the playoffs)

Dallas Stars NHL member team since 1993 (previously known as Minnesota North Stars)

Dallas Stars Tonight Dallas Stars' game-night program

damaged 1. hurt, injured 2. **~ goods** injured player; also, one who frequently misses games after returning from injury, and whose performance is a shadow of what it once was

Damkronor (Swedish) name of Sweden's women's national hockey team

dance 1. fight 2. skate beautifully 3. **~ in on goal** deke skilfully towards the goal 4. **the big ~** slang for the NHL

Dandurand's Dandies alternative nickname for the Montreal Canadiens during the years when Leo Dandurand managed the team (1921-35)

dandy 1. great player 2. **~ chance** great

scoring opportunity 3. **~ opportunity** var. of ***dandy chance***

dangerous 1. constant scoring threat 2. **~ equipment** illegal equipment 3. **~ pass** pass that has a high probability of being intercepted, creating a good scoring chance for the opponent 4. **~ play** play in which a scoring opportunity by the opponent might result, or one in which serious injury might occur

dangerously close 1. describes a puck which almost goes into the net 2. of a player: narrowly avoiding a serious injury

dangle 1. stickhandle with great skill 2. loiter near the opponent's blueline when the puck is in the defensive zone (i.e., goal suck)

dark opposite of white, sweater style used in pickup hockey to distinguish teams

dash rush

dasher 1. player who rushes the puck up ice 2. base of the boards around the entire rink, usu. yellow

dashing 1. good-looking (player) 2. exciting (player)

date game ("Detroit has a date with the Leafs on Saturday night")

Dawson City Yukon-based challengers for the Stanley Cup in January 1905

day 1. **~ off** day when the team neither plays nor practises 2. **~-to-day** player who is injured, but not seriously, and who may or may not be available to play upcoming games

Daymen alternative nickname for Toronto Maple Leafs in the days of coach Happy Day

dazed stunned, as a result of being hit hard

dazzling exciting, skilful

dead-end kids players with little talent who gain little respect (i.e., underdogs)

deadline date before something must be completed, usu. in reference to trading players

deadlock 1. a tie game 2. to tie a game

deadly shot hard, dangerous shot

deadly shot

dead-on very accurate, usu. of a shot or prediction

dead-puck era years in the NHL at the end of 20th century and beginning of 21st century marked by stifling defence, few scoring chances, and fewer goals (replaced by the *New NHL* in 2005)

deal 1. trade 2. negotiate 3. contract

debatable 1. controversial (as a call by an official) 2. of suspect quality (as a trade)

debris refuse thrown onto the ice by angry fans, usu. popcorn boxes, plastic cups, etc., from concession stands

debut initial appearance

decided by margin of victory

deciding goal game-winning goal

decisive victory victory that is convincing either because of lopsided play or lopsided score

deck hit hard, usu. with a punch

decoy player who appears to be wide open for a scoring chance but whom the puck carrier ignores in favour of a teammate with an even better chance of scoring

deep 1. part of the rink farthest from a team's own goal ("get the puck deep") 2. of a team: rich with talented players at all positions

deer hair material used in the making of early shin pads

defaulted game game in which one team forfeits, usu. because of extreme controversy or invocation of rule for the safety of players or fans

defeat 1. a loss 2. to win

defeated down and out

defence 1. team's strategy vis-à-vis preventing the other team from scoring ("their defence has had an excellent game") 2. pair of defencemen ("Smith and Williams are on defence for this power play") 3. a team's play inside its own blueline 4. ~ **pairing** two defencemen who usu. play together 5. ~ **partner** player with whom a defenceman regularly plays 6. ~ **player** (archaic) defenceman 7. **team** ~ team's play inside its own blueline

Defence model of stick produced by Doolittles of St. Marys, Ontario

defenceman player who plays behind the forwards and whose primary concern is preventing goals

defenceman

defender var. of *defenceman*

defending champions usu. Stanley Cup champions from previous year

defending the flags defending the goal (reference to early days when goal posts had flags at the top to identify them)

defending zone area inside team's blueline

defensive 1. ~ **defenceman** defenceman who possesses limited offensive ability (i.e., puck carrying, smooth skating) but who is very effective in his own zone (i.e., taking the man, hitting) 2. ~ **forward** forward who excels at backchecking and checking the opposition forwards 3. ~ **lapse** breakdown inside the defensive end 4. ~ **liability** player whose checking skills inside his own blueline are lacking 5. ~ **shell** conservative style of play, usu. adopted when a team has a lead late in the game 6. ~ **specialist** forward whose particular skill is to prevent goals rather than score them 7. ~ **zone** area inside blueline 8. ~-**zone breakdown** mistakes inside the blueline that lead to scoring chances for the opposition 9. ~-**zone coverage** defensive play by all five skaters inside their blueline to prevent goals

deficit 1. number of goals by which a team is trailing (e.g., a three-goal deficit) 2. shortfall in team budget

deflect redirect a shot, usu. skilfully, as a scoring tactic near opponent's net

deflection shot whose direction is changed by skilful use of stick

deflector (archaic) blocker

deft skilful ("Harrison displayed some deft stickhandling in the corner to retrieve the puck")

defunct no longer in operation (as in a team: "the Montreal Maroons played in the NHL in the 1930s but are now defunct")

degenerative joint disease weakening of bones through wear and tear

deke feint or fake; deceptive move designed to draw an opponent out of position or to skate by an opponent while maintaining control of the puck

deke

delay 1. do anything to run time off scoreclock or prevent a faceoff from occurring as quickly as the referee or opponent would like 2. ~-of-game minor infraction called against a player who deliberately shoots the puck out of the rink or who freezes the puck unnecessarily—punishable by a two-minute penalty

delayed 1. ~ offside situation where an attacker enters the offensive end ahead of the puck and is, therefore, offside, but does not touch the puck before the defensive team takes possession; linesman raises his arm to signal the offside but does not stop play if the defending team clears the puck out or if the offensive player comes back outside the blueline 2. ~ penalty a. infraction committed by a member of the team that does not have control of the puck; referee will raise his arm but will not stop play and assess the penalty until the penalized team touches the puck b. third minor penalty against one team, held in abeyance until one of the first two expires (no team can play three men short, in other words) 3. ~ whistle whistle not yet blown in the case of a delayed offside or penalty

deliberate attempt to injure any action intended to cause injury to an opponent; punishable by an automatic gross misconduct

deliberate illegal substitution any attempt to make a player change while play carries on which is deemed by the referee to be both deliberate and illegal because too many men are on the ice

deliberately shooting puck out of rink lifting the puck out of play, punishable by a two-minute penalty (also called "delay of game")

deliver 1. execute, usu. a check or hit 2. ~ a goal score at an opportune time 3. ~ a hit check an opponent 4. ~ a pass successfully complete a pass 5. ~ a victory of a player: win a game almost single-handedly

deltoid ligament ligament that stabilizes the tibia to the ankle

deltoid muscle triangular muscles at the top of the arm near the shoulder which aid movement of the shoulder

deluge prolonged offensive surge

demand 1. public's desire to buy, usu. tickets 2. requirement expressed by a player during contract negotiations

demolish beat badly

demote send to minor-league or junior team

Denmark IIHF member nation since 1946

dental work injury to the mouth (often the loss of a tooth)

deny 1. of a goalie: make a great save 2. of a team official: refute, usu. trade rumour

depart 1. leave via trade 2. leave game or practice early, usu. because of injury

department category ("the team needs to improve its defence—that's one department that has hurt them all year")

departure player's absence due to a trade ("his departure will leave a huge hole at centre")

depleted of a roster: reduced in manpower (often because of injury)

deposit score (i.e., deposit puck into the net)

depth significant skill at any one position ("they've got great depth on the blueline")

depth chart ranking of a team's players, by position and in order of importance

derby league

desert abandon, usu. goalie ("the

defence deserted Palmateer on the play and he had to face three quick shots")

Desert Dogs alternative nickname for Phoenix Coyotes

deserving of mention praiseworthy

designated 1. ~ **goon** player who acts as the enforcer on a team 2. ~ **tough guy** var. of *designated goon*

desperate bid last-ditch effort

desperate hockey 1. final attempts to tie game late in the third period 2. all-out efforts in the final days of the regular season in an attempt to qualify for the playoffs

details of play (archaic) detailed description of action, rush by rush, in old newspaper reports

Detroit Cougars original name of Detroit Red Wings, 1926-30 (changed name to Detroit Falcons)

Detroit Falcons name of Detroit team in NHL, 1930-32 (changed name to Detroit Red Wings)

Detroit Red Wings NHL member team, 1932-present (formerly Cougars and Falcons)

Detroiters (archaic) players on the Detroit Red Wings

Deutschland Cup national team tournament held annually in Germany

Devils nickname of New Jersey's team in NHL

Dey's Arena original home arena of Ottawa Senators in NHL, 1919-22

diamond formation penalty-killing strategy which requires one player to cover the point, one player the front of the net, and two to either side of the goalie in the high slot

die-hard fan lifelong supporter of a team

diet 1. food ingested by player 2. ice time

dig 1. jostle for loose puck 2. work hard in corners with or without puck

3. ~ **it out** claim puck after scrum along the corner boards 4. ~ **the puck free** pry puck loose from a mass of sticks and skates to gain possession 5. ~ **the puck loose** var. of *dig the puck free*

digger player adept at successfully fighting for the puck in the corners

dime slang for $1,000

dimensions parameters agreed to by teams for various aspects of play, notably size of rink and nets, and size and weight of puck

ding 1. hit or hurt ("Floyd dinged Abrahams coming in over the blueline") 2. hit the post ("he dinged it off the iron before the goalie could move")

dipsy-doodle tricky stickhandling or skating

direct 1. deflect 2. control play, usu. in the slot 3. ~ **traffic** use superior muscle to establish position and communicate positioning with teammates

director 1. member of a team's executive that decides on all personnel and financial matters 2. ~ **of player development** person in charge of overall player training from junior to the farm team and NHL team 3. ~ **of player personnel** person in charge of team's players, including decisions 4. ~ **of scouting** person in charge of all team's scouts, co-ordinating assignments and ensuring all potential players are evaluated for talent and skill

Directorate Awards awards presented by IIHF directorate after every international tournament: Best Goalie, Best Defenceman, Best Forward

Directors' Lounge area underneath platinum seats at Air Canada Centre, Toronto, to which Maple Leafs' board of directors and other team dignitaries and guests repair during inter-mission

dirty 1. style of play and conduct on ice that is violent or disreputable 2. ~ **hit** check which is marked by violence or illegal tactics 3. ~ **seventies** decade of the 1970s, which commonly featured bench-clearing brawls and other nefarious acts detrimental to the game's reputation

disagreement pushing and shoving

disallow wave off, usu. a goal

in the playoffs

disciplinary hearing meeting between NHL officials and a player who has committed a flagrant foul on ice, to determine if a suspension is warranted

discourse slang for heated exchange

discover of a scout: find and recruit a player

discussion 1. meeting, usu. about a player's future with team 2. trash talking between players

disallowed

disallowed goal puck that crosses the goal line but is nullified by a subsequent decision by the referee or video goal judge

disappearing act sudden instance of poor play, usu. by a player who stars in the regular season but does not play nearly as well in the playoffs ("Yashin pulls his disappearing act every spring")

disband permanently withdraw (a team) from league play

disc puck

discard 1. release, usu. an unwanted player 2. unwanted player

discipline self-control, required to draw penalties but not commit fouls, usu.

disgruntled unhappy, usu. player or fans

dish off pass puck more or less laterally

dish out administer, usu. a check

disinterested party objective observer (as a referee)

dislocate displace a bone from its socket or natural position

dislodge the net move net off its moorings unintentionally—or intentionally—requiring play to be halted

disorganized scrambly play with few passes being completed

Dispersal Draft distribution of players among existing teams from a team that has disbanded

display 1. exhibition, usu. of skill or

talent 2. ~ **of knuckles** fight 3. **put on a ~** perform with excellence

dispute argue, usu. a call by a referee

disputed goal goal which is allowed to stand but which lacks legitimacy if viewed on video replay

distinguish oneself make an impression to coach or fans through impressive play

distraction any side element to a team, usu. in the dressing room, which detracts from the team's overall performance ("his whining about ice time has proved to be a distraction")

disturbance fight

dive unsportsmanlike embellishment of a routine play wherein a player falls to the ice at the slightest touch in order to try to draw a penalty

diver player who tries to draw a penalty by faking an infraction ("Domi is the biggest diver in the league")

diving 1. repeated taking of dives ("the diving in this game is a disgrace to real hockey") 2. ~ **pokecheck** sensational last-ditch effort whereby a player lunges as far as possible to knock the puck away from an opponent 3. ~ **save** spectacular save made by lunging to cover the exposed side of the net to block a shot

diving

division 1. group of teams within a league, smaller than a conference 2. ~ **finals** playoff series designed to crown a division champion

Division I in international competition, the second-highest tier of countries

Division II in international competition, the third-highest tier of countries

Division III in international competition, the fourth-highest tier of countries

do-or-die describes a game in which one team must win or be eliminated from the playoffs

do the splits of a goalie making a save: spread both legs out as far as possible

doctor professional who assesses and treats injuries

dodge deke or avoid a check

dogfight battle, usu. for playoff position

doghouse state of disfavour with the coach, usu. for deficient play and resulting in reduced ice time ("he's been in the coach's doghouse ever since that giveaway in the first period led to a goal")

dogs feet

doldrums slump

dominate 1. overpower 2. ~ **the boards** play with superiority when the puck is along the boards 3. ~ **the faceoff circle** win the vast majority of faceoffs in a game or period

Dominion Pro type of hockey stick

don 1. put on, usu. skates ("don the blades") 2. ~ **a uniform** put on team's sweater

done 1. at an end, usu. a player's career 2. ~ **like dinner** certain to lose, expression made famous by Dave "Tiger" Williams ("if we play our game, they're done like dinner")

donnybrook brawl or multiple-player fight

Doolittles stick manufacturer in St. Marys, Ontario, notable for models such as Excelsior, Special, Progress, Hockey King, Arena, Amateur Practice, and Boys

doormats last-place team

doorstep area directly in front of the goalie

dope 1. slang for a player who makes a bad play 2. slang for the inside scoop on a story

doping 1. use of banned substances to improve performance 2. ~ **control** method of testing for use of illegal substances by analyzing sample of player's urine (usu. at international competitions) 3. ~ **station** private room where doping control is carried out

dose amount, usu. of ice time

dot short for *faceoff dot*

double 1. ~**-enders** type of skate common before introduction of tube skates 2. ~**-header** two games in one day, usu. junior game in the afternoon followed by NHL game in the evening 3. ~ **minor** two minor penalties assessed simultaneously against one player but served consecutively, for a total of four minutes 4. ~ **minor penalty** var. of *double minor* 5. ~**-referee system** early term to distinguish a game with two referees from a game with one referee 6. ~ **runners** type of skate 7. ~ **shift** stay on the ice to play with new linemates after original linemates have left the ice 8. ~**-team** assign two defending players to check one offensive player, usu. a top scorer

doubtful 1. questionable, usu. penalty 2. status of player unlikely to play on a given night 3. ~ **starter** var. of *doubtful*

doughnut 1. shutout 2. ~ **line** friendly jab describing a forward line weak at the centre position—it has two wingers, but no centre (opposite of

helicopter line, which has no wings)

Dowling's Grill famous greasy-spoon restaurant inside Maple Leaf Gardens where players and media frequently dined and whiled away the hours prior to a game

down 1. trailing, losing a game ("the Senators are down 2-0 after the first period") 2. to defeat 3. ~ **a man** short-handed 4. ~ **low** (in the offensive end) position on ice in the corners or behind the net 5. ~ **the ice** toward the opposite end of the ice 6. ~ **the middle** a. centre part of the ice (as opposed to along the boards) b. centre position on a team

downplay trivialize, usu. friction between teammates or coach and player

downside weakness in player's game ("Lyon's downside is his defensive work")

downstairs term used by announcers in broadcast booth to describe position of colleague at ice level ("let's go downstairs where Bill is talking with the team's GM")

D pool designation used by IIHF until 2000 to denote fourth and lowest class (after A, B, and C pools) of teams in international hockey

draft 1. system of evenly distributing rights to players 2. **Amateur** ~ see *Amateur Draft* 3. **Dispersal** ~ see *Dispersal Draft* 4. ~ **choice** a. player selected by a team in a draft b. right to select a player in a draft 5. ~**-eligible** player who is available (i.e., of age) to be drafted 6. ~ **lottery** random draw to determine order of first few draft selections among non-playoff teams to prevent teams from intentionally losing games so as to secure the top choice 7. ~ **order** sequence in which teams select players 8. ~ **pick** var. of *draft choice* 9. ~

selection var. of ***draft choice*** 10. ~ **year** the year in which a particular player will become draft-eligible ("Tavares's draft year isn't until 2009") 11. **Entry** ~ see ***Entry Draft*** 12. **Expansion** ~ see ***Expansion Draft*** 13. **Inter-league** ~ see ***Inter-league Draft*** 14. **Intra-league** ~ see ***Intra-league Draft***

drag move stickhandling move whereby the puck carrier pulls the puck toward his back skate with the toe of his blade, moves to his side, and carries on after the defenceman has reached for the puck and been drawn out of position

drama events in a game ("the night's drama peaked in the second period when the Slovaks had a five-on-three")

draped covered thoroughly (by defenders)

drastic changes extreme measures necessitated by a team's long-term poor play

draw 1. faceoff 2. tie game 3. (archaic, late 19th C.) term used by referees in western Canada to commence play ("Draw!") 4. ~ **an assist** earn an assist on a goal 5. ~ **a bead on** close in on, usu. an opponent or a record 6. ~ **blood** commit an act, usu. a high stick, which cuts an opponent 7. ~ **a crowd** engage in mischievous or dirty play, causing opponents to gather and jostle with a player 8. ~ **the goalie from his net** fake a shot or make a move such that the goalie comes too far out of his net and leaves some part of it exposed for a good scoring chance 9. ~ **out of position** take an opponent away from where he should be 10. ~ **a penalty** make a play or move which requires an opponent to commit a foul

drawing card attraction, usu. star player

dress 1. be in uniform and ready to play 2. put on equipment 3. uniform 4. ~ **quickly** a. change out of full equipment to street clothes with great haste after certain games to catch a plane to another city b. put equipment on with haste to get on the ice as fast as possible 5. ~ **rehearsal** regular season (i.e., as preparation for playoffs, the *real* show)

dressing room private room where players put on their equipment and prepare for a game

dribble (archaic, U.S. 1970s) stickhandle

dribble

dribbler 1. slowly moving shot or pass 2. (U.S.) player who stickhandles well

drift light shot on or near goal

drifter shot that floats harmlessly toward the goal

drill 1. hit a man 2. shoot hard 3. practice exercise designed to develop a specific skill 4. ~s series of practice exercises to develop specific skills

drive 1. hard shot 2. go hard to the net 3. inspiration 4. ~ **the puck** take a shot

Drôlet stick manufacturer in Quebec

drop 1. hit someone so hard he falls 2. scratch from lineup 3. release a player outright 4. lose game ("they dropped a 3-2 decision last night") 5. ~ **back** of a forward: move back to the defensive position when a defenceman has joined the rush 6. ~ '**em** fight, var. of *drop the gloves* 7. ~ **the gloves** fight 8. ~ **in front of a shot** block a shot 9. ~ **in the standings** lose ground in the standings as a result of a loss or another team's victory 10. ~ **a man** (archaic) take a man off the ice after the other team has lost a man to injury 11. ~ **pass** pass the puck back to a teammate trailing the puck carrier 12. ~ **the puck** a. action by on-ice official to commence play b. exhortation to officials to begin play 13. ~ **to the ice** block a shot

drought stretch of several games without scoring or winning

drub defeat soundly

drubbing bad loss ("they suffered an 8-2 drubbing last night in Selkirk")

drug policy regulations specifying punishment for use of performance-enhancing substances

drum-beating support

Drumheller Miners Allan Cup champions in 1966

Drumondville Eagles Allan Cup champions in 1967

dry-land training off-ice training, usu. in summer

dry scrape partial resurfacing of ice by removing snow and watering the area lightly to create a new surface (done prior to a shootout)

dual role usu. person who is both coach and general manager or player and coach

ducats tickets

duck 1. avoid a hit or a high puck or high stick 2. ~ **soup** (archaic) team or player in trouble

Ducks nickname of Anaheim team in NHL

dud poor player, esp. after obtained in a trade

duds uniform or, more generally, equipment

duds

due diligence care taken by a league to ensure that everything about a particular deal is legal and in the best interest of the league, usu. when a team is sold

duel 1. game 2. stick fight 3. **goaltenders'** ~ var. of *goaltenders' battle*

duke it out fight

Dukes alternative nickname for OHL Toronto Marlboros (Marlies)

dull 1. of a skate blade: in need of sharpening 2. of a game: listless

dumb penalty penalty incurred by a player away from the play or far from the defensive goal, handicapping his team for no good reason

dump 1. trip 2. defeat 3. ~-**and-chase** upon reaching centre ice, shooting the puck deep into the opposition end and chasing after it 4. ~ **it in** shoot puck deep into the opposition end ("dump it in and head off") 5. ~ **it out** lift puck out over the defensive blueline 6. ~ **the puck in** var. of *dump it in*

Duquesne Gardens home arena of NHL's Pittsburgh Pirates, 1925-30, and AHL Hornets, 1935-56

durability impervious to injury

Durene slightly shiny, heavy-knit fabric made from a blend of nylon and cotton, used in manufacture of hockey sweaters, early 1960s to early 1980s

dust-up fight

Dutchies alternative nickname for Kitchener-Waterloo Dutchmen

duties task of playing, usu. of a goalie

dying moments last few seconds of a game

dynamite highly skilled ("that kid is dynamite out there!")

dynasty any team that wins its league championship at least three times in succession

Dynamite Line Boston forward trio featuring Cooney Weiland, Dutch Gainor, and Dit Clapper, which flourished in the late 1920s

Ee

ECAC Hockey League NCAA Division I conference, made up of colleges in New England, New York, and New Jersey (formerly affiliated with Eastern College Athletic Conference)

ECAHA *Eastern Canada Amateur Hockey Association*

ECHA 1. *Eastern Collegiate Hockey Association* 2. *Eastern Canada Hockey Association*

ECHL 1. *Eastern Canada Hockey League* 2. *East Coast Hockey League*

EHL 1. *Eastern Hockey League* 2. *European Hockey League*

EN abbreviation for *empty-net goal*

EPHL *Eastern Professional Hockey League*

ESP official IIHF abbreviation for Spain

EST official IIHF abbreviation for Estonia

Eagles nickname of St. Louis team in NHL, 1934-35

early 1. near the beginning of a game 2. ~ **goal** goal scored during the first stages of a game 3. ~ **hockey** hockey in its formative years (i.e., late 1800s) 4. ~ **lead** lead taken during the first stages of a game 5. ~ **stages** the first part of a game (or period, overtime, power play, etc.) 6. ~ **tee time** fate of a team in danger of missing the playoffs or being quickly eliminated from them (reference to golf) 7. **go down** ~ of a goalie: fall to his knees prematurely to block a shot

earn 1. deserve (compliment about one's play) 2. receive a dubious distinction ("she earned a trip to the penalty box for that slash") 3. ~ **a spot in the lineup** play well enough in training camp, the minors, or a tryout with the big club to warrant playing on a regular basis 4. ~ **an assist** be credited with an assist on a goal 5. ~ **a victory** work hard to win a game

East Division one of two divisions in the NHL from 1967-74, originally made up of the "Original Six" teams

East Coast Hockey League second-tier minor-pro league, founded in 1988; name changed to ECHL in 2003 following merger with West Coast Hockey League

east-west from one wing to the other (as opposed to north-south, which refers to offensive end to defensive end)

Eastern Canada Amateur Hockey Association premier amateur hockey league in Canada, 1906-08; became a pro league for 1908-09

Eastern Canada Hockey Association successor league to Eastern Canada Amateur Hockey Association; active only in 1908-09; succeeded by *Canadian Hockey Association*

Eastern Canada Hockey League minor-pro league based in Nova Scotia; active only in 1914-15

Eastern code var. of *Eastern rules*

Eastern Collegiate Hockey Association non-NCAA college hockey league, made up of club teams affiliated with U.S. universities

Eastern Conference one of two conferences in the NHL since 1993, the other being the Western Conference

Eastern Hockey League minor-pro league which operated 1954-73; known as Eastern Amateur Hockey League, 1938-53

Eastern Professional Hockey League minor-pro league (1959-63) based primarily in Eastern Canada

East European Hockey League league which operated 1995-2005, with teams from Ukraine, Belarus, Latvia, Lithuania, and Poland

Eastern rules six-man hockey, as opposed to the seven-man game played in the West, which required early Stanley Cup series to alternate rules from game to game

Easton brand of hockey equipment

eat lose money on ("the scalper couldn't give away his tickets to the game—he had to eat them")

eat crow accept that one has made a bad prediction after the opposite transpires

eclipse beat, better, or set record

edge 1. sharpened portion of a skate blade 2. win by narrow margin 3. **catch an ~** put skate onto ice in an awkward manner, resulting in a fall 4. **~ in play** slight advantage over an opponent

Edmonton Coliseum former name (1995-98) of Edmonton Oilers' home arena (renamed Skyreach Centre)

Edmonton Eskimos Stanley Cup challengers in December 1908

Edmonton Flyers Allan Cup champions in 1948

Edmonton Oilers NHL member team since 1979; played in WHA (originally as Alberta Oilers), 1972-79

Edmonton Oil Kings Memorial Cup champions in 1963 and 1966

Edmonton Mercurys gold medallists at 1952 Olympic Winter Games and the 1950 World Championships

effective efficient in a particular area, usu. penalty killing or checking ("he's most effective when used as a penalty killer")

effort 1. performance 2. shot on goal

effortless seemingly without exerting any outward strain (esp. of a player's skating or scoring ability)

eggbeater player adept with his stick in close quarters, usu. in the corner to stick check an opponent and claim the puck

Eishockey Almanach small guide book produced for the IIHF from the 1970s through 2003

Eishockey magazine German magazine which focuses on European hockey

Eishockey News German magazine which focuses on European and international hockey

eject 1. expel from game 2. expel from faceoff circle

elbow illegal use of that body part to check or injure an opponent

elbow

elbow pad equipment used to protect that part of the body

elbowing illegal use of that part of the body, punishable by a two-minute (and in some instances five-minute) penalty

elder statesman veteran player who generally has played many years for one team

electric clock timepiece used to keep time of a game or track a player's ice time

electric lamps lamps used to light arenas in early days

electric man early play-diagramming board used to design game strategies

elephant neck nickname given to the long-necked Stanley Cup of the 1950s (also called the Stove Pipe Stanley Cup)

eliminate 1. ~ **(a team) from the play offs** win a playoff series, forcing the opponent out 2. ~ **man from play** check man so that he is no longer a threat to contribute to a rush

elimination round IIHF term for series of round-robin games that determine which teams advance to the playoff round and which must go to the relegation round

elite 1. top level 2. ~ **league** European term for top professional league(s) 3. ~ **player** term first coined by Hockey Canada to differentiate an NHL player from the best of the best (i.e., an Olympic-quality player)

Elmer Ferguson Memorial Award annual award presented by Hockey Hall of Fame to distinguished newspaper reporters or columnists who cover hockey

elude 1. deke or skate past an opponent 2 ~ **a check** avoid contact with an opposing player who is trying to hit the puck carrier

elusive capable of eluding opponents

EL-WIG hockey stick manufacturer in Durham, Ontario

Elysium early 20th century arena in Portland, Oregon

embarrass make an opponent look bad as a result of a clever play

embattled involved in a dispute, usu. over a contract

embellish try to make a foul appear all the more flagrant by diving or feigning injury

emerge 1. develop quickly 2. ~ **as the team to beat** play very well very early in the season and become a favourite to win the championship

emergency recall player promoted temporarily from the minors to take the place of an injured player

emergency replacement player who joins a team on an emergency recall basis

employees players (modern term preferred by NHL Commissioner Gary Bettman and NHLPA executive director Bob Goodenow)

employers management (modern term preferred by NHL Commissioner Gary Bettman and NHLPA executive director Bob Goodenow)

empty-net goal

empty 1. ~**net** goal not being defended by a goalie, because he is either out of position, sitting on the bench to allow for an extra attacker on a delayed penalty call, or has been pulled late in a game in which his team is trailing 2. ~~**net goal** goal scored, generally in the closing minutes of play, by a team in the lead when the opponent has pulled the goalie for an extra attacker; or, rarely, on a delayed penalty call when the team accidentally scores into its own net 3. ~-netter colloquial for *empty-net goal* 4. ~ seats feature of an arena that is well short of a sellout for a game

encounter 1. game 2. collision 3. fight

end 1. part of the rink inside the blueline 2. ~ of a game *or* period the conclusion of a game or period of play 3. ~ of a shift few seconds before a player leaves the ice 4. ~ of a stick either the top or bottom of a hockey stick

end boards sections of boards behind the end red lines

end zone 1. area inside the blueline 2. ~ faceoff spot two red circles inside each blueline, where most faceoffs occur

end-to-end 1. of any aspect of a game: marked by quick, frequent transitions from one end of the ice to the other 2. ~ action fast-paced hockey with few whistles 3. ~ run var. of *end-to-end rush* 4. ~ rush dash by a player from his own end of the rink to the other, maintaining puck possession the whole time and dazzling fans

enemy opponent

energy guy fourth-liner or other player who lacks star quality as a scorer but brings other qualities to the team, namely hard work and tenacity

enforcer 1. player whose prime purpose is to fight opponents who check or hit a team's star players 2. goon

engage become involved in a fight

engagement game

engineer create goal or scoring chance

engraving name stamped on the Stanley Cup (erroneously but commonly called engraving)

enjoy have, such as a lead or a day off

enliven the proceedings raise a mundane game so that it is more entertaining, usu. through exciting play,

great scoring chances, or sometimes fighting

enter 1. ~ a game be assigned to take part in a game after it has started (usu. of the second goalie who replaces the starter) 2. ~ the fray join a fight

entertain host a game (e.g., "the Leafs entertain the Senators tonight at the ACC")

entertainment enjoyable, fast-paced action

enthusiasts fans

entrant team

entry team

Entry Draft annual procedure by which rights to unsigned players (usu. shortly after their 18th birthday) are distributed among NHL teams; originally known as Amateur Draft; name changed in 1979 to reflect the drafting of 18-year-olds (previously the limit was 20, then 19)

entry level contract first contract signed by a player yet to play in the NHL, subject to limits on salary, signing bonus, and performance incentives

equal 1. tie 2. ~ to the task up to the challenge

equalize 1. (late 19th and early 20th C.) drop player from the ice to even up the sides after one team suffered an injury (dates to the days when the only players on the team were those who played the full 60 minutes) 2. tie the score

equalizer goal that evens the score

equipment 1. any articles used by players, esp. protective gear 2. ~ manager person whose main function is to ensure that all equipment gets from city to city, arena to arena, in a safe and timely manner 3. ~ room area inside the dressing room which houses various equipment and parts to repair equipment 4. ~ trunk carrying cases for equipment

era period of history marked by a prominent player ("i.e., the Gretzky era") or event ("the expansion era")

erase 1. eliminate (i.e., a lead) 2. hit hard

errant pass wayward pass, usu. intercepted by the opposing team

erratic 1. ~ **behaviour** inconsistent actions by a player on ice or off, to the detriment of a team 2. ~ **pass** wayward pass

escort 1. of an official: guide a player off the ice, usu., after he has been assessed a game misconduct after a violent outburst ("the linesman escorts Probert to the penalty box")— also escort (a player) off the ice or escort (a player) to the dressing room 2. ~ **to the train station** (in the "Original Six" era) provide police accompaniment for a team in order to make a late train after a game

Esso Cup 1. men's tournament, first contested in Quebec in 1986, for the unofficial midget hockey championship of the world (also known as World Under-17 Hockey Challenge) 2. tournament for the women's hockey championship of Canada (also known as Esso Women's Nationals)

establish 1. ~ **oneself** earn a position on a team or a special-teams unit 2. ~ **position** stand in front of a goalie to screen him or disrupt him

establish position

Estonia IIHF member nation; joined in 1937 before being subsumed by the Soviet Union; resumed status as independent member in 1992

"et le but" French for "he scores"

etiology study of the causes of injuries and diseases

Euro slang for European player

Europa Cup see *European Cup*

European 1. player from Europe 2. pejorative for cowardly player who avoids physical play or contact

European Champions Cup tournament (founded 2005) between champions of the top six European hockey leagues as ranked by IIHF

European Championship 1. title awarded to highest-placing European team at World Championships, 1930-31 and 1933-91 2. separate tournament for the hockey championship of Europe, 1910-29 and 1932

European Cup tournament (1965-97) between champions of European leagues

European Draft draft of European midget-age players held by the three major junior leagues in Canada

European flow style of play marked by circuitous movement of the puck and routes to the net rather than direct skating to the opponent's goal

European Hockey League European international club competition (1996-2000) involving between 16 and 24 teams

European ice surface rink measuring 200 feet long by 100 feet wide, compared with the North American standard of 200 feet by 85 feet

European Junior Championships international tournament for the under-20 championship of Europe

European scout scout who assesses talent of players playing in European leagues

European-trained of a player: born in Europe or developed and learned the game there

evaluation camp training-camp sessions in which coaches and scouts discuss the merits of young players, usu. junior-age players

even 1. tie the game ("Calgary evens the score") 2. tied ("the game is even, 3-3") 3. **on ~ terms** tied (as a game or series) 4. **~ the count** tie the game 5. **~ the score** tie the game

even money 50-50 chance, equal odds

even strength 1. describes a situation when both teams have five skaters on ice ("Jones comes back onto the ice and the teams are playing at even strength") 2. **~ goal** goal scored when both teams have the same number of players on the ice

even-up 1. **~ call** penalty call against team currently or recently on a power play 2. **~ penalty** var. of *even-up call*

evenly played describes a contest in which both teams play at about equal skill and success

Everlast sporting goods manufacturer based in New York

ex 1. former (e.g., ex-Leaf) 2. **~-NHLer** player no longer in the league

Excelsior brand of hockey stick produced by Doolittles of St. Marys, Ontario

exchange 1. trade 2. **~ blows** fight 3. **~of possession** giveaways 4. **~ pleasantries** ironic var. of *exchange words* 5. **~ scoring chances** play in a way that results in end-to-end action 6. **~ words** engage in heated discussion with an opponent

excuse exempt from attending, usu. practice ("Johnson has been excused from practice this morning to attend to his sick mother")

excuses weak justifications offered for poor play or a loss

execute perform under game conditions those plays and strategies that have been well practised

execution performance of practised plays and strategy

executive top club official

executive vice-president club official who reports to the vice president

exercise room area in dressing room or arena where players can lift weights, ride a stationary bike, and perform other workouts

exertions (archaic) great attempts

exhibition 1. display of skill 2. **~ game** match, usu. pre-season, that doesn't count in the standings

exile banish, usu. by trading a player to a weak team

expansion 1. increase in the number of teams in a league, usu. to the detriment of the game and quality of play 2. **~ team** a. team recently added to a league b. pejorative for weak team

expel penalize with a game misconduct or suspension

expendable status of a player whose performance is no longer satisfactory and deemed tradeable (as opposed to *untouchable*)

experience knowledge of the game that can be acquired only through more and more play

experience difficulty euphemism for feeling great pain ("Smithson is experiencing difficulty as he heads to the bench")

experiment 1. try something new, usu. concerning line combinations, lineup, or style of play

experts pejorative for critics

expire reach the end (of a penalty, period, or other part of the game that is timed)

explode score many goals in succession ("the Czechs have exploded for four, third-period goals")

exploits 1. (usu. sarcastic) on-ice play ("his exploits into the offensive end usually result in a two-on-one going the other way") 2. achievements

explosive powerful, usu. offence

Expo Hall home arena of Tampa Bay Lightning during its first season, 1992-93

exponent of hockey fair, classy player

expose 1. leave a player available in any draft 2. of a goalie: leave any part of the net open ("Taylor could see Plante exposed the far side") 3. reveal ("Montreal's forechecking has exposed a weakness in Ottawa's defence")

extend 1. force extra exertions ("they're extending Thompson's abilities") 2. stretch, usu. referring to a goalie ("Hasek had to extend his pad full out to make that stop") 3. force another game in a playoff series ("and with the win, Edmonton extends this series to a sixth game")

extension strain to a joint or muscle caused by pushing it beyond its natural limits

extra 1. ~ **attacker** sixth skater; appears on ice after goalie has been pulled, at the end of a game when a trailing team is trying to tie the game, or during a delayed penalty call 2. ~ **man** advantage enjoyed by a team on the power play 3. ~ **minor** second minor penalty when a player has been assessed a double minor at the same time an opponent is penalized for only two minutes 4. ~ **move** manoeuvre by the puck carrier, usu. at the blueline, resulting in an offside as a teammate anticipates play and crosses the blueline ahead of the puck

carrier 5. ~ **period** overtime 6. ~ **play** var. of *extra period* 7. ~ **session** var. of *extra period* 8. ~ **time** var. of *extra period* 9. ~ **two** var. of *extra minor* 10. ~-**curricular activity** pushing and shoving after the whistle

Extraliga name for national league in both the Czech Republic and Slovakia

eye 1. desire ("the Leafs are eyeing first place after their win tonight") 2. **keep an ~ on the puck** focus on the puck's whereabouts 3. **keep one ~ on the scoreboard** watch carefully how out-of-town opponents are performing (generally late in the season as playoff races intensify)

eye-opener surprising result or event that provides a wake-up call for a player or team

eyelash distance by which a shot narrowly misses the goal

eyelets holes into which skate laces are inserted along the top of the boot

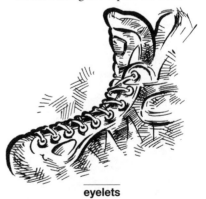

eyelets

eyes 1. ~ **in the back of his head** attribute of a player who sees the whole ice at once and can make accurate passes without looking 2. **puck has ~** attribute of a shot that finds its way into the net through a maze of players

Ff

F abbreviation for forward

FAHL *Federal Amateur Hockey League*

FIN official IIHF abbreviation for Finland

FRA official IIHF abbreviation for France

Fabulous Forum popular name for Los Angeles Kings' home rink

face 1. play ("Canada will face Russia tonight in the finals") 2. ~ **a goalie** play against a particular goalie 3. ~ **a shot** of a goalie: make or attempt to make a save 4. ~ **of the post** the front of the post 5. ~ **the puck** (late 19th and early 20th C.) drop the puck to start play

face mask 1. protective plastic shield or cage affixed to the front of the helmet 2. full-protection helmet worn by goalie to prevent injury

face mask

face massage rubbing of one player's glove into the face of an opponent

face shield protective plastic shield affixed to the front of the helmet

face wash var. of *face massage*

facelift significant changes to a team's roster

faceoff 1. dropping of the puck by an official to begin play 2. ~ **circle** red circle marked on ice where faceoffs are generally held—two in each defensive zone, one at centre ice 3. ~ **dot** red dot in the centre of a faceoff circle where the puck is dropped; also the two red dots outside each blueline where faceoffs occur after offside calls 4. ~ **interference** illegal check, usu. by one centre or wing against his opponent, which prevents player movement after the drop of the puck and can result in a two-minute minor penalty 5. ~ **percentage** ratio of faceoffs won to faceoffs taken 6. ~ **specialist** player who is particularly adept at winning faceoffs 7. ~ **spot** var. of *faceoff dot*

Faceoff game-night program for Anaheim Ducks and Chicago Blackhawks

facial protection var. of *face mask* or *cage*

fail 1. ~ **to click** miss a pass or fail on a power-play opportunity 2. ~ **to connect** usu. missed a pass or a shot on a good scoring chance 3. ~ **to get the puck out** of the defensive team: be unable to clear the puck beyond the blueline 4. ~ **to impress** of a player: be unable to make a favourable impression (on a coach, scout, etc.) 5. ~ **to produce** lack the ability to score goals or win games

fair 1. ~ **game** of a goalie: be vulnerable to a check upon leaving the crease 2. ~ **market value** player's worth relative to other players of similar calibre around the league   3. ~-**minded** unbiased   4. ~ **play** sportsmanlike play by a player or usu. team

Fair Play Cup honour bestowed upon team in any international tournament that has drawn the fewest penalties in minutes without having incurred a major foul

fair shake fair chance

faithful fans (e.g., "the Jets' faithful")

fake 1. deke   2. ~ **an injury** fall to the ice or remain on the ice, feigning pain or injury so as to stop play, draw a penalty, or prevent a good scoring opportunity by the opponent   3. ~ **a man** beat an opponent with a clever move   4. ~ **pass** manoeuvre by which puck carrier pretends to pass to one man so as to throw off a defender and be able to pass more easily to a teammate or keep the puck

fall 1. descend entirely to the ice   2. euphemism, often pejorative, for dive   3. lose to ("Detroit fell to Vancouver tonight")   4. ~ **back** usu. of a forward: play back on defence, taking the place of a defenceman joining the rush   5. ~ **behind** trail in a game or in the standings   6. ~ **down** (archaic) of a goalie: drop to one's knees to cover the puck (illegal tactic until early 1920s)   7. ~ **on the goalie** action by an opponent, often deliberate, to disrupt a goalie's concentration by falling on him at a whistle or during play if pushed by a defenceman   8. ~ **on the puck** cover the puck quickly to force a whistle, usu. in the defensive end when an opponent is attacking   9. ~ **to the ice** a. deliberate fall b. go down to block a shot

false face face mask

false faceoff faceoff incorrectly executed, usu. because of premature

movement by a player, forcing the draw to be retaken

falter lose momentum in game or during season

familiar note describes repetition of a habit, often negative

familiar position negative situation, such as losing or playing poorly ("they find themselves in a familiar position again tonight")

famine period during which a player or team has trouble scoring; slump

fan 1. avid spectator   2. miss completely when trying to take a shot   3. of a goalie: miss an easy save and allow a goal

fan

fanatic particularly ardent or passionate fan

fancy 1. ~ **jig** dance to celebrate a goal   2. ~ **skates** (archaic) blades that attached to boots to create skates (only later did the term refer to figure skates)   3. ~ **skating** demonstration of expert skating, usu. involving twirls, jumps, and tricks on skates

fandom group or base of fans

fan favourite player who is particularly popular

far 1. ~ **boards** boards on the opposite side to where the action occurs (term usu. used by play-by-play broad-casters) 2. ~ **post** goalpost farthest from the shooter 3. ~ **side** area of ice opposite to where the action occurs

Fantasy NHL road show, affiliated in particular with the All-Star Game

fantasy hockey hockey pool, usu. in the form of public contest with prizes awarded for winners

fare perform

farm 1. minor-league affiliate 2. ~ **system** group of minor-league teams which comprise all of the players under contract to any NHL team 3. ~ **team** minor-league affiliate team which develops and supplies players to the parent club

farmhand minor-league player

fashion 1. manner 2. record ("he fashioned a three-point night last time in Atlanta")

fast clip action marked by great speed

fast 1. speedy (of a skater) 2. ~ **glycolysis** metabolic process which results in production of lactic acid 3. ~ **hockey** game action with few whistles, exciting plays, and displays of excellent skill 4. ~ **ice** ice that is smooth, without holes or bumps and conducive to fast hockey 5. ~ **one** quick shot 6. ~ **pace** a high tempo, a feature of *fast hockey*

Fast Ice ice-resurfacing system that lays down water in a mist, rather than a continuous stream

fastest skater competition contest among players to determine who is the speediest at going from one end to the other or completing a lap of the rink

fat percentage proportion of tissue on one's body made up of fat (also *body fat percentage*); an indicator of physical fitness

fat rebound puck that, when saved by a goalie, bounces in the direction of an opponent

fate team or player's future

father-son combination instance of a father and son playing in the same league or on the same team ("they're one of a few father-son combinations to play for the Leafs")

fatigue lacking energy, usu. owing to excess travel or late arrival in a particular city the previous night

favour 1. treat an injury gingerly ("he's favouring his left knee") 2. **in ~ of** out of preference for ("Harris is playing in favour of Davidson")

favourable 1. ~ **impression** good feeling (usu. about a player's performance or work ethic) 2. ~ **showing** performance that would give an observer a favourable impression

favouritism of referees, esp. in early days: bias towards one team

fearless 1. play without regard to one's safety or well-being 2. ~ **shot blocker** player who willingly blocks shots regardless of body position or identity of the shooter

feather make a beautiful pass between two objects in close proximity (usu. sticks or skates)

feather duster stick check performed at a distance so as to avoid physical contact

feather duster

feature important aspect of a game

Federal Amateur Hockey League league that operated in eastern Canada, 1903-06; rival to Canadian Amateur Hockey League and later ECAHA

Federation short for *International Ice Hockey Federation*

feeble attempt weak effort

feed make a pass

feeder 1. developmental team or system 2. ~ **pass** forward pass to a teammate

feel the effects experience pain after a hit or injury

feign pretend, usu. to be injured

feint deke or fake a man

feisty pugnacious

felled injured by a shot or check

fellow (archaic) term used by a coach to refer to a player

felts sections of blue felt measuring 2.2" x 12" which players placed beneath skate laces, enabling skates to be tightened, and which extended like tongues over the toes of skate boots to protect them

femur thigh bone (and the longest bone in the body)

fence 1. term from the days prior to 1948 when chain-link fencing enclosed the playing area rather than

fend off

the modern Plexiglas ("he ran him into the fence") 2. **on the** ~ in the penalty box ("they scored while he was on the fence") 3. penalize ("referee Jones fenced Horner for two minutes")

fencing engaging in stick battle

fend off fight off, usu. a check

feud rivalry or antipathy between two players, coaches, or teams during a game, season, or career

feuding engaged in a feud

fever 1. excitement ("playoff fever is in the air") 2. ~ **pitch** fast pace

feverish encounter exciting game

few surprises of game or situation: predictable outcome

fibreglass material (brand name Fibreglas) used in manufacture of sticks and other pieces of equipment (esp. goalie masks of the 1960s and '70s)

fibula smaller of two lower leg bones that runs on the outside from the knee to the ankle

field hockey hockey on grass played with eleven players per side and using smaller hooked sticks

fielding average (1950s) goalie's save percentage

50-goal scorer player who records 50 goals in a season

50-goal season a season in which a player records at least 50 goals

"Fifty Mission Cap" song by The Tragically Hip celebrating the life of Bill Barilko

fight 1. fistic encounter 2. ~ **for a job** compete for one of relatively few roster openings during training camp 3. ~ **for position** jostle to establish superior position to score or check 4. ~ **for the puck** battle for the puck between two or more players 5. ~ **off** a check var. of *fight off a man* 6. ~

off a man elude a check through physical strength and wile 7. ~ **strap** strip of fabric sewn into back of sweater, equipped with snap and Velcro fasteners, designed to ensure that sweater remains in place during a fight; mandatory under NHL rules (also "fighting strap" and "tie-down strap")

fighter 1. player known for his pugilist skills 2. competitive player

fighting 1. dropping gloves and throwing punches at an opponent, punishable by a five-minute major penalty 2. ~ **the puck** usu. of a goalie: having trouble making routine plays; also, of a skater: having trouble controlling the puck as he usually might be expected to

Fighting Irish alternate nickname for Montreal Shamrocks

figure in participate in ("he figured in the Cup team of 1907" or "he figured in the sixth Vancouver goal")

fill in 1. replacement for an injured player 2. hit an opponent particularly hard ("Jones filled in Thompson along the boards")

films video records of games, studied by teams to prepare to play opponents

final 1. score upon completion of a game ("it's a 4-3 final here in Calgary tonight") 2. ~ **cuts** those players who are the last to be dropped from a team, usu. at the end of training camp 3. ~ **documentation** complete tournament statistics for any international competition 4. ~ **gong** final bell, buzzer, or siren to signal the end of a game 5. ~ **playoff spot** lowest ranking team in regular-season standings that qualifies for playoffs 6. ~ **score** result at end of game 7. ~ **seconds** last moments of any period or game

finale last game (of a series or regular-

season schedule)

finals championship series, usu. best-of-seven

finances team payroll or other issues pertaining to the monetary aspect of running a team

find 1. player who proves to be surprisingly talented or was somehow overlooked by most scouts 2. ~ **a way to win** win a game despite being outplayed by the opposition 3. ~ **the back of the net** score 4. ~ **the handle** a. control a loose puck b. score 5. ~ **the loose puck** gain control of a puck that is up for grabs 6. ~ **the open man** make a nice pass to an unchecked player 7. ~ **the range** score 8. ~ **the target** var. of *find the range*

finesse 1. puckhandling skill 2. ~ **player** player capable of executing the basics of the game with style and skill 3. ~ **move** quick, skilled manoeuvre

finger penalize

Finland IIHF member nation since 1928

fine monetary penalty

fine work good shift or game

finer points of the game details or fundamentals of good play

find 1. spot a player in the open 2. ~ **one's bearings** recover from injury, usu. to the head 3. ~ **one's legs** start to skate well ("if they don't find their legs, they won't have a chance against this smooth-skating team")

finish 1. score ("he made a nice move and then finished things off with a great shot") 2. ~ **a check** take a man out of the play by checking him after he has made a pass or is no longer part of the action

finished no longer skilled ("he's washed up, finished")

fire 1. shoot the puck hard and quickly

2. dismiss from employment 3. ~ **a goal** score 4. ~ **a pass** make a hard, accurate pass 5. ~ **home** score 6. ~ **in** var. of *fire home* 7. ~ **into the boards** check an opponent into the boards, usu. from behind 8. ~ **on all cylinders** of a team: play well in all aspects of the game 9. **on** ~ playing extremely well 10. ~ **sale** trading of several players at the trade deadline, with little regard for fair value in return, usu. to rid a team of expensive contracts

fireplug small, tenacious player

fireplug

firepower scoring ability

firewagon hockey style of hockey featuring end-to-end rushes, exciting scoring chances, and wide-open play

fireworks action marked by plenty of fighting or scoring chances

firm grip a commanding grasp, whether on first place in the standings or on a man's stick

first 1. ranked number one 2. ~ **assist** player credited with an assist that leads to a goal (as opposed to second assist, which goes to player who passes to first-assist player) 3. ~ **blood** initial goal of the game ("and Winnipeg draws first blood less than a minute into the game") 4. ~ **call** Montreal's right of first refusal on all French-Canadian players (see *reservation of French-Canadian players*) 5. ~-**class**

hockey skilled, fast hockey without any intimidating tactics 6. ~ **goal** a. initial goal of game b. initial goal of career 7. ~ **half** a. (archaic) from 1917-20, first part of NHL season, champion of which earned a berth in NHL playoffs b. (archaic) earlier of two 30-minute periods (in days when games were divided into two halves) c. general reference to initial half of any season 8. ~ **intermission** respite between first period and second period 9. ~ **line** top forward combination on a team 10. ~ **overall** ranked number one in the standings 11. ~ **period** initial 20 minutes of play 12. ~ **place** top ranking in any division, conference, or grouping 13. ~ **power-play unit** top five players who combine to start most man-advantage opportunities 14. ~ **punch** blow thrown by a player to begin a fight or melee 15. ~ **save** initial save of a flurry of chances around a goalie 16. ~ **shot** initial shot of a flurry of chances around a goalie 17. ~ **star** top player in a game 18. ~-**string goalie** goalie who plays in the majority of a team's games

first star

First All-Star Team team comprising the best players at each position (one goalie, two defencemen, three forwards—centre, left wing, right wing), selected after end of season

First Team All-Star player selected as the best at his position at the end of a season

First Union Center former name of Philadelphia Flyers' home arena, 1998-2003

Fischler Report private newsletter compiled by writer Stan Fischler providing news about teams, players, and other inside information

fish retrieve, usu. the puck, out of the net after a goal has been scored

fist war fight

fistic 1. ~**encounter** fight 2. ~ **exchange** var. of *fistic encounter*

fisticuffs fighting

fit 1. play well together 2. in game shape 3. ~ **in** coalesce on new team

Fitkin's Follies Christmastime revue orchestrated by Maple Leafs publicist Ed Fitkin at Maple Leaf Gardens, in which members of the media poked fun at the league and players—specifically the Leafs

fits and starts inconsistently; irregularly ("the team has been successful only in fits and starts")

fitness test series of exercises designed to evaluate the physical condition of a player

five short for five minutes ("he's going to get five for fighting")

Five for Fighting U.S. rock band named for the colloquial term for a five-minute major penalty for fighting

five hole area between a goalie's pads (usu. of those who play the butterfly style)

500-goal club group of players who have scored 500 goals in their careers in the league

.500 team 1. team that wins and loses an approximately equal number of games 2. mediocre team

five-man unit group of five players who play together

five-minute major five-minute penalty

five-minute overtime overtime period, five minutes in duration

five-on-five situation in which both teams play at full and even strength

five-on-four power-play situation

five-on-three two-man advantage situation

fix dilemma

fixture 1. (archaic) game 2. mainstay of team's lineup ("he's been a fixture on the Americans' defence for ten years now")

flag 1. pennant emblematic of league champion 2. ~**s** (archaic) goalposts

flair for the dramatic quality of player who embellishes his skill or who has the uncanny ability to score important goals or make great plays at critical times

Flames nickname of Calgary (and, 1972-80, Atlanta) team in NHL

flamingo cowardly player who lifts one leg while playing defence so as to avoid blocking a shot

flamingo

flank wing

flare break out ("fights flared in the third period")

flare-up fight

Flarrow manufacturer of hockey sticks, first in Martintown, later Martinville, Ontario

Flash (archaic) nickname for a speedy or spectacular player, usu. in conjunction with player's place of birth (e.g., the Stratford Flash)

flash the leather of a goalie: make a great glove save

flashes of brilliance occasional bursts of superlative play (often of a player who has not completely lived up to potential)

flashy cocky or showy display of skill

flask bottle containing a sample for drug-testing purposes

flat-footed prone to being badly beaten on a play ("Jansen was caught flat-footed and Potter walked around him with ease")

flat 1. listless ("they came out flat in the first, and that cost them the game") 2. ~ **pass** pass in which the puck doesn't wobble or ripple 3. ~ **puck** puck that lies entirely on the ice for ease of stickhandling and passing

flatten hit hard

Fleet Center former name of Boston Bruins' home arena (now TD Banknorth Garden)

fleet of foot of a skater: fast

flex 1. bend, usu. a stick ("Sakic's stick has a lot of flex, which helps his shot") 2. ~ *muscles* of a team or enforcer: establish a clear preference for physical play; dominate

flexible pegs pegs that affix a goal net to its position but release upon hard contact to help avoid serious player injuries

flexibility suppleness; ability to bend or stretch

flick 1. quick, short movement (as a pass or shot) 2. ~ **of the stick** quick shot ("and with the flick of a stick the game is tied, 2-2")

flickering hopes faint chance of overcoming a deficit in a game or series ("this power play revives their flickering hopes as they trail by two goals with a minute to play")

Flin Flon remote small town in Manitoba, named after fictitious prospector Josiah Flintabbatey Flonatin, that has produced notable NHLers including Bobby Clarke

Flin Flon Bombers Memorial Cup champions in 1957

flip 1. lift quickly, usu. the puck 2. ~ **(the puck) in** score 3. ~ **(the puck) out** lift puck out over the defensive blueline 4. ~ **pass** pass made by lifting the puck quickly to a teammate 5. ~ **shot** shot made by lifting the puck quickly, usu. into the top part of the net

flirt with disaster play in a careless way that suggests disregard for negative consequences

float skate lazily

floater 1. player interested only in scoring goals 2. weak shot

floatfest game lacking a physical dimension, usu. any league's All-Star Game

Flocky Hockey (1980s) style of hockey named after NHLer Ron Flockhart characterized by determination, persistence, and skill

flood 1. resurface the ice 2. ~ **the zone** send several players into one area of the ice to force a turnover or pressure the opposition

floor hockey hockey played on a floor, usu. in a gymnasium, with a ball instead of puck and minimal equipment

flop 1. failure 2. of a goalie: fall to the ice to make a save

flopper style of goaltending marked by flopping to the ice (contrast with *stand-up goalie*)

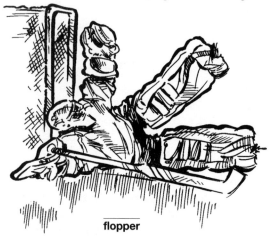

flopper

floral wreaths (archaic) metaphoric symbol of condolence to be sent to a team eliminated from playoffs (used by journalists)

Florida Panthers NHL member team, 1993-present

floundering of a team: mired in a slump

flow rhythm of a game marked by up-and-down play, few whistles, and numerous scoring chances

fluke 1. lucky break 2. ~ **goal** goal scored more because of luck than skill 3. ~ **injury** injury that occurred in unpredictable, strange manner

flurry 1. burst of action 2. ~ **of activity** burst of activity, usu. at trade deadline or draft

fly 1. skate fast 2. ~ **into the net** lose one's balance or be checked into the goalie or the goal net 3. ~ **into the boards** lose one's balance or be checked—and fall heavily into —the boards 4. ~ **down the wing** skate quickly down the left side or right side of the rink and become

a scoring threat as a result

Flyers nickname of Philadelphia's NHL team

flying 1. moving speedily ("he's been flying down the wing all night long") 2. ~ **start** fast start, usu. to game or season

Flying Fathers hockey team started by Father Les Costello, former NHLer-turned-priest, that played charity games the world over

Flying Frenchmen alternative nickname for the Montreal Canadiens, esp. during the 1930s

foe opponent

fog blanket of mist rising from the ice in a warm, humid arena, making it almost impossible to play

Fog Game Philadelphia-Buffalo playoff game of May 20, 1975, which was delayed several times because of heavy fog above the ice caused by extreme humidity

fold collapse; lose

follow 1. watch; keep an eye on—usu. the development or progress of a player 2. ~ **the play** keep an eye on the puck or play as it unfolds 3. ~ **through** continue the shooting motion after releasing a shot 4. ~ **up**

seek an update on a situation 5. **puck**
~s him quality of a player whom the
puck always seems to be near because
he anticipates the play well and is able
to react faster than others ("the puck
seems to follow Gretzky wherever he
goes")

followers fans

fool 1. make a nice deke or deft play 2.
~ **a goalie** score

foot 1. ~ **race** race between two players
to get to a loose puck first 2. ~ **sol-**
dier player lacking in skill but who
plays with perseverance and all-out
effort 3. ~ **speed** skating ability

footwork use of skates to make quick
turns or rapid adjustments

foozle (archaic) miss, muff, blow, usu. a
shot

For 'Em Club Detroit Red Wings fan
club that thrived during the 1950s

for sale player who is trade candidate
("Harrison is for sale if the price is
right")

force 1. hasten an opponent 2. player
who dominates a game 3. extend the
game into overtime 4. require a goalie
to make a great save ("that hard shot
forced Labonte to come up with a big
save") 5. ~ **a bad pass** check the puck
carrier quickly so he doesn't have time
to make a good play 6. ~ **a turnover**
check the puck carrier quickly so that
he makes an errant pass or loses possession because he has been rushed

forecast predict

forecheck 1. skate deep into the offensive end to check the defensive puck
carrier aggressively in hopes of forcing
a turnover 2. ~, **backcheck, pay-**
cheque mantra of the hard-working
player (as opposed to superstar)

forechecker player who forechecks

forehand natural side a player shoots
from (as opposed to backhand)

forehand

foreign ice site of a road game

foreigner designation for players in
European leagues who play in countries from which they don't hold a
passport or citizenship and for which
there is a maximum number allowed
per team

forfeit concede a game

forget neglect to cover an opponent
(usu. in past tense: "he forgot to
watch Jones in front and it was Jones
who slid the loose puck home")

form calibre of play ("he's in top form
tonight")

former was previously, as a member of a
team

Fort Frances Canadians Allan Cup
champions in 1952

Fort William War Veterans Memorial
Cup champions in 1922

48th Highlanders Canadian militia
regiment whose pipe band has
marched onto the ice in Toronto prior
to the Maple Leafs' home opener
every season since 1931, when Maple
Leaf Gardens opened

40-goal scorer player who scores 40
goals in a season

40-goal season season during which a
player scores at least 40 goals

Forum 1. former home arena of Montreal

Canadiens (1926-96) 2. former home arena of Los Angeles Kings (1967-99)

forward 1. one of three players on a team—centre, left wing, right wing—whose primary role is to score 2. ~ **line** three-man unit consisting of a centre, left winger, and right winger 3. ~ **pass** any pass made to a player who is in front of the passer

Forward model of hockey stick produced by Doolittles in St. Marys, Ontario

Foster Hewitt Memorial Award annual award presented by Hockey Hall of Fame to distinguished hockey broadcasters

foul 1. infraction or violation of the rules 2. commit a foul 3. ~ **language** abusive language directed usu. at an official

fouling (archaic) committing a foul ("the fouling in this game has been frightful")

four 1. ~ **minutes** double minor penalty ("he's going to get four minutes for that high stick") 2. **playing ~ forwards** coaching strategy, usu. on the power play, which calls for a team to substitute one of its defencemen for an extra forward 3. **rolling ~ lines** coaching strategy whereby a coach distributes ice time relatively equally among four forward lines rather than concentrating it among the top three lines

Four Nations Tournament 1. periodic tournament in women's hockey featuring the national teams of four countries (sometimes Three Nations Tournament) 2. European under-20 tournament; preparation for European Junior Championship

four-on-four 1. game situation in which both teams are playing one man short (particularly regular-season overtime in NHL) 2. ~ **hockey** var. of *four-on-four*

four-on-three game situation in which one team is playing one man short and the other is playing two men short

four-point game game between teams that are close in the standings or in the same division; a win by the lower-ranked team brings it two points closer, while a loss leaves it two points farther back

fourth 1. ~ **forward** defenceman skilled at rushing the puck 2. ~ **line** weakest, least skilled line, usu. given ice time to allow the other three lines to catch an extra respite on the bench

fourth-line 1. ~ **centre** defensive-minded centre or weakest centre on the team 2. ~ **forward** one of the least skilled forwards on a team 3. ~**r** player who is relegated to the weakest line and will likely play the fewest minutes in a game 4. ~ **winger** one of the least skilled wingers on a team

Fox 40 pealess whistle; official whistle of the NHL

FoxTrax puck short-lived (1996-98) experimental puck created by Fox television network; contained sensors that enabled the puck's speed and location to be tracked, so that TV

FoxTrax puck

crew could highlight it on screen and add a red trail when its speed topped 112 kilometres per hour

fracas fighting, or pushing and shoving

fracture 1. breaking of a bone, either a simple (one break) or compound (multiple breaks) 2. (archaic) break a record

fragile 1. ~ **body** easily injured 2. ~ **confidence** lack of consistent belief in one's skills

frame period

France IIHF member nation since 1908

franchise 1. team 2. elite player on a weak team, or the cornerstone of any team

Frank J. Selke Trophy annual NHL trophy awarded to the league's best defensive forward

frantic desperate

fraternization rule rule instituted by NHL President Clarence Campbell in 1948 which forbade members of opposing teams from socializing in any way with other players

fray melee or fight

freak 1. ~ **accident** injury which occurs under strange or unpredictable circumstances 2. ~ **injury** var. of *freak accident*

free 1. in the open 2. ~ **agent** player whose contract with his team has expired and who is not bound in any way to play for that team again 3. ~-**for-all** brawl 4. ~ **hand** hand not being used by a fighter against an opponent and which can have a devastating effect if he is able to punch with it 5. ~ **shot rule** experimental rule (used by NHL only during pre-season in 1974-75) that allowed a player on the attacking team a free shot on goal from within either faceoff circle if the defending team was guilty of freezing

the puck 6. ~ **the puck** poke and jab at a puck from a scrum of players or from underneath the goalie before the whistle to keep it in play 7. ~**wheeling** skating at high speed with plenty of open ice 8. ~**wheeling hockey** var. of *firewagon hockey*

freeze 1. ~ **the goalie** of the puck carrier: hold the puck a split second longer than the goalie anticipates, thereby making him hold his position a bit longer and gaining the advantage over him 2. ~ **the puck** any attempt to force an official to blow his whistle and stop play

Frenchmen (archaic) colloquial for Montreal Canadiens

French press pejorative for negative, anti-English media in Quebec, usu. Montreal

fresh 1. well rested 2. ~ **face** rookie 3. ~ **ice** newly flooded ice at the beginning of a period, marked by its smoothness and speed 4. ~ **legs** a. line change b. attribute of a player who is well rested or who has spent most of the game on the bench 5. ~ **troops** players with fresh legs

Friendship Tour pre-season exhibition games played in Moscow in 1989 and 1990 between Soviet teams and NHL teams

fringe benefits bonuses

fringe player player of marginal skill

frisk off penalize

front 1. ~ **of the net** area directly in front of the goal (also the slot) 2. ~ **office** executives, and other decision-making staff (such as the general manager) of a team 3. ~ **ranks** forwards 4. ~-**runner** a. team leading in the standings b. player who plays well only when his team is in the lead 5. **in** ~ directly ahead of the goalie (i.e., in the slot or crease areas)

frontier justice revenge exacted on an opponent through a wildly vicious or dangerous assault

front-liner 1. forward 2. starting player

frozen chemical state that water must be in for hockey to be viable

Frozen Four tournament for the championship of the NCAA

frozen pond idyllic setting for hockey: outdoors on a naturally frozen body of water

frozen pond

frustrate 1. check persistently 2. of a goalie: make one great save after another against the same shooter or team

full 1. ~ **flight** top speed 2. ~ **head of steam** var. of *full flight* 3. ~ **measure** deserving of ("the Generals were full measure for their win over

full speed

the Petes") 4. ~ **of surprises** unpredictable (coach or player) 5. ~ **skate** all players in attendance on a given night of shinny 6. ~ **speed** var. of *full flight* 7. ~ **slate** date when all of league's teams are scheduled to play ("it's a Saturday night, so there's a full state of games across the league") 8. **at ~ strength** a. five skaters on the ice b. injury-free 9. ~ **stride** longest possible stride 10. ~ **tilt** at high speed; all out

fumble mishandle, usu. the puck

fundamentals basics of the game at which any professional is thoroughly proficient

funnel power-play formation in which the puck is kept in the middle of the ice inside the offensive end, from the middle of the point to the goal-crease area

funny 1. ~ **bounce** bounce of the puck in an odd or unpredictable manner, often resulting in a goal or good scoring chance 2. ~ **hop** var. of *funny bounce*

furious fast (of game action)

furnish provide

future great promise ("he's only 19, but it's clear he's got a future in this league")

future considerations component of a trade that is yet to be determined, but which rarely amounts to a significant player or addition to the team

future Hall of Famer player of outstanding skill, usu. a veteran who will likely be inducted into the Hockey Hall of Fame after his retirement

futures var. of *future considerations* ("Ottawa traded him to Florida for futures this afternoon")

Gg

G 1. abbreviation for goalie 2. abbreviation for goals scored by a player

GA abbreviation for goals against, as listed in league standings

GAA abbreviation for goals-against average

GBR official IIHF abbreviation for Great Britain

GER official IIHF abbreviation for Germany

GF abbreviation for goals for, as listed in league standings

GM abbreviation for general manager

GP abbreviation for games played

GRE official IIHF abbreviation for Greece

GWG abbreviation for game-winning goal

GTHL Greater Toronto Hockey League, name (since 1998) of world's largest amateur league, founded in 1911

gain 1. ⁓ **the blueline** carry the puck to the blueline despite defence's efforts to prevent just that 2. ⁓ **control** take or claim puck and start to move it up ice 3. ⁓ **the lead** score goal that puts a team ahead in the game 4. ⁓ **possession** var. of *gain control* 5. ⁓ **speed** accelerate in open ice 6. ⁓ **a tie** play to a tie score 7. ⁓ **the zone** var. of *gain the blueline*

gallery gods fans in the highest reaches of an arena (esp. in Boston Garden)

Gallivan, Danny famed Montreal Canadiens play-by-play announcer who coined many descriptive phrases (e.g., cannonading, spinarama) in the course of his hockey commentary

Galt Ontario-based team that challenged for Stanley Cup in January 1910

Galt Hornets Allan Cup champions in 1969 and 1971

Galt Terriers Allan Cup champions in 1961

gamble 1. pinch at the blueline by defenceman 2. dangerous play that could result in a good chance by the opponent

gambling attempting to win money by predicting the results of scores of games or details pertaining to the playing of game

game 1. hockey match 2. (archaic) a goal ("he scored his second game of the period to give his team the lead") 3. competitive spirit 4. ⁓ **action** play while the puck is being competed for and the scoreclock is running 5. ⁓ **conditions** shape of the ice (usu. for outdoor games) 6. ⁓ **day** day of a game 7. ⁓**-day skate** morning practice (usu. light and quick) the day of a game 8. ⁓ **face** serious, competitive attitude prior to a game 9. ⁓ **in hand** having played one fewer game than an opponent 10. ⁓ **misconduct** player's expulsion for the remainder of a contest 11. ⁓ **night** evening of a game 12. ⁓**-night host or hostess** person, usu. woman, who entertains fans during stoppages in play and intermissions 13. ⁓ **notes** thoughts and comments for a game, compiled either by coaching staff or media members 14. ⁓ **on** expression used in detailed descriptions of early game to announce resumption of play 15. ⁓ **plan** strategy for a particular game 16. ⁓ **played** official statistic player is credited with upon stepping on the ice during game action 17. ~ **report** official summary of all aspects of the running of a game 18. ~ **seven** last possible game of a playoff series 19. ~ **shape** a. excellent physical condition b. state of being fit to play 20. ~-**skate decision** decision, made immediately prior to a game, as to whether a player who has recently returned from injury is fit to play 21. ~ **summary** statistical capsule of a game's events 22. ~ **time** scheduled time of opening faceoff 23. ~-**time decision** var. of *game-skate decision* 24. ~ **timekeeper** official who sits between penalty boxes and operates the scoreclock 25. ~-**tying goal** goal which secures a team a tie in the game 26. ~-**winner** goal which gives a team victory 27. ~-**winning goal** var. of *game winner*

Game, The best-selling book by Ken Dryden detailing life in the NHL as a member of the 1970s Montreal Canadiens

Game Night game-night program for Los Angeles Kings and Buffalo Sabres

Game On NHL slogan

gamer competitive player

gamester hockey player

gang 1. team 2. ~ **attack** (archaic) five-man offensive foray 3. ~ **play** var. of *gang attack*

gap opening

gaping net wide-open net

gaping net

Garage unofficial nickname for Vancouver's GM Place

garbage 1. rebounds and loose pucks from near the opposition goal 2. ~ **collector** player whose forte is to score goals from in close on rebounds and deflections 3. ~ **goal** goal that lacks in quality and skill, as in banging in a rebound, crashing the net, or any play that lacks aesthetic flair 4. ~ **man** var. of *garbage collector*

garments equipment

garner 1. record, earn—usu. goal or assist 2. ~ **attention** earn praise from team personnel, media, or fans

garter belt soft belt-like attachment worn on waist, designed to hold up socks

gash cut

Gashouse Gang nickname for Toronto Maple Leafs during the 1930s because of their colourful off-ice behaviour

gas lamps means by which early rinks were lit

gate get the ~ be penalized

gate receipts revenue earned from ticket sales

gather 1. ~ **the puck** collect the puck 2. ~ **speed** accelerate through open ice 3. ~ **steam** var. of *gather speed*

gathering 1. crowd attending a game 2. players milling about, pushing and shoving

Gaul (archaic) French-Canadian players on Montreal Canadiens

gauntlets (archaic) hockey gloves

Gaylord Center Nashville Predators' home arena

gel come together, usu. as a team

gem star player

general manager team official responsible for acquiring players, negotiating contracts, and other business functions

General Motors Place Vancouver Canucks' home rink, 1995-present

general opinion public consensus

general public non-subscribers who buy tickets for a game

Generalettes cheerleaders at the Greensboro Coliseum in North Carolina in 1959-60

genna Ethiopian term for Christmas, named after a ball-and-stick game played on dirt or grass, similar to hockey

George name of Portland Rosebuds' pig mascot in 1915-16

Germany IIHF member nation since 1909

Gerry Cosby and Co. New York-area seller of hockey sticks to the Rangers, named after the goalie for gold medal-winning USA team at 1933 World Championship

get 1. ~ **all of it** take a hard shot 2. ~ **around** deke or manoeuvre past an opponent 3. ~ **away** fast break 4. ~ **away with one** commit foul that goes unpenalized 5. ~ **back** backcheck quickly 6. ~ **back** into the game score goal that makes the score close again 7. ~ **by** var. of *get around* 8. ~ **the call** a. benefit from an official's decision b. of a player: be called up from the minors c. of a goalie or official: be assigned to start a particular, usu. important, game 9. ~ **the face** (archaic) win the faceoff 10. ~ **the gate** be penalized 11. ~ **a goal** score 12. ~ **in front** go to the slot 13. ~ **in front of a shot** block or redirect a shot out of harm's way 14. ~ **involved** play with extra intensity or greater physical presence 15. ~ **it in deep** shoot the puck deep into offensive end 16. ~ **it up** shoot the puck to the top areas of the net 17. ~ **off the ice** go to the bench on a line

change 18. ~ **on him** forecheck or check an opponent doggedly 19. ~ **one back** score a goal when trailing, thus reducing the size of the lead 20. ~ **a piece of an opponent** make partial body contact 21. ~ **a piece of the puck** partially block or deflect a pass or shot 22. ~ **the puck** gain possession of the puck 23. ~ **the puck to sit** cradle rolling puck until it lies flat on the ice 24. ~ **rid of the puck** a. shoot quickly b. pass quickly 25. ~ **set** of a goalie: prepare to face an offensive foray or a shot 26. ~ **a stick on the puck** partially block or redirect pass or shot 27. ~ **there first** beat opponents to the puck 28. ~ **together** fight; melee 29. ~ **to the puck** var. of *get there first* 30. ~ **wood on the puck** let go a hard shot

gift easy goal

gilt-edged play high-quality play

give 1. ~**-and-go** passing combination in which a player makes a pass, heads for open ice, and gets the puck right back from his teammate 2. ~ **the blueline** of the defence: allow the puck carrier to cross the blueline before trying to check him 3. ~ **chase** pursue puck carrier or other opponent 4. ~ **him a look** make an implied threat of revenge 5. ~ **a lesson** outplay an opponent 6. ~ **a pass** pass the puck 7. ~ **room** a. of a defenceman: allow a forward the chance to move into open ice b. of a goalie: leave part of the net unguarded as a target for shooter 8. ~ **them the broom** sweep an opponent in a playoff series 9. ~ **up** a. allow a goal b. allow a scoring chance c. trade a player

given a rest penalized

giveaway turning over of puck to an opponent because of a mistake

gladiators players—more specifically, fighters

glance 1. quick look 2. graze 3. ~ **off post** of a shot: just barely hit the post

glass 1. short for Plexiglas or protective glass between ice and fans 2. ~ **partition** var. of *glass*

glassy surface ice

glide coast on skates

glitter game (archaic) slang for All-Star Game

Globe Arena principal arena in Stockholm, Sweden

glorious 1. ~ **chance** excellent scoring opportunity that does not result in a goal 2. ~ **opportunity** var. of *glorious chance*

glove 1. goalie's catching glove 2. make a glove save ("St. Pierre gloves the puck and holds it for a faceoff") 3. ~ **hand** hand on which the goalie wears his glove 4. ~ **pass** pass made using the glove, illegal anywhere on the ice except within the defensive zone 5. ~ **the puck ahead** advance puck to a teammate with the glove, causing a stoppage in play 6. ~ **save** stop made by the goalie using his glove hand 7. ~ **side** side of the net nearest goalie's glove hand 8. ~**s** hand protection worn by skaters 9. ~**s off** fighting

GM meetings meetings between the team's general managers to discuss the state of the game

GM Place see *General Motors Place*

Gnash Nashville Predators' mascot

go 1. play 2. rush with the puck 3. engage in fisticuffs 4. ~ **after** a. chase down loose puck b. track down an opponent c. start a fight 5. ~**-ahead goal** goal which gives a team the lead 6. ~ **around** deke or manoeuvre past a man 7. ~ **at it** fight 8. ~ **back** skate into defensive end to collect puck after opponent has cleared it out

of its end 9. ~ **down** of a goalie: fall to the ice to make a save 10. ~ **down early** of a goalie: fall to the ice even before a shot has been taken 11. ~ **down low** play with the puck in the corners of the offensive zone 12. ~ **for a skate** a. of a goalie: wander

go down

from the crease b. take part in recreational skating c. rag the puck to kill off a penalty 13. ~ **hard** skate with determination, usu. to the net or to the puck carrier 14. ~ **in alone** be on a breakaway 15. ~ **off** a. deflect b. leave the ice c. earn a penalty 16. ~ **off a skate** var. of *go off* (15a) 16. ~ **offside** skate across the offensive blueline before the puck 17. ~ **on the power play** gain a man advantage when opponent is penalized 18. ~ **on the road** embark on a road trip 19. ~**-to guy** key player on a team 20. ~ **to the net** skate to the goal without the puck so as to create traffic or accept a pass 21. ~ **to the puck** skate to where the puck is 22. ~ **up** take the lead ("if they can score here, they'll go up 2-0") 23. ~ **up ice** make a long pass from defensive zone to offensive zone 24. ~ **upstairs** a. shoot the puck to one of the top corners of the net b. of a referee: call for the video goal judge to help make a ruling 25. ~ **with** a. play regularly with b. of a coach: decide how many forwards or defenceman to use in a game ("Quinn is going with seven defencemen tonight")

goad 1. ⁓ **into a fight** provoke opponent into fighting 2. ⁓ **into taking a penalty** frustrate an opponent into committing a foul for no significant reason

goal 1. any play on which the puck crosses the goal line, the last man on the scoring team to touch the puck being credited with scoring it 2. long- or short-term objectives of a player, team, or coach 3. the net into which pucks must enter for a goal to be scored 4. ⁓ **box** (archaic) goal net 5. ⁓ **cage** var. of *goal net* 6. ⁓ **cover** position on ice, most often in Maine hockey in late 19th century, of a player who protected the goalie 7. ⁓ **crease** area directly in front of the net, demarcated by red lines and blue ice 8. ⁓ **differential** the figure attained by subtracting goals allowed from goals scored 9. ⁓ **distribution** analysis of how many players on a particular team score the team's goals 10. ⁓ **frame** var. of *goal* 11. ⁓ **the game** starting goalie ("Lumley will goal the game") 12. ⁓ **getter** a. player who is credited with scoring a goal b. player who scores frequently 13. ⁓ **hanging** lingering in offensive end; banned in 1930, when the NHL's first offside rule banned a player without the puck from entering or occupying the offensive end before the puck carrier has entered 14. ⁓-**hungry** team or player who has had a difficult time scoring goals 15. ⁓ **judge** official who sits behind the goal and signals when the puck has entered the net 16. ⁓ **light** red light located at the top of the Plexiglas directly behind the goal net

which is lit when a goal has been scored 17. ⁓ **line** red line that extends from goalpost to goalpost, over which the puck must cross for a goal to be counted 18. ⁓ **maker** top scorer on a team or in a league 19. ⁓ **minder** goalie 20. ⁓ **mouth** var. of *goal crease* 21. ⁓-**mouth pileup** group of fallen players in the area immediately in front of the net 22. ⁓-**mouth scramble** battle for possession of the puck immediately in front of the net 23. ⁓ **pads** thick leg protection worn by the goalie alone 24. ⁓ **poles** nets 25. ⁓ **post** one of two upright steel poles which are joined by the crossbar to form the frame of the goal 26. ⁓ **production** team's offensive output 27. ⁓ **register** score ("ring the goal register") 28. ⁓-**scoring drought** inability of a team or player to score 29. ⁓-**scoring streak** series of consecutive games during which a player scores at least one goal 30. ⁓ **stick** special stick with extra-thick blade and shaft used only by a goalie 31. ⁓ **suck** player who doesn't skate back into his own end and is concerned primarily with his own scoring chances 32. ⁓ **tend** (archaic) goaltender ("Roach is the goal tend tonight") 33. ⁓ **umpire** (archaic) judge who stood on the ice behind the goal and signalled scores by waving a kerchief

Goal 1. model of stick made by Doolittles of St. Marys 2. model of stick from Hilborn made by Salyerds of Preston, Ontario

Goal Magazine magazine used by many American NHL teams in the 1970s

goaler 1. var. of *goalie* 2. ⁓'s **book** statistical record for goalies (minutes played, goals against)

goalie 1. player whose job it is to prevent the puck from entering the net

2. ~ **coach** coach whose sole job is to train and practise with the goalie 3. ~ **cut** special type of sweater made especially for goalies featuring sleeves that are wider, shorter, and taper less than on a skater's sweater, as well as provide slightly more room in the chest 4. ~ **instructor** var. of *goalie coach* 5. ~ **mask** special protective mask that covers the entire head, often colourfully decorated, worn by a goalie 6. ~ **pads** special protective covering for the legs that extends over the knees 7. **reflex** ~ goalie who relies more on agility and quick reactions than positioning and playing angles 8. ~ **skates** special skates with flat blades and more durable boot 9. ~ **stick** special stick of extra thickness in the blade and shaft 10. ~**'s worst nightmare** opposition's top scorer

goaling playing goal ("Hewitt is goaling for the Blues tonight")

goalkeeper 1. var. of goalie 2. ~ **interference** act of preventing the goalie from moving freely or making a save, punishable by a two-minute penalty

goalkeeping play of a goalie ("his goalkeeping has been impeccable tonight")

goalless draw game in which the result is 0-0

goals 1. play goal ("he goals tonight again") 2. ~ **against** number of goals a goalie or team has allowed in a game or over the course of a series or season ("he's allowed just four goals against in his last five games") 3. ~**-against average** goaltending statistic calculated by dividing a goalie's goals allowed into his total minutes played and multiplying that figure by 60

goaltender 1. player whose job it is to prevent the puck from entering the net (spelled goal-tender in early days)

2. ~ **interference** var. of *goalkeeper interference* 3. ~**'s battle** game in which both goalies play very well, resulting, usu., in a low score

goaltending 1. the job of being a goalie 2. ~ **coach** coach whose sole job is to practise with and instruct the goalie

goalward towards the goal, usu. the puck or a player

goat player who makes a costly mistake

gobble up gain possession, usu. of puck ("he gobbled up the puck at centre and went in alone")

gods short for gallery gods

go-getter energetic player

gold medal award for first place in any international competition

gold medal

Gold Medal Goal model of stick made by Columbia

Golden Helmet promotional feature in many European leagues which sees the league's leading scorer wear a special yellow helmet to denote his status

Golden Hockey Stick award presented to the MVP of the Czech league

golden opportunity excellent scoring chance that does not result in a goal

Golden Seals nickname of California's NHL team, 1970-76 (previously

Oakland Seals and California Seals; later moved to Cleveland)

Golden Skate award presented to Sweden's best player in an international game

golds best seats in the house at Maple Leaf Gardens

golf swing at the puck in the defensive end with both hands together on the stick in an attempt not to control the puck but simply to clear it away

golfing euphemism for being eliminated from the playoffs

gondola broadcast booth suspended above the ice at Maple Leaf Gardens, made famous by Foster Hewitt

gone 1. assessed a game misconduct ("he's gone from the game after that fight") 2. on a breakaway 3. time having elapsed in a game or period ("ten minutes have gone in the period and we still haven't had a goal") 4. fired 5. unable to finish a game, usu. because of injury ("he's gone for the night but will be re-evaluated in the morning") 6. ~ **fishing** having lost focus or concentration in a game

gong 1. (archaic) noise made to signal start or finish of a period 2. ~ **show** situation which is ridiculous or completely unprofessional 3. ~ **to gong** start to finish

"Good Old Hockey Game" song by Stompin' Tom Connors (a.k.a. "The Hockey Song") celebrating hockey

Goodall Cup trophy awarded to champions of Australian league play

good 1. ~ **bet** likely ("it's a good bet Hainsworth will get the start in goal again") 2. ~ **conduct** clean play 3. ~ **form** skilled and disciplined play 4. ~ **game** praise offered for a fine performance 5. ~ **hustle** diligent effort, usu. to backcheck or check an opponent 6. ~ **job** fine play 7.

~ **penalty** infraction which is worth the two minutes' punishment because it prevented a sure goal or great scoring chance 8. ~ **showing** fine performance 9. ~ **wood** hard shot ("he got good wood on that blast")

good wood

goodwill ambassador any player, active or retired, who carries himself in an exemplary manner and promotes his team and the game in the finest ways

Goodman, Paul, High-Scoring Trophy see *Paul Goodman High-Scoring Trophy*

Goodwill Games international sports competition staged six times (1986-2000); only the 1990 Games in Seattle featured a hockey tournament (top six national teams from Europe as well as teams from Canada and the U.S.)

goon 1. talentless player employed by a team strictly to engage in fights and intimidate 2. ~ **coach** coach who favours the use of goons and intimidation tactics as a means of winning

3. ~ **it up** of a losing team late in a game: try to instigate fights to defend its honour and make the winning team pay for the embarrassing defeat

Gordie Howe hat trick game in which a player records a goal and an assist and engages in a fight

gorilla style of goaltending (perfected by Terry Sawchuk, who played hunched over to appear larger and block as much of the net as possible); see also *crouch*

gossip usu. trade talk

grand larceny 1. one-sided trade 2. spectacular save by a goalie

Granites nickname of Toronto team that won Allan Cup in 1922 and 1923 and won gold medal at 1924 Olympic Winter Games

Grapes nickname of TV personality and former coach Don Cherry

graphite shaft shaft of a stick made of composite of graphite and other materials such as Kevlar

graze the post of a puck: deflect off the post after hitting it only lightly (as opposed to hitting it flush)

graze the post

Gothamites alternate nickname for New York Rangers

gouret (Fr., archaic) 1. hockey (game of) 2. hockey stick

governor executive who represents a team at NHL meetings

grab 1. claim or acquire a player 2. hold onto an opponent 3. ~ **the lead** take the lead in a game 4. ~ **the puck** recover a loose puck or rebound

graduate player who is no longer eligible for junior hockey

Granby Predateurs Memorial Cup champions in 1996

grandfather clause exemption from a new rule (e.g., from the 1979 rule making helmets mandatory)

Great Britain IIHF member nation since 1908

great 1. ~ **hands** attribute of player who has excellent passing and shooting skills 2. ~ **save** of a goalie: outstanding job of preventing the puck from going into the net

Greece IIHF member nation since 1987

Green Dragons name for fans of Olympija Ljubljana, Slovenian club team

green ice ice as it appears early in the morning before it is game-ready

green light 1. permission (usu. a coach allowing his defenceman to rush the puck—"he's got the green light to go

with it whenever he sees an opening")
2. one of two coloured lights at the
top of the glass behind the net, green
to signal the end of a period, red to
signal a goal

greens seats at Maple Leaf Gardens
that were the second-farthest from
the ice

Greensboro Coliseum home rink of
Carolina Hurricanes, 1997-99

Green Unit the most famous of the
Soviet Union's five-men units, consisting of defencemen Viacheslav
Fetisov and Alexei Kasatonov and forwards Vladimir Krutov, Igor Larionov,
and Sergei Makarov

Gretzky's eponymous restaurant in
downtown Toronto, located at 99
Blue Jays Way

Gretzky's office area directly behind
the net, made famous by Wayne
Gretzky for his uncanny ability to
pass and score from that area

grey elm kind of wood used in the
making of hockey sticks

greys seats farthest from the ice at
Maple Leaf Gardens

grim warriors any team that is superior
to its opponents

grind 1. long schedule 2. ~ **down** wear
down through checking, hard
skating, or perseverance 3. ~ **out a
win** win a game that has been physically or mentally exhausting

grinder less-skilled player who works
hard and checks more than he scores

grip 1. hold onto an opponent 2. firm
possession of a spot in the standings
("they have a grip on third place") 3.
~ **the stick tightly** metaphor for tendency of player in a scoring slump to
try too hard

grippe influenza

grit hard-nosed play

gritty demonstrating grit

groan disappointed audience reaction

groggy euphemism for having suffered
a concussion

groin 1. area where the thigh connects
to the abdomen, notably the muscles
that allow the hip to twist and flex 2.
~ **injury** common injury, suffered
most frequently by goalies

groom develop, usu. a prospect ("they'll
groom him in the AHL for a year or
two before bringing him up")

groove 1. any cut into the ice made by
skates which is either dangerous or
detracts from fast, quality play 2. **in
a** ~ play well over a stretch of time

gross 1. ~ **injury** serious injury 2. ~
misconduct game misconduct
penalty for dangerous play

group 1. division 2. in international
hockey, a collection of teams that play
one another in preliminary rounds
leading to playoffs

group race fight among better teams
for first place in standings

Group I Player under the NHL's collective bargaining agreement, any rookie
who falls under the entry-level contract system

Group II Player any player who is
neither a Group I nor Group IV
player, nor an unrestricted free agent;
when such a player's contract expires,
he becomes a restricted free agent

Group III Player any player between 30
and 32 years of age, with four years in
the NHL; when such a player's contract expires, he becomes an unrestricted free agent

Group IV Player player who has never
signed an NHL contract and is a free
agent after having defected from his
birth country

Group V Player player whose contract
has expired, who has played at least
ten NHL seasons, and who did not

earn the average salary in the final year of his contract

Group VI Player player who is older than 25, without a contract, who has played fewer than a specified number of NHL games (28 games for goalies, 80 games for skaters)

Growl Florida Panthers magazine

Grumpy Old Men nickname for Kirk Muller, John MacLean, and Mike Keane in Dallas, a trio of veteran players toward the end of their careers, known for their competitive spirit

guard 1. protect the net   2. (U.S.) watch an opponent closely   3. play goal

gugahawat Indian form of shinny

Guelph Biltmores Memorial Cup champions in 1952

Guelph Platers Memorial Cup champions in 1986

guess of a goalie: make a judgement based on instinct

guide force in one direction, usu. toward the boards ("he ignored the puck and simply guided his man into the boards")

Guldpucken "Gold Puck"; Swedish player-of-the-year award as presented jointly by the Swedish Ice Hockey Association and the newspaper *Expressen*

gullet part of the goal stick where the thin part of the shaft connects to the broader part

gullet

gum confection included in packs of hockey cards

gun 1. take a hard shot 2. ~ **for a goal** try to score 3. ~ **shy** of a goalie: afraid of the puck to the point that his play is adversely affected

gunk colloquial name for skin rash that afflicts some players for unknown reasons, though it is apparently connected to the wearing of sweaty equipment; the condition is known to end careers

gunner top scorer

gut-check time that moment in a game or season when a team must play better or face elimination or loss

gut it out play with all energy and reserve

gutless cowardly

gutsy play a high-risk play, such as blocking a shot or making a pass just as an opponent is about to deliver a check

Hh

H.A. Proulx hockey stick maker and retailer in Ottawa, Ontario

HE Hockey East

HHOF Hockey Hall of Fame

HNIC *Hockey Night in Canada*

HP Pavillion name (since 2002) of San Jose Sharks' home rink (formerly known as Compaq Center)

HSBC Arena name (since 2000) of Buffalo Sabres' home arena (formerly Marine Midland Arena)

HUN official IIHF abbreviation for Hungary

Habitants Fr., early alternative nickname for Montreal Canadiens, later shortened to Habs

habituees Fr., frequent visitors, *fans*

Habs short for *Habitants*

hack 1. slash 2. player who uses his stick frequently 3. a less-skilled player ("he's such a hack—I don't want to play with him")

hacker player who is a *hack (2)*

hackey slang, often derogatory or playful form of hockey

hacking slashing

hacksaw tool used to cut sticks, usu. butt end, down to size

had him beat had an opponent badly out of position, usu. goalie ("How did Smith miss that one? He had him beat.")

half 1. (archaic) 30 minutes of playing time (from days when games consisted of two 30-minute halves) 2. ~ boards modern term for the boards, midway between the blueline and the end red line 3. ~-hearted weak (of an attempt or effort) 4. ~ shield clear face shield for helmets that extends only about as low as the bridge of the nose (contrast with full shield, which extends to the jaw and neck areas) 5. ~time intermission of a game in days when a regulation game consisted of two 30-minute halves 6. ~ visor var. of *half shield*

halfway mark 1. midway point of game or period 2. midway point of season

Halifax Rules generally accepted to be the first and most enduring rules of the game in its infancy, named for the Nova Scotian city where the game was likely first played in its modern form

Halifax skates first true hockey skates ever made (c. 1863)

Halifax style style of hockey in which the two goal posts faced the side boards rather than the ends of the rink; the attacking team could score from either side of the posts

Halifax Wolverines Allan Cup champions in 1935

Hall of Fame short for *Hockey Hall of Fame*

Hall of Famer 1. honoured member of the Hockey Hall of Fame 2. player who demonstrates skill akin to a truly great player

halt 1. end, usu. a streak 2. timeout 3. any stoppage in play

Hamilton Fincups Memorial Cup champions in 1976

Hamilton Red Wings Memorial Cup champions in 1962

Hamilton Tigers 1. Allan Cup champions in 1919 2. NHL member team, 1920-25

hammer hit hard

hamper 1. slow down; obstruct; interfere with 2. ~ **by checking** cause an opponent's performance to suffer as a result of close checking 3. ~**ed by injuries** of a player: unable to play his best because of an injury, although he continues to play nonetheless

hamstring muscles that run from the buttock to the knee along the back side of the body

hand 1. ~ **(them a) defeat** win ("Ottawa handed Vancouver its third defeat of the week") 2. ~ **(it to them) on a platter** surrender a goal because of a bad mistake ("they handed Wickenheiser the goal on a platter") 3. ~ **off** pass (the puck) 4. ~ **out** a. deliver, as a hit ("he's handing out checks tonight with carefree abandon") b. assess, as a penalty ("Udvari is handing out another penalty, this time to Clancy") 5. ~ **pass** directing of the puck to a teammate using one's glove 6. ~ **puck** var. of *hand pass* 7. ~ **signals** visual means by which referees indicate the type of penalty being assessed (introduced by referee Frank Udvari, 1940s) 8. ~ **the puck over** give up the puck; commit a turnover

hand pass

handcuffed of a goalie: had trouble handling a shot on goal ("Reece should have made the save, but the puck seemed to dip at the last minute and handcuffed him")

handicapped at a disadvantage

handkerchief piece of material used to signal a goal in hockey's earliest days, when goal judges stood on the ice directly behind the net

handle 1. of a coach: take charge of a team ("Burns will handle Montreal again this season") 2. shaft of a goal stick 3. ~ **the bell** (archaic) referee a game (in days when referee used a bell instead of a whistle) 4. ~ **the chores** of a goalie: start the game 5. ~ **the game** referee a game ("Armstrong will handle the Detroit-Toronto game tonight") 6. ~ **himself** fight or exercise self-defence when necessary ("he can handle himself if the going gets rough") 7. ~ **a man** ("Stevens is so good in his own end because he ignores the puck and handles the man") 8. ~ **the puck** a. of a goalie: play the puck, usu. after an opponent's shoot-in ("Johnston comes out to handle the puck before anyone else can get to it") b. of a goalie: overall puck-handling skills ("Brodeur handles the puck better than any goalie in the league") 9. ~ **responsibilities** take on an assignment ("Savard is going to handle the goalie responsibilities tonight") 10. **get a ~ on the puck** control the puck ("he couldn't get a handle on the puck, and Messier just took it away from him")

hang 1. of a player: position oneself near opposition goal, even when the puck is in one's own end; goal suck 2. ~ **back** play cautiously or defensively 3. ~ **him on the glass** hit a man very hard along the boards 4. ~ **on** a. preserve a lead, usu. late in the game b. refuse to relinquish the puck; maintain possession of the puck patiently c. play beyond one's prime, often changing teams frequently, when it might be wiser to retire 5. ~ **up the skates** of a player: retire 6. ~ **up the stick** (archaic) retire 7. ~ **up the whistle** of an official: retire

Hangar unofficial nickname for Toronto's Air Canada Centre

Hannigans (1950s) veterans on the Leafs team in training camp

Hanson brothers three wild and brawling brothers who played for Charlestown Chiefs in the movie *Slap Shot*

hapless unlucky

harangue (archaic) verbally abuse

hard 1. ~ **after** chasing hard 2. ~ **around** shoot-in along the side boards just beyond centre ice (thus avoiding an icing call) that goes around the back of the net to an onrushing player on the other side of the rink 3. ~ **cap** salary cap that may not be exceeded under any circumstances 4. ~ **drive** fast shot 5. ~**-fought** tough, as a game between two evenly matched opponents 6. ~ **ice** thoroughly frozen rink, ideal for a fast game (as opposed to soft ice) 7. ~ **luck** bad luck 8. ~**-nosed** gritty, tenacious 9. ~ **rock** of a player: tough 10. ~ **shot** shot with great velocity 11. ~ **to swallow** difficult to accept, usu. a loss ("that defeat was hard to swallow after they led 4-0 early in the third period")

hardest shot 1. player with the fastest, most powerful shot on his team 2. winner of the competition at the All-Star Game in which players' shots are measured for speed

hardware trophies or awards

harmless-looking shot weak shot that nonetheless finds the net from a long distance or bad angle ("it was a harmless-looking shot, but it seemed to handcuff Cloutier and squirt through his pads and into the net")

harm's way a dangerous position ("he clears the puck out of harm's way and goes off")

Hart Memorial Trophy annual NHL award for most valuable player

Hartford Civic Center home arena of New England Whalers (WHA) and Hartford Whalers (WHA and NHL)

Hartford Whalers NHL member team, 1979-97 (previously New England Whalers of WHA; later moved and renamed Carolina Hurricanes)

Hartford Whalers Magazine Hartford Whalers' game-night program

Hartwall Arena principal arena in Helsinki, Finland

Harvey the Hound Calgary Flames' mascot

has-been player who is past his prime

hash marks short lines that jut out from the four faceoff circles inside each end, dissecting them, designed to separate opposing wingers from each other prior to faceoffs

hash marks

hassle fight

hat short for *hat trick*

hat trick 1. three goals in a game by one player 2. **natural** ~ three goals in succession by one player 3. **pure** ~ var. of *natural hat trick*

hatchet man goon or violent player

haul down trip, hold, or grab a player with such force that he falls to the ice

haunt of an error: have lasting negative impact ("that goal will haunt Salo for a long time")

have 1. ~ **the answers** of a goalie: seem unbeatable 2. ~ **an eye on** scout 3. ~ **a hand in** contribute, usu. to a goal or victory 4. ~ **the puck** maintain possession of the puck ("he has the puck coming in over the blueline") 5. ~ **a word with** engage in a harsh discussion (usu. between a coach and his players or the referee)

hawkey 1. early spelling of "hockey" 2. stick used to play hockey 3. ~ **bats** (archaic) hockey sticks

hawkie (U.S.) early bowdlerized spelling of "hockey"

Hawks abbreviated nickname of Chicago's NHL team (Blackhawks)

haze perform a ritual, often cruel or embarrassing, to welcome a new player to a team (usu. in junior or university hockey)

"He shoots! He scores!" signature phrase coined by Foster Hewitt to announce a goal

head 1. ~ **athletic therapist** primary team therapist 2. ~ **butt** hit an opponent on the head with one's own head 3. ~ **butting** act of committing a head-butt offence 4. ~ **check** check to the head, illegal in minor hockey, women's hockey, and international hockey 5. ~ **checking** infraction of checking to the head, punishable by a five-minute major and game misconduct penalty

6. ~ **coach** person responsible for developing a team's strategy and deciding who plays 7. ~ **down** of a player: watching the puck while it's on one's stick, leaving oneself very vulnerable to being hit 8. ~ **down the ice** skate toward opposition end 9. ~ **fake** deke using the head only 10. ~ **off** a. intercept a pass b. leave the ice 11. ~ **off the ice** a. go to the bench b. go to the penalty box 12. ~ **shot** vicious hit to the head of an unsuspecting opponent; deliberate attempt to injure 13. ~ **to** skate to (i.e., bench, penalty box, dressing room) 14. ~**-to-head** series of games between two teams 15. ~ **to the bench** skate off the ice 16. ~ **to the dressing room** leave the ice or players' bench to go to the dressing room 17. ~ **to the net** skate towards the goal 18. ~ **to the penalty box** incur a penalty

headache what a great player can be to opposition

headgear helmet or other protective covering for the head

headhunter dirty player who tries to check opponents to the head instead of the body

headlong fast, furious

headman play the puck to a point slightly ahead of a teammate so that he skates into the pass and collects it while in flight

headman

heads-up play smart play

headset two-way communication device worn by assistant coach on the bench to communicate with another assistant coach who is watching the game from the press box

headway momentum, progress

headwork game smarts

heady smart

healthy 1. fit and ready to play 2. ~ **run** charge at a player with intent to injure 3. ~ **scratch** player who is physically able to play but is not in uniform because of a coach's decision

heap 1. standings 2. pile of players in front of goal

hearing disciplinary session regarding an incident that might warrant a suspension

heated 1. ~ **argument** shouting match between players, often escalating into a fight 2. ~ **discussion** var. of *heated argument* 3. ~ **exchange** var. of *heated argument*

Heaton brand of hockey equipment

heavy 1. overweight ("Fuhr came to training camp heavy, so the coach sent him home") 2. ~ **going** rough game or action 3. ~ **hit** fierce physical contact initiated by one player 4. ~ **hitter** player known for delivering hard checks 5. ~ **ice** bad ice, slow and thick 6. ~ **shot** hard shot using a stiff and weighty stick 7. ~ **workload** of a goalie: assignment to play vast majority of a team's games

heavyweight tough fighter

hecklers fans who boo or jeer a player, often from the opposition but sometimes a disliked player on the home team

heel 1. ~ **cup** fortified area of the back of skate, made of plastic, to absorb force of contact with the back part of foot 2. ~ **of foot** part of foot placed

into the heel of a skate 3. ~ **of goalie glove** part of the glove closest to the wrist 4. ~ **of skate** rearmost part of skate boot

hefty 1. mighty 2. epithet for a player who weighs a lot

helicopter line forward unit that has a star centre and lesser-known wingers (i.e., a centreman who has no wings)

helm to coach

helmet 1. protective covering for the head 2. ~ **and gloves** see *locker boxing* 3. ~ **head** matted-down, dishevelled hair as a result of wearing a helmet (or, outdoors, a toque)

help 1. new player ("they're getting help on the blueline tomorrow when Anderson arrives from the minors") 2. ~ **out** assist, usu. in covering or checking an opponent ("he came over to the side of the net to help out")

helper an assist (on a goal)

helpless of a goalie: down and out with no chance of making a save

hem in forecheck or maintain possession in the offensive end for an extended period of time

hematoma buildup of clotted blood

hemp guardian goalie

hen fruit (archaic) slang for eggs, often tossed at enemy players or on-ice officials

herniated disk disorder of lower back whereby a vertebral disk presses on the nerves in the spine

Hendy's Hockey Guide annual register of hockey information published by James Hendy, 1933-51

herd hang onto the puck

hero player who scores the winning goal, makes a big play, or makes a game-saving play

Herculite original type of glass used to separate fans from action on ice (followed by Plexiglas)

Hespeler brand of hockey stick made in Hespeler (Cambridge), Ontario

Hespeler St. Marys Wood Specialty Products see *Hespeler*

Hewitt, Foster original play-by-play broadcaster at Maple Leaf Gardens who gave hockey many of its first famous expressions (notably, "He shoots! He scores!"); see also *Foster Hewitt Memorial Award*

hex jinx on a team

hexagon early slang for puck, in reference to its shape

hey-rube fight

hickory 1. (archaic) stick, at a time when sticks were made primarily from that wood 2. kind of wood used in the manufacture of hockey sticks, primarily the shaft

high 1. of a player: in front of the net and in a position to get a good shot 2. ~ **and wide** of a shot: over the net and off target 3. ~ **drive** shot aimed at the top of the net 4. ~ **five** celebratory gesture whereby players slap upraised gloves 5. ~**-flying** offensively talented (of a team or player) 6. ~ **gear** top speed 7. ~ **hard one** hard shot aimed at the top of the net 8. ~ **heat** hard shot aimed at the top of the net 9. ~ **over the glass** shot that carries over the glass and forces a whistle 10. ~**-powered** offensively talented 11. ~**s** positive emotions (as opposed to *lows*) 12. ~ **shot** shot aimed at the top of the net 13. ~ **slot** part of the slot area farthest from the goal (i.e., near the top of, and in between, the faceoff circles) 14. ~**-stick** a. strike an opponent with a stick in the upper body b. make contact with the puck above the shoulders 15. ~**-sticking** infraction resulting in two-, four-, or five-minute, or game misconduct penalty depending on the severity of the foul

highlight 1. key moment in a game 2. snippet of television footage showing a key moment from a game 3. ~**-reel** of a play or goal or great play: worthy of being celebrated as a highlight

highly coveted much sought after by one or more teams, either via trade or free agency

highly touted subject of a great deal of publicity (as a rookie or prospect)

Hilborn brand of stick manufactured by Salyerds in Preston, Ontario; notable models included Junior, Boys Expert, Practice, Varsity, Championship, and Goal

hint 1. rumour 2. suggestion ("he shows a hint of rust when he's handling the puck, but he hasn't played in two weeks, so it's understandable") 3. advice ("here's a hint for being more successful on faceoffs")

hinterland site of a team or league far removed from the glamour of the NHL

hip check physical contact made by thrusting the hip out and checking an opponent

hip check

hip pointer injury to the iliac crest

historical record see *rule book*

history experiences between players or teams that intensify a rivalry ("there's a lot of history between these two teams")

hit 1. strike an opponent 2. make a successful pass to a teammate ("Jones hit him with a perfect pass breaking out of his own end") 3. strike the goal post with the puck 4. check hard 5. ~ **the blueline** reach the blueline ("he hit the blueline and dumped the puck in") 6. ~ **from behind** dirty and illegal hit wherein a player is checked in the back while near the boards and falls dangerously into the boards 7. ~ **hard** check with extra force 8. "~ **him!**" cry from fans, demanding that a player make contact with the puck carrier, usu. a star player who excels at stickhandling and avoiding contact 9. ~**s** NHL statistic tracking the number of times a player makes significant contact with an opposing player 10. ~ **the net** take a shot on goal ("she has the ability to hit the net with every shot from the point") 11. ~ **the wall** bump into the boards

hitch problem or difficulty

hitter player who engages in physical contact with an opponent

hitting physical element of a game ("the hitting continues non-stop in this period")

HKG official IIHF abbreviation for Hong Kong

Hobb's Gold Medal model of stick produced by Columbia

Hobey Baker Award annual award presented by the NCAA to the best player in U.S. college hockey

hockey 1. game played with a puck and sticks, the object of which is to score into the opponent's goal 2. ~ **bag** any pliable receptacle for carrying hockey equipment, famous for its continuous and particularly malodorous smell

3. ~ **circles** those involved in hockey business 4. ~ **club** team that has a regular group of players competing in an organized league 5. ~ **dad** father of young hockey player(s), who watches them play, offers suggestions, and dreams of success for them 6. ~ **days** that part of a player's life which constitutes his career 7. ~**dom** var. of *hockey circles* 8. ~ **equipment** protective gear worn by players 9. ~ **fever** general excitement for the game 10. ~ **hair** mullet hairstyle predominant in early 1990s 11. ~ **hotbed** any city in which hockey plays a prominent role or is especially popular 12. ~ **manufacturer** business that makes hockey equipment 13. ~**-minded** possessed of an aptitude for, or interest in, hockey 14. ~ **mom** mother of young hockey players who drives them to the arena and otherwise participates in her children's enjoyment of the game 15. ~ **operations** a. department of a hockey team in charge of team's performance, including coaches, scouts, general manager, trainers, and athletic therapists b. NHL department, largely responsible for enforcement of rules and disciplining players who violate rules 16. ~ **pool** contest, usu. between work colleagues or friends, in which participants draft "teams" of NHL players and earn points based on the players' performances in games 17. ~ **puck** dim-witted person (epithet coined by comedian Don Rickles) 18. ~ **school** short camps or clinics where youngsters may practise the game's fundamentals, usu. during summer or other school breaks 19. ~ **smart**s hockey skills 20. ~ **special** train or bus that takes fans to a team's road game 21. ~ **stick** a. piece of equipment used to shoot and pass the

puck b. name given to a graph which takes the shape of a hockey stick and shows clearly the dramatic climate change from 1900 to present 22. ⁓ **talk** conversation based on any aspect of the game's current events

Hockey Toronto Maple Leafs' game-night program during the 1970s

Hockey Business News monthly publication devoted to business aspects of the game

Hockey Canada successor to Canadian Hockey (and CAHA) as of 2003

Hockey, Colonel member of a prominent Nova Scotia family, reputed to have advanced the game in the 19th century to the point that hurley became known as hockey

Hockey Digest pocket-sized publication since early 1970s

Hockey East NCAA conference including teams principally from Massachusetts, Maine, and New Hampshire

Hockey Hall of Fame museum and archives located in Toronto which also honours the game's greatest personalities

Hockey Hall of Fame

Hockey Hall of Fame Game NHL game played at Air Canada Centre, hosted by Toronto Maple Leafs, on the Saturday night of induction weekend

Hockey Hall of Fame Induction ceremony held annually to honour the greats of the game

Hockey Hall of Fame Induction Committee group of men who meet annually to consider candidates for induction into the Hockey Hall of Fame

Hockey Hints important early hockey book by Lloyd Percival

Hockey Illustrated hockey magazine which began publishing in early 1960s

Hockey King brand of hockey stick made by Doolittles in St. Marys, Ontario

Hockey Magazine 1. Boston Bruins' game-night program 2. New York Rangers' game-night program

Hockey News weekly newspaper established in 1947

Hockey Night in Canada 1. weekly telecast of NHL games, broadcast over CBC since 1952 2. weekly radio broadcasts of NHL games by Foster Hewitt, from 1933 through 1950

Hockey Night in Toronto Toronto Maple Leafs' game-night program during the 1990s

Hockey Pictorial magazine published in mid-1950s

Hockey Quebec Quebec Nordiques' game-night program

Hockey Sweater, The popular Roch Carrier children's story about a boy who is a Montreal Canadiens fan but who mistakenly receives a Toronto Maple Leafs sweater for Christmas

Hockey Times magazine published briefly in early 1970s

Hockey Wax Pack first hockey cards sold in wax wrappers and issued by Goudey Sport Kings

hockeyist (archaic) hockey player

hockeyite var. of *hockeyist*

hockeys (archaic) stick

Hockeytown 1. competition held by CBC/Kraft to determine the best hockey town in Canada 2. Detroit Red Wings' game-night program 3. self-ascribed nickname for Detroit

Hod Stuart Memorial Game benefit game played in Montreal in January 1908, between Montreal Wanderers and an all-star team, to raise funds for the widow and children of the Wanderers' late star player

Hoffman, Abby, Cup see *Abby Hoffman Cup*

hog 1. selfish player 2. **ice ⁓** player who stays on the ice for too long 3. **puck ⁓** player who never passes the puck, instead trying to deke through the opposition every time he has it ("Berezin is a skilled stickhandler but a puck hog all the same")

ho-gee (apocryphal) term used by Iroquois, meaning "it hurts," while playing unnamed game

Hohaco model of stick for boys, produced by Columbia

hoist 1. lift puck high in the air, usu. to clear the puck out of the defensive end 2. **⁓ the Stanley Cup** raise the Stanley Cup over one's head after winning it

hoister player (usu. defenceman) known for hitting incoming forwards hard

hoisting clean check that results in a player being lifted into the air

hold 1. grab onto an opponent to impede his progress 2. **⁓ down** maintain, usu. a position on the team ("he's been able to hold down the job as their main penalty killer for most of the year") 3. **⁓ in check** prevent opposition from excelling to the fullest of its capacity 4. **⁓ a lead** maintain superior goals total in a game 5. **⁓ off** prevent, usu. a late rally ("the Leafs held off a late charge from the Canucks to win, 4-3") 6. **⁓ off the scoresheet** shut out, usu. star player ("they've managed to hold Gretzky off the scoresheet through two periods") 7. **⁓ onto the puck** maintain possession of the puck for an extended period of time 8. **⁓ a pass** control the puck after receiving a pass 9. **⁓ scoreless** prevent opposition or top player from scoring a goal 10. **⁓ the zone** of a defenceman: ensure that the puck stays in the offensive end 11. **⁓ their own** of a weaker team: compete successfully with a superior opponent 12. **⁓ up** interfere with through centre ice 13. **⁓ the upper hand** maintain an advantage

holder 1. plastic fitting underneath the boot of the skate that keeps the blade and boot connected 2. most recent winner of the Stanley Cup or other title

holding 1. infraction for grabbing onto an opponent and preventing him from skating, punishable by a two-minute penalty 2. **⁓ the stick** infraction for grabbing an opponent's stick and preventing him from skating away or using the stick for shooting or passing, punishable by a two-minute penalty

holding

holdout player who has a contract but is unhappy and wishes to renegotiate the terms or be traded

holdover player who was with the same team the previous year during a time of much change

holler 1. call for the puck 2. scream loudly at an opponent or official 3. ~ **guy** screamer or talker on team

Holy Grail Stanley Cup

home 1. designation on the scoreboard for one of two teams (as opposed to visitors) 2. net ("he saw the opening and drilled the puck home") 3. ~-**and-away** consecutive games played just a day or two apart, between two teams, one at each team's arena 4. ~-**and-home** var. of *home-and-away* 5. ~ **free** on a breakaway 6. ~ **game** game played in a team's own arena 7. ~ **ice** arena where a team plays half of its games 8. ~-**ice advantage** a. privilege of playing one more game of a playoff series in the team's own arena than in the opposition's ("because they finished first in the standings, they have home-ice advantage throughout the playoffs") b. increased likelihood of a win for the home team because of a supportive crowd 9. ~ **opener** first game of the season on home ice 10. ~-**road book** statistical register kept by the NHL of every player in the league, breaking down his totals in home games and road games 11. ~-**run hitter** goal scorer 12. **tap it** ~ score 13. ~ **uniforms** sweaters worn at home instead of on the road (i.e., dark uniforms as opposed to white)

homebrew 1. player who was born in the same city or region as he plays 2. player who was developed in his current team's minor or junior system

homemade Stanley Cup amateur rendering of the Stanley Cup, usu. out of tin foil

homemade Stanley Cup

homer 1. someone (announcer, sportswriter, referee) who favours the home side 2. ~**s** team that plays very well at home and equally poorly on the road

homesters home-team players

Honda Center name (since 2006) of Anaheim Ducks' home rink (formerly Arrowhead Pond)

honest worker player who may lack in pure skill or talent but makes up for it with consistent, dogged effort

Hong Kong IIHF member nation since 1983

honour competitive spirit without gamesmanship such as diving, faking injury, etc.

Honorary Members stars of the past who are acknowledged by the IIHF for their contributions to international hockey

Honoured Member inducted into the Hockey Hall of Fame

honoured number distinction used exclusively by the Toronto Maple Leafs to raise a great player's number to the rafters but not take that number out of circulation

hoodlum goon

hoodoo (archaic) jinx

hook 1. illegally obstruct an opponent by using the stick 2. pull goalie during a game because of poor performance 3. ~ **check** originated by Jack Walker, check that entails taking the puck from an opponent from behind using the inside crook of the blade to sweep it off his stick

hook

hoosegow penalty box

hoot scream; jeer

hop 1. move quickly over the boards and onto ice 2. tendency of a bouncing puck 3. ~ **over stick** puck that appears to be heading for the stick of a player but bounces over it at the last moment

hopeful aspiring player ("some 42 hopefuls will attend training camp this September")

hoquet Fr., "shepherd's crook" and, apocryphally, a source for the word "hockey"

horn instrument used to signal the start and end of each period

hornbeam tree native to Nova Scotia, used to make first hockey sticks (also called ironwood)

hors de combat (archaic) out with an injury ("James is *hors de combat* until his charley horse heals")

horse apple piece of frozen horse manure, used as a puck in early days (usu. small towns)

horse puck var. of *horse apple*

horses strength ("he's got the horses to go to the net with two men draped all over him")

horseshoes symbols of luck

Horton, Tim, Trophy see *Tim Horton Trophy*

hospital list injured list

host play game in home arena ("Montreal will play host to Boston on Monday night")

hot 1. angry 2. playing very well 3. ~ **dog** player who performs tricky manoeuvres when simple ones would suffice 4. ~ **game** violent game 5. ~ **goalie** goalie who is playing very well 6. ~ **hand** goalie who is playing very well ("Hlinka will go with Vokoun, who has the hot hand, instead of the struggling Hasek") 7. ~**ly contested** competitive and physically charged game 8. ~ **one** hard shot 9. ~ **seat** under pressure as a result of poor play ("the coach is on the hot seat after the team's seventh straight loss") 10. ~ **shot** a. hard shot b. show off c. fast skater 11. ~ **streak** period during which a team wins several games in succession 12. ~**-tempered** of a player: prone to lapses of discipline 13. ~ **under the collar** angry, upset

Hot Stove League radio and television feature at Maple Leaf Gardens (1930s to 1950s) during which personalities discussed hockey issues before and after a game and during intermission

Hot Stove Lounge members-only restaurant/club at Maple Leaf Gardens

hound 1. harass an opponent 2 player who harasses an opponent, (i.e., a checking forward)

house 1. home rink 2. ~ **cleaning** process of making drastic changes to a roster to eradicate a team's poor play 3. **~ goalie** (1950s-1960s) emergency goalie provided by every home team in case of injury to either team's starting netminder 4. **~ league** youth or minor hockey organization for players who participate solely for recreation

Howes brand of hockey stick

Howie Morenz Memorial Game all-star game played at the Forum in Montreal the night of November 3, 1937, to benefit the widow and children of the late Canadiens' star

howitzer very hard shot

howl jeer

Howler Colorado Avalanche mascot

Hub slang for the city of Boston

hubbub fighting or brawling

huddle meeting

Hudson's Bay rules game in which anything goes (i.e., no rules)

hug the post of a goalie: lean the whole side of his body against the post so that no puck can slip past him on that side

hug the post

hull underside of a skate blade which is slightly concave to a lesser or greater degree (the hull of a goalie skate blade is minimal; the hull of a skater's blade can be quite pronounced)

Hull Olympiques Memorial Cup champions in 1997

hummer exciting game

hunch 1. intuitive sense of what will work ("acting on a hunch, Cherry started Reece, even though the goalie hadn't played in two months")

Hungary IIHF member nation since 1927

hungry eager or desperate to win

hunting grounds the minors

hurl shoot

hurley 1. European game played outdoors on large bodies of frozen water under rules similar to hockey 2. (archaic) hockey stick 3. **~ stick** stick used in hurley that somewhat resembles a hockey stick

hurling playing hurley

hurrahs cheers, words of praise

Hurricanes nickname of Carolina's NHL team

hurry 1. move quickly 2. force an opponent to act hastily 3. **~ back** backcheck with extra swiftness 4. **~ a pass** pass the puck before one wants to because of opponent's pressure

hurt 1. injured 2. damaged ("giving up that third goal really hurt Ottawa's chances of winning this game")

hurting injured

husky (archaic) big, usu. a defenceman

hustle 1. skate with determination 2. **~ back** backcheck with determination

hustler player who never stops skating or trying

hydrotherapy treatment using water

hyperbaric chamber cabin into which air with a higher-than-average concentration of oxygen is pumped, to speed up the recovery of a player from injury

hyperextend extreme extension of a bone or muscle

Ii

"I" nickname for International Hockey League ("he played in the 'I' all of last year")

IHL International Hockey League

IIHF International Ice Hockey Federation (formerly Ligue Internationale de Hockey sur Glace)

IND official IIHF abbreviation for India

IR injured reserve—short for *injured reserve list*

IRL 1. official IIHF abbreviation for Ireland 2. injured reserve list

ISL official IIHF abbreviation for Iceland

ISR official IIHF abbreviation for Israel

ITA official IIHF abbreviation for Italy

ice 1. surface the game is played on 2. space, or lack thereof (i.e., "there's not much ice out there") 3. synonym for game (i.e., "we have ice tomorrow night") 4. ~ **carnival** fancy-dress parties often held in rinks during the early years of the indoor game, featuring dancing, costume balls, and other formal events 5. ~ **cleaner** generic term for Zamboni 6. ~ **cop** tough guy; fighter; goon 7. ~ **cream bar** frozen snack sold during games 8. ~ **doctor** Dan Craig, the NHL's facilities operation manager and long-time ice-maker for the Edmonton Oilers 9. ~ **fever** (U.S.) disorder suffered by players who get nervous playing before a large crowd 10. ~ **flooding machine** generic term for Zamboni 11. ~ **game** hockey 12. ~ **general** player, usu. defenceman, who takes charge of play while on the ice 13. ~ **hockey** U.S. and European term for hockey 14. ~ **hounds** players 15. ~ **hurley** early version of hurley played on ice instead of a grass field 16. ~ **hurling champions** name given to 1837 winners of first-ever hockey game 17. **"~ it!"** exhortation to a teammate to clear the puck the length of the ice for an icing call when their team is under siege by the opposition 18. ~ **lanes** hockey rink 19. ~ **palace** hockey rink 20. ~ **polo** (U.S.) early var. of *hockey* 21. ~ **the puck** shoot the puck from behind centre to beyond the far end red line 22. ~ **a team** assemble enough players to participate in a game or tournament 23. ~ **thickness** measurement used by ice-maintenance crews to determine the quality of ice 24. ~ **thug** goon 25. ~ **time** the amount of time a player spends on the ice (statistic kept officially by the NHL)

ice cleaner

Ice Breaker Phoenix Coyotes' game-night program

Ice Dogs reference to Victoria Cougars, Stanley Cup champions in 1924-25

Ice Palace 1. first hockey rink in USA, opened in New York City in 1894 2. former name of Tampa Bay

Lightning's home arena (now known as St. Petersburg Times Forum) 3. principal arena in St. Petersburg, Russia

Ice Time St. Louis Blues' game-night program

Ice Times official newsletter of IIHF

Iceburgh Pittsburgh Penguins' mascot

Iceland IIHF member nation since 1992

icers hockey team; players

icing 1. shot from a player's own side of centre ice that goes, uninterrupted, past the end red line of the other team, resulting in a faceoff back in the shooting team's end 2. ~ **call** stoppage in play, called when puck has been iced 3. ~ **charge** var. of *icing call* 4. ~ **line** end red line, beyond which the puck must pass for an icing call to be made 5. **no-touch** ~ rule which calls for an automatic icing call if the puck crosses the end red line after having been shot from the team's own side of centre ice (opposed to touch icing) 6. **touch** ~ rule which demands the non-offending team touch the puck first after it crosses the end red line after having been shot by the opponent from its own side of centre ice to effect a whistle and a faceoff deep in the offending team's end

idle of a team: not playing ("the Majors are idle tonight")

idol (archaic) superstar

Igloo, The nickname of Pittsburgh Penguins' home arena

ignite begin great things, usu. a rally

IIHF Super Cup IIHF competition between winners from the European Hockey League and European Cup (later Continental Cup), started 1997

ill effects repercussions from a hit or injury

illegal 1. not permitted 2. ~ **check** unnecessary physical contact in women's hockey, punishable by a two-minute penalty 3. ~ **equipment** any protective gear, usu. a goalie's, that does not meet the standards set out in the rulebook 4. ~ **curve** blade of a stick which has a bend in it greater than that permitted in the rule book 5. ~ **puck** puck that is thrown from the stands or benches 6. ~ **stick** usu. var. of *illegal curve*, but can also refer to length of a stick as well 7. ~ **substitution** situation in which a skater steps onto the ice before the one he is replacing has stepped off; if neither is involved in the play, a faceoff is called rather than a penalty

illegal curve

imbroglio melee or series of fights

impact player star player

impartial unbiased (essential quality of a referee)

impose 1. call a penalty 2. ~ **a fine** punish a player monetarily for conduct unbecoming

impossible angle a position close to the end red line, from which it is extremely difficult to score a goal

in 1. goal ("and it's in!") 2. ~ **alone** on a breakaway 3. ~ **and out** puck that is shot so hard and travels so quickly that it enters the net and comes back out before the goalie can stop it 4. ~ **balance** term used to describe game sheets that are perfectly accurate 5. ~ **behind** a. stationed beyond the end red line and goal net b. unmarked by a defenceman 6. ~ **the books** of a game: complete 7. ~ **the box** penalized 8. ~ **the clear** var. of *in alone* 9. ~ **the community** performing charity work 10. ~ **control** a. having unchallenged possession of the puck b. dominating the game entirely 11. ~ **the corner** along the boards deep in the offensive or defensive end 12. ~ **the crease** a. play immediately in front of the net b. violation of rule prohibiting player in to be in the blue ice 13. ~ **the doghouse** of a player: out of favour with the coach 14. ~ **front** in the slot 15. ~ **front of the net** var. of *in front* 16. ~ **goal** playing goal 17. ~ **hand** a. controlling play b. having played fewer games ("Toronto has two games in hand over Montreal") 18. ~ **the hole** a. goal b. in net 19. ~**-line hockey** hockey played on Rollerblades 20. ~ **the market** trying to acquire talent 21. ~ **the nets** playing goal 22. ~ **on goal** close to the goalie, with a clear scoring chance 23. ~ **the pink** physically fit 24. ~ **a rut** not performing up to capabilities 25. ~ **a slump** var. of *in a rut* 26. ~ **tight** of a scoring chance: very close to the goalie 27. ~ **tough** on the brink of losing; facing adversity 28. ~ **vain** to no effect ("Ference tried in vain to slow big Thornton down") 29. ~ **your face** of a team's play: aggressive, marked by trash talking and other attempts at intimidation 30. ~ **the zone** colloquial description of a player who is mentally sharp and playing extremely well

inactive list old term for *disabled list*

incensed angry

incentives monetary bonuses, included in a player's contract, for meeting certain personal and team statistical milestones during a season

incident 1. any event during a game, usu. one that is detrimental to the game 2. **ugly** ~ instance of dirty or violent play

incidental contact contact between two players away from the play that is so harmless that no penalty need be called

incidents of the match game report

incorrect lineup situation in which the starting players on the ice are not the same as those listed in the roster report, punishable by a two-minute penalty

incur 1. ~ **an injury** suffer injury 2. ~ **a penalty** be penalized

India IIHF member nation since 1989

Indian file (archaic) describes three defending players in a straight line—something to be avoided

indicate signal (usu. icing, by linesman)

indifferent play 1. uninspired play 2. (archaic) lax play, in the (often fluid) judgment of a coach, usu. punishable by a fine ("Shore fined White $50 for indifferent play over the weekend")

indisposed unavailable

individual 1. one player, usu. to refer to selfish play 2. ~ **effort** excellent attempt by one player to create a scoring chance or maintain puck possession

indoor arena covered rink

indoor polo (U.S.) early hockey played indoors with polo rules

industrial league recreational hockey,

usu. played at night in community arenas

ineffective 1. weak; without result 2. ~ **player** player who does not contribute to a team's success 3. ~ **power play** power-play unit unable to score or even generate scoring chances

ineligible player player who cannot play in a game because he does not meet the league's criteria to participate (citizenship, registration, etc.)

infirmary area near dressing room where injured players are tended to by team doctor

initial save of a goalie: saving of the first shot of a flurry of shots

initial shot first shot of a flurry of activity around goalmouth

initiate 1. be aggressive in one's play 2. ~ **contact** bodycheck an opponent before being hit 3. ~ **play** play with confidence and in a way that prevents the opposition from playing the way it wants

injection 1. addition, usu. to the lineup ("there's been an injection of enthusiasm in the dressing room with the acquisition of Oates") 2. ~ **of youth** addition of young players to a team

infirmary

inflammation swelling of a part of the body as a result of injury to that area

influenza epidemic outbreak of influenza in 1918 and 1919 that prevented the latter year's Stanley Cup finals from being completed

infraction foul; violation of rules or code of conduct

infringement infraction

ingredient 1. specific contribution to a team's success 2. **missing** ~ some essential aspect of a team's play that is deficient ("an effective power play is a missing ingredient they'll have to find if they hope to do well")

injured hurt

injured reserve list list of players who are unable to play for an extended time due to injury; teams who put a player on this list are allowed to call up a player to take his place without exceeding the roster limit

injury 1. physical hurt or damage 2. ~**ies** a. series of physically disabling problems for one player or a team b. common explanation given for a team's poor performance over a number of games 3. ~ **bug** series of injuries that hits a team in a short period of time 4. ~ **department** area in which injuries are concerned ("they're not doing very well these days in the injury department") 5. ~ **front** var. of *injury department* 6. ~ **report** report issued by a team on the status of its players' health 7. ~-**riddled** of a team's roster: depleted by many injuries

ink sign to a contract ("the Canucks inked Luongo to a three-year deal yesterday")

insert add player to the lineup

inside 1. area closer to the goal than to the boards ("he made a move inside and took a quick shot") 2. ~ **edge** part of a skate 3. ~ **hockey** play up the middle of the rink 4. ~-**out** describes a fancy move in which the puck carrier fakes a move to the inside, then shifts quickly to the outside to get around the defenceman 5. ~-**out hockey** practice game in which the nets are placed at the bluelines, facing the end boards

Inside the Blue Shirt title of the New York Rangers' media guide in the 1940s

inspiration motivation to perform better, the source being a team leader or an adverse event that affects the entire team

instigate start, usu. a fight

instigator 1. player who starts a fight 2. ~ **rule** rule that calls for the instigator of a fight to receive additional penalty time

instructions 1. game plan 2. order given to a player, usu. by coach, to fight ("you know he had instructions on the bench, and two minutes later he was fighting")

insurance 1. additional players, usu. called up from the minors, for playoffs 2. ~ **goal** goal that increases a team's lead to two or three goals

3. ~ **marker** var. of *insurance goal*

insurmountable that which cannot be overcome, usu. a lead ("with the score 6-0 now, they've built an insurmountable lead")

intended expected but not completed, as the recipient of a pass ("Everley was the intended target, but the puck never got to him")

intentional 1. deliberate, as the shooting of the puck over the glass to cause a stoppage of play 2. ~ **offside** deliberate play to cause a whistle as a result of offside

intercept take control of a puck intended to be played between two opponents

inter-conference play games played between teams in differing conferences

inter-divisional play games played between teams in differing divisions

interesting euphemism for violent ("with Barnaby and Probert out there, things could get interesting pretty quickly")

Inter-League Draft draft (held 1948-72) in which NHL teams could claim players from minor-league rosters

interference 1. obstructing the progress of an opponent, punishable by a two-minute penalty 2. ~ **by spectators** any attempt by members of the audience to interfere with a player or the progress of a game

intermediate hockey level of hockey between professional and junior

intermission 1. intervals (usu. 15 minutes each) between periods when the ice is flooded and players have a chance to rest 2. ~ **feature** any in-arena entertainment or segment broadcast on television during the first or second intermission of a game

international hockey hockey played between countries

International Hockey Hall of Fame hall of fame and museum founded in 1943 and located in Kingston, Ontario

International Hockey League 1. minor-pro league (1945-2001) 2. first full-fledged pro league (1904-07)

International Ice Hockey Federation worldwide governing body for hockey and inline hockey, which sanctions international competitions such as the Olympics and World Hockey Federation for games between national or club teams from different nations

interpretation adjudication of rules

interpreter translator between two languages

inter-sectional games played between teams in different divisions

interval intermission

interview recorded conversation between player and member of media

interview

Championships for men and women; 65 nations are members

International Ice Hockey Federation Hall of Fame official IIHF honour roll of great players and builders who, through the years, made an outstanding contribution to the game at the international level

international ice surface rink that measures 200 feet by 100 feet (compared with the North American standard of 200 feet by 85 feet)

international play games played under international rules

international rules code of conduct prescribed by the International Ice

intestinal fortitude ability to perform effectively under the most difficult circumstances

intimidate use highly physical play in an attempt to render the opponent timorous

into a crowd of a shot: directed to an area of the rink where several players are jostling for position (usu. in front of net)

Intra-League Draft draft (established by NHL in 1952) in which a team may claim unwanted players from other teams in the league (renamed Waiver Draft in mid-1970s)

invade play a road game ("Toronto invades Montreal this Saturday")

invaders visitors

inverted power play power-play formation which sees two offensive players stationed along the red line instead of at the blueline

inverted triangle three-man formation used to kill penalties wherein one player watches both point positions while two defencemen guard the area nearest the goal

investigation research into on-ice or off-ice incident detrimental to the reputation of the game

investment time, money, and patience provided a young player who shows promise of becoming a star

irate extremely angered

Ireland IIHF member nation since 1997

Irish nickname for Toronto St. Pats and the Toronto St. Michael's Majors of junior hockey

iron post or crossbar ("he rang a shot off the iron last shift")

iron blades (archaic) skate blades made of iron

Iron Dukes Toronto Wellingtons of 1902

iron out solve, usu. problems on a team ("they've ironed out their power play

and have scored twice with the extra man tonight")

ironwood see *hornbeam*

Islanders nickname of one of New York's NHL teams

Islanders Magazine New York Islanders' game-night program

Isles short for New York Islanders

Israel IIHF member nation since 1991

issue slang for game ("and that goal decided the issue")

Italo slang for any non-Italian player playing in Italy—who, after at least three years there, is no longer considered an import in the league, which limits the number of foreign-born players each team may use in any game

Italy IIHF member nation since 1924

ITECH manufacturer of visors

Izvestia Cup trophy presented the winner of the Izvestia tournament

Izvestia tournament annual tournament sponsored by Soviet newspaper *Izvestia*, a tournament started in 1967 and played in mid-December, featuring a number of international teams (renamed Baltica Cup in 1997)

Jj

JPN official IIHF abbreviation for Japan

jab 1. poke 2. ~ **at the puck** try to free or gain control of puck in traffic

Jack Adams Award annual NHL award for the league's best coach

Jackets short for Columbus Blue Jackets

jam 1. nasty, rough play 2. grit 3. stuff ("he jammed the loose puck into the net before the goalie could cover up") 4. ~ **along boards** fight for the puck (usu. with several others) along the boards 5. ~ **on the brakes** stop suddenly, usu. when a player sees he is about to be hit hard 6. ~ **shot** (1960s) in-close shot

jamb metal piece used to support sections of Plexiglas

James Norris Memorial Trophy annual NHL award given to the league's best defenceman

jammed to the rafters of an arena: sold out

Japan IIHF member nation since 1930

Japan Cup tournament held in May 1989 and 1990 in Tokyo featuring Japan and two European nations

jar hit hard

jarring hit hit that shakes up the recipient

jaunt shift on ice

jaw 1. talk back to referee 2. trash talk with opponent

Jennings, William M., Trophy see *William M. Jennings Trophy*

jersey (U.S.) sweater

Jet Ice company that makes paint used to mark lines on ice, as well as water-treatment equipment used in ice-making

Jets nickname of Winnipeg team in NHL (1979-96) and WHA (1972-79)

Jets Magazine Winnipeg Jets' game-night program

jewels privates (a.k.a. family or crown jewels); groin

jig fight ("these two are doing a jig for the second time tonight")

jig time (archaic) quickly

jill protective equipment for women's groin

jinx uncontrollable force that causes one team to lose frequently to another

jock protective cup for men's privates

jockstrap elastic that goes around the waist and keeps the jock stationary

jock strap

Joe, The colloquial nickname for Joe Louis Arena in Detroit

Joe Louis Arena home arena of Detroit Red Wings since 1979

Jofa brand of equipment

John Ross Robertson Cup 1. emblematic of amateur supremacy in Toronto 2. trophy presented to playoff champions of Ontario Hockey League

Johnny-come-lately newcomer; player

who develops into a quality performer at a later age than expected

Johnny-on-the-spot player who happens
to be in the right place at the right
time, usu. to score a goal

Johnson, Bob, Memorial Award see
Bob Johnson Memorial Award

join 1. ~ **a fight** assist a teammate who
is fighting an opponent 2. ~ **a team**
become a member of a new team 3.
~ **the rush** defenceman who continues up ice after passing the puck to
a forward in the hopes of creating a
scoring opportunity

jolt 1. hard hit 2. bad news

Jr. Pro a model of hockey stick produced by EL-WIG in Durham,
Ontario

Jubilee Rink Montreal Canadiens'
home arena, 1917-18

judgement call decision made by the
referee which is more a matter of
interpretation than a strict factual
assessment

judge-of-play (archaic) game referee

juggle 1. of a goalie: make a save but fail
to control the puck 2. ~ **lines** of a
coach: mix up the forward lines 3. ~
the lineup make changes to lineup in
hope of producing better results

jolt

jostle 1. push and shove 2. ~ **for position**
push and shove while play goes on in
the hopes of achieving superior positioning to an opponent 3. ~ **for the
puck** battle with opponent for puck
possession 4. ~ **after the whistle**
push and shove once play has been
whistled dead

journey travel to opponents' city

journeyman player who never stays
with one team for very long yet
always finds someplace to play

joust 1. stick fight 2. fight for position

juicy rebound loose puck which the
goalie can't control after making a save

jump 1. life; emotion; spark 2. ~ **into
the rush** defenceman who moves
deep into the opposition end after
passing the puck up to his forwards
3. ~ **on a rebound** pounce on a loose
puck 4. ~ **over** bounce inoppor-
tunely, as a puck over a stick 5. ~
over the boards begin a shift 6.
make the ~ graduate ("he made the
jump to the NHL straight from
junior")

junior 1. short for *junior hockey* ("he played two years in junior before making the NHL") 2. ~ **hockey** amateur hockey for players age 16-20, usu. with a focus on developing players for the NHL 3. ~ **leaguer** pejorative for weak NHLer 4. ~**s** var. of *junior hockey* 5. ~ **scout** assessor of talent who specializes in junior leagues

Junior 1. model of hockey stick produced by Doolittles of St. Marys, Ontario 2. model of stick produced by the Monarch Hockey Stick Company 3. model of hockey stick produced by Clark's in Breslau, Ontario 4. model of hockey stick under the Hilborn model produced by Salyerds of Preston, Ontario 5. ~ **Goal** model of hockey stick produced by the Monarch Hockey Stick Company

Junior A 1. from 1933 to 1970, highest level of junior hockey in Canada, comprising teams eligible for the Memorial Cup 2. since 1970, second-highest level of junior hockey in Canada (after major junior— sometimes called Provincial Junior A) 3. in U.S., highest level of junior hockey

Junior B 1. from 1933 to 1970, second-highest level of junior hockey in Canada 2. since 1970, third-highest level of junior hockey in Canada

Junior C lowest level of junior hockey, primarily regional in scope

Junior Hockey Junkies group of crazed hockey fans based in Calgary who attend the Memorial Cup tournament annually

junket road trip

just missed describes a shot that came close to going into the net but didn't

juvenile 1. level of hockey for players age 18-19 2. **overage** ~ level of hockey for players age 20

Juvenile 1. model of hockey stick under the Wally brand produced by the Ingersoll Hockey Stick Company 2. model of hockey stick produced by Monarch Hockey Stick Company

Kk

KAZ official IIHF abbreviation for Kazakhstan

KO knockout

KOR official IIHF abbreviation for Korea

Kamloops Blazers Memorial Cup champions in 1992, 1994, and 1995

kangaroo leather (1940s) durable material used to make tube skates

Kansas City Scouts NHL member team, 1974-76

kayo knockout (from KO in boxing)

Kazakhstan IIHF member nation since 1991

Kazmaier, Patty, Award see *Patty Kazmaier Award*

keen enthusiastic ("keen following")

keep 1. hold onto (the puck, a player) 2. ~ **at bay** play solid defence, usu. under intense pressure 3. ~ **one's head up** skate and stickhandle with head up and looking ahead, not down at the puck 4. ~ **it simple** mandate by coaches to players to play effective but unspectacular hockey 5. ~ **pace** win at the same rate as other teams in the division or conference 6. ~ **the puck in** maintain puck possession in the offensive zone by blocking clearing attempts at the blueline 7. ~ **the puck out** mount a desperate defensive effort to prevent the puck from crossing the goal line 8. ~ **punching** motto of Red Dutton to keep trying in the face of all adversity

keepaway game of hog in which the player with the puck tries to maintain possession as many others try to check him

keeping goal (archaic) playing goal

Kemper Arena home arena of Kansas City Scouts, 1974-76

Kenesky pads early goalie pads named after their creator, Emil "Pop" Kenesky

Kenora Thistles Stanley Cup champions, January-March 1907

key 1. important 2. ~ **game** game of special significance 3. ~ **matchup** duel between players on opposite teams, with ability to determine which team will win the game 4. ~ **player** player who is most valuable to a team

Khodynka Arena principal arena in Moscow, Russia

kick the puck

kick 1. energy; motivation ("we had no kick tonight") 2. ~ **ahead** move puck ahead by using a skate 3. ~ **in** illegal method of scoring whereby a skate intentionally directs the puck over the goal line 4. ~ **loose** use a skate to knock the puck free from a scrum or other situation that would cause play to be whistled dead 5. ~ **an opponent** dirty tactic whereby a player uses a skate to try to injure an opponent 6. **~ out** save made by a goalie with his pad 7. **~ plate** yellow plastic border along base of boards to ensure smooth travel of the puck on shoot-ins or other plays along the boards 8. **~ the puck** use a skate to propel the puck in any way 9. **~ save** save made by a goalie by kicking the puck away from the goal with his pads or skate 10. **~ shot** early version of slap shot

kicking any soccer-like use of the skates to make contact either with the puck or an opponent

kid hockey grassroots hockey

Kid Line 1. Toronto Maple Leafs threesome of Joe Primeau, Charlie Conacher, and Harvey Jackson of the 1930s 2. any forward line whose players are all young and potential stars

kidder practical joker

Kiel Center name of St. Louis Blues' home arena, 1994-2000 (renamed Savvis Center)

kill 1. short for *penalty kill* 2. defeat soundly 3. **~ a penalty** prevent opposition from scoring a power-play goal

Kimberley Dynamiters Allan Cup champions in 1936 and 1978

King, The brand of hockey stick produced by Crown

King Clancy Memorial Trophy annual NHL award for humanitarian contributions

Kings nickname of Los Angeles's NHL team

Kingston one of the earliest cities where hockey was played and home to *International Hockey Hall of Fame*, established in 1945 by Captain James Sutherland

Kirkland Lake Blue Devils Allan Cup champions in 1940

kissing your sister experience to which a tie game was often compared

(i.e., unpleasant)

Kitchener hockey stick manufacturer

Kitchener Hockey Club Allan Cup champions in 1918

Kitchener Rangers Memorial Cup champions in 1982 and 2003

Kitchener-Waterloo Dutchmen Allan Cup champions in 1953 and 1955 and Olympic participants in 1956 and 1960

kitty-bar-the-door stifling defensive style of play based on preventing goals and preserving leads

klieg sunshine (archaic) spotlight

knack sixth sense; uncanny ability

knee brace

knee 1. use the knee to make contact with an opponent (usu. dirty and dangerous) 2. **~ bend** exercise to strengthen or rehabilitate the knee by bending it from a standing position 3. **~ board** piece of equipment used by goalies which protects the inner knee but also helps to cover the five-hole 4. **~ brace** medical apparatus attached to a knee for reinforcement or to prevent further injury 5. **~ lift** exercise to strengthen the knee in which the leg, bent at the knee, is lifted to a position where the thigh is parallel to the ground 6. ~-on-knee hit dangerous hit whose perpetrator uses his knee to hit an opponent on the knee 7. ~ pad protective equipment, obsolete for skaters but still worn by goalies

kneehunter dirty player who tries to hit an opponent at the knees

kneeing using the knee to trip, interfere with, or attempt to injure an opponent, punishable by a two-minute penalty

knickers (archaic) pants that extended below the knees; worn prior to the introduction of kneepads, which necessitated shorter pants and long stockings

knife 1. ~ away clear the puck quickly out of harm's way 2. ~ the puck in take a quick jab at the puck that ends up going into the net

knob protective attachment at the top of the stick, made either of tape wrapped many times around the butt end or a plastic fitting

knock 1. criticism ("the knock against him is that he can't play defence") 2. ~ down a. cause an opponent to fall b. bat puck out of the air 3. ~ down with a high stick hit puck in the air, but with the stick above the level of the crossbar, thus causing play to stop 4. ~ it in score from in close 5. ~ a

knock the net off its moorings

man off the puck check puck carrier in such a way that he loses possession of the puck 6. ~ the net off its moorings push net in such a way that it becomes dislodged, forcing play to stop 7. ~ out a. render an opponent unconscious with a punch b. be forced to leave game ("the leg injury has knocked him out of the game") 8. ~ the puck away clear puck from a scoring area in the defensive zone or check man off the puck in other areas of the ice 9. ~ the puck off his stick check puck carrier off puck

knot tie (the score)

knotting manner in which goal net mesh is wound

knuckleball shot that lacks velocity but wobbles crazily towards the goal, making it difficult for the goalie to stop

knuckler var. of *knuckleball*

knuckle chucker fighter

knuckle-chucking fighting

Koho brand of hockey equipment

Koln Arena principal arena in Cologne, Germany

Kolven early Dutch sport combining hockey and golf played in winter

Koora ancient hockey-like game played annually at Christmastime in Algeria up to 1930s

Kootenay Ice Memorial Cup champions in 2002

Korea IIHF member nation since 1964

Krajala Cup tournament between Europe's top four national teams, held in Finland since 1995

Kraut Line (1930s) Boston Bruins' threesome of Woody Dumart, Milt Schmidt, and Bobby Bauer, all of whom came from Berlin (now Kitchener), Ontario

Kubok Stanley Russian for Stanley Cup

Ll

L 1. loss, usu. a column heading in the standings or a goalie's statistics 2. to indicate a player shoots left

LAT official IIHF abbreviation for Latvia

LCL lateral collateral ligament; tissue that connects the femur to the fibula

LD short for left defence

LIHG Ligue Internationale de Hockey sur Glace (established in 1908 and later re-named International Ice Hockey Federation)

LNH French abbreviation for NHL (Ligue Nationale du Hockey)

LTU official IIHF abbreviation for Lithuania

LUX official IIHF abbreviation for Luxembourg

LW short for left wing

La Suisse formal name for the Swiss national team

label 1. take an accurate shot 2. capsule description of a player, usually negatively (i.e., too small, too slow) 3. hit hard

laboratory facility where doping tests are carried out for international play

lace 'em up 1. put skates on 2. play hockey

laces fabric string that holds skates to the feet

lacklustre uninspired

lactic acid acid produced by muscles during rigorous exercise; can be offset by aerobic activity such as riding a stationary bike

lads players

Lady Byng wife of Viscount Byng, governor general of Canada (1921-26) and donor of eponymous trophy awarded annually to the NHL's most gentlemanly player

Lady Byng Trophy trophy donated by Marie Evelyn Moreton, Lady Byng, in 1924 to be given annually to the NHL's most gentlemanly player; renamed the Lady Byng Memorial Trophy in 1950, following Lady Byng's death

Lady Luck good luck

l'affaire Lindros French name for the controversy surrounding the 1991 drafting of junior player Eric Lindros by the Quebec Nordiques after Lindros told that team he would never play for it

lag skate slowly or show fatigue

lagging loafing (e.g., "lagging offside")

laid up injured

lamp short for goal lamp

lamp

lamplighter top-notch goal scorer

lance stick

land 1. acquire ("the Flames have landed a fine two-way centre in Conroy") 2. ~ **on** fall on

lane 1. narrow opening where players should skate to get in the clear and accept a pass 2. **passing** ~ any gap between players such that teammates can make and receive a pass unobstructed 3. **skating** ~ that area where a player can skate freely to get into the open

Lange brand of skate introduced in the 1970s featuring heavily padded interior boots for extra comfort and safety

lanky tall and thin

lapse mental gaffe

larceny great save

large come up ~ of a goalie: make a great save

larger ice surface Canadian reference to European ice surface which is 15 feet wider

larrup (archaic) check

larynx exposed area of the throat, usu. protected by clear plastic attachment to goalie mask

lash shoot (the puck)

last 1. at the bottom of the standings (also dead last) 2. ~ **chance** final opportunity (to score or tie game) 3. ~ **change** advantage given to home team whereby it can make line changes after the visiting team prior to all face-offs 4. ~-**ditch effort** desperate effort to score and usu. try to tie game 5. ~-**gasp effort** var. of *last-ditch effort* 6. ~ **man** rearmost player as a team advances towards the opposition goal, usu. in reference to a giveaway by that player leading to a great chance by the opponent ("he made a dangerous pass out of his own end when he was the last man back") 7. ~ **minute of play** announcement made over arena public-address system to signal the final minute of each period of play 8. ~-**minute shopping** trade discussions made as trade deadline nears

late 1. ~ **bloomer** player who develops not at 18 or 19 years of age but after

a few years of professional play 2. ~ **call** whistle by linesman or referee that seems to come several seconds after the related infraction or play 3. ~ **cut** player cut from a team towards the end of a training camp or tryout period 4. ~ **goal** goal scored towards the end of a game or period 5. ~ **hit** hard bodycheck that occurs several seconds after a player has lost possession of the puck (euphemism for dirty hit) 6. ~ **man** final player on the attacking team to cross the opposing blueline 7. ~ **penalty** penalty called late in a period or game 8. ~ **pick** low draft choice; player drafted in the last few rounds (eighth, ninth, tenth) of the Entry Draft 9. ~ **rally** comeback by a team with little time left in the game 10. ~-**round draft choice** var. of *late pick* 11. ~ **scratch** player who is removed from the starting lineup by the coach just minutes before the start of a game 12. ~ **stages** latter part of a game or season 13. ~ **start** game that starts either late at night in the local time zone or late in the Eastern time zone 14. ~ **whistle** var. of *late call*

lateral movement side to side movement (usu. for goalies)

Latvia IIHF member nation; joined in 1931, and again in 1992 after gaining independence from the former Soviet Union

launch 1. begin an offensive thrust 2. ~ **a rocket** take a hard shot

laurels 1. crown or championship 2. praise 3. **rest on their** ~ be complacent; bask in previous success

laws rules

lay 1. ~ **the body on** bodycheck 2. ~ **the lumber on** slash 3. ~ **a perfect pass** make a pass right onto the tape of a teammate's stick

layering (illegal) addition of extra padding to goalie equipment

layoff time off between games

lazy of a player's performance: sloppy; lacking of effort

Le Gros Bill nickname for Jean Beliveau, star player of Montreal Canadiens (1950-1971)

lead 1. to be ahead in the score 2. ~ **pass** forward pass to a teammate, delivered before he has reached the place where he will receive it 3. ~ **a rush** usu. of a defenceman: carry the puck up ice to begin an offensive thrust 4. **long ~ pass** var. of *lead pass*, but of extra length

leader captain, or any player who takes charge in dressing room or on bench

leadership 1. ability to motivate teammates through words and actions 2. ~ **skills** skills marked by the ability to lead a team

leading 1. first in a league or division 2. ahead in the score of a game

Leafian livery Toronto Maple Leafs' uniform (alliterative phrase used by print journalists in the "Original Six" days)

Leafs short for Toronto Maple Leafs

Leafs, The Toronto Maple Leafs' game-night program during 1970s

LeafsTV television station owned by Toronto Maple Leafs, whose programming focuses on the team and its affiliates

league 1. formal grouping of teams that compete for a championship 2. ~ **disciplinarian** usu. Colin Campbell, NHL official in charge of deciding whether a player should be suspended for a flagrant foul on ice 3. ~ **game** game that is counted in the standings of league play 4. ~ **headquarters** NHL term, usu. refers to head office in New York (formerly Montreal) 5.

~ **leaders** first-place team 6. ~ **leadership** var. of *league leaders* 7. ~ **mark** logo or insignia developed for the purposes of licensing and promotion 8. ~ **monogram** NHL shield 9. ~ **rivals** teams that play each other frequently 10. ~ **standings** ranking of teams in a league in order of points accumulated through results of games played (i.e., wins and losses)

lean 1. in shape 2. ~ **on** bother; check closely; frustrate

leap 1. advance from minors to NHL 2. move up several places in the standings

leapfrog move up in standings, overtaking one or more rival teams

leather 1. material used in making equipment, mostly shin pads or goalie pads 2. **flash the ~** of a goalie: make a great glove save 3. ~ **helmet** early helmet made of leather (used infrequently because it became heavy when wet with sweat) 4. ~**-lunged** of a coach or fan: loud, vocal

leave 1. go off; vacate—usu. the ice or dressing room 2. depart from a team 3. ~ **the bench** step onto the ice, usu. to join the fight, punishable by automatic suspension 4. ~ **the puck** a. make a drop pass b. overskate puck

left 1. short for left wing 2. time remaining in period or game ("there is 2:40 left in the second period") 3. ~ **defence** defenceman whose primary assignment is to cover the left side of the ice 4. ~**-hand shot** player who places the stick on the ice to the left of his body 5. ~ **point** player (usu. defenceman) who positions himself inside the blueline near the left-hand side boards (usu. on a power play) 6. ~ **side** that part of the ice 7. ~ **wing** forward who plays primarily to the left of the centreman 8. ~**-wing lock**

defensive system developed in Sweden and Russia but now employed by many NHL teams, designed to force turnovers by assigning two forwards to pursue the puck carrier and make him move toward the left winger, who is stationed near the blueline 9. **~-wing man** (archaic) left winger

left-hand shot

legal permissible under rules of play

leg 1. **~ cut** gash to the lower body, common in 1950s 2. **~ drag** slew foot; illegal and dangerous method of tripping an opponent 3. **~ gash** var. of *leg cut* 4. **~ guards** (archaic) a. shin pads of any sort b. goalie pads 5. **~ kick** type of save by a goalie 6. **~ pads** early term for goalie pads 7. **~s** player with good speed or endurance 8. **~ save** stop made by the goalie by kicking out a leg to stop the puck 9. **~ sweep** circular motion made with one leg while the other is bent, used to maintain balance while turning to cover or defend a man in the defensive end 10. **~ weary** tired

Leland Hotel hotel frequented by teams visiting Detroit during the "Original Six" era

length of the ice distance from one end of the rink to the other, usu. refers to icing of the puck ("and she shoots it the length of the ice to relieve pressure")

lengthy absence extended period during which a player is not in the lineup, usu. because of injury

Les Canadiens Montreal Canadiens' current game-night program

Les Glorieux alternative nickname for Montreal Canadiens

Les Habitants early alternative nickname for Montreal Canadiens; later shortened to *Habs*

Lester B. Pearson Award trophy given to the best player in the league as determined by a vote by the players themselves

Lester Patrick Trophy award presented by NHL and USA Hockey to men who have made an outstanding contribution to hockey in the United States

let them play expression of frustration by fans or commentators when they think the referee is calling too many penalties in a game

Let's Play Hockey hockey magazine

lethargic lazy, tired, or sloppy (of a player's or team's performance)

letter A or C sewn on a sweater, indicating status as alternate captain or captain ("he has a letter on his sweater for a reason")

letter

level 1. hit hard 2. ~ **best** utmost effort ("The Axion are doing their level best to tie the game")

licensed product merchandise with league's official seal of approval

licensee company that produces licensed products for retail sale or promotion

lick 1. defeat soundly 2. ~ **their wounds** suffer defeat

lid slang for helmet

lie angle of a stick from the shaft to the blade when the latter sits on the ice

life renewed energy ("that goal has given the Oilers new life")

lifeless boring (of a game)

lifetime career

lift 1. (archaic) lob the puck out of harm's way or down the ice (from the days before forward passing was allowed) 2. pull (the goalie from a game) 3. inspire; enable 4. ~ **shot** shot that involves hoisting the puck out of one's own zone 5. ~ **the Stanley Cup** win Stanley Cup 6. ~ **his stick** check an opponent by raising the opponent's stick off the ice with one's own, preventing the opponent from receiving a pass, deflecting a shot, or otherwise making a play on the puck

lifter skilled practitioner of the lift shot

ligament tissue that connects bone to bone or bone to cartilage and acts as a support and strengthener for joints

light 1. fleet of foot 2. ~ **the cage** score 3. ~ **the lamp** var. of *light the cage* 4. ~ **it up** score frequently 5. ~ **practice** on-ice workout intended to get the blood flowing and loosen the body as opposed to an all-out, intense practice

Lightning nickname of Tampa Bay's NHL team

lights short for goal lights

Ligue Internationale de Hockey sur Glace precursor to International Ice Hockey Federation

Ligue Nationale de Hockey French name for NHL

Ligue Nord-Americaine de Hockey Quebec-based semi-pro league with a reputation for fight-filled games

limited action infrequent ice time (in a game or season)

limp 1. skate weakly off the ice after a leg or foot injury 2. weak (as a team's performance) 3. **on the** ~ suffering from a leg or foot injury

line change substitution of one forward line for another, either during a stop in play or while play continues

Lindsay Miracle Goal Net goal net designed by goaltender Bert Lindsay (circa 1920s), meant to collapse on impact, thus preventing injury

line 1. three-man forward unit 2. short for blueline or red line 3. ~ **matchup** strategy employed by coaches to pair one forward unit against an opponent's, often a checking line against a top-scoring line, for greater effect 4. **shut-down** ~ forward unit, usu. fourth line, whose prime objective is to prevent the opponent's top line from scoring

line up 1. play ("Edmonton lines up against Calgary tomorrow night") 2. assume position prior to a faceoff 3. prepare to hit ("he lined the forward up as he crossed the blueline") 4. ~ **across the blueline** play a defensive game 5. ~ **with** play for ("he lined up with Vancouver last year before moving east to start this season")

liner 1. hard shot 2. slang for linesman

linemate teammate who plays on the same forward unit as another

linesman the two on-ice officials who drop the puck for most faceoffs, call offside and icing infractions, and assess some penalties, such as too many men on the ice

linesman

lineup team's complete roster, submitted by the coach prior to a game

liniment preparation used to relax sore or inflamed muscles

linkage term employed by NHL Commissioner Gary Bettman primarily during the cancelled 2004-05 season, to describe the connection between salaries and league revenues

lip 1. top of crease 2. rude language to official

Lipstick Hockey Tournament North American Ladies Championship tournament in the 1960s

listless 1. of a game: boring 2. of a player: lacking energy

Lithuania IIHF member nation since 1992

Little Lord Fauntleroys childishly clean players

Little Men of Iron Stanley Cup-winning Montreal AAA team of 1902, so-called because of their unwavering

tenacity and courage of play

lively 1. of boards: active, producing dangerous caroms and rebounds 2. of play: exciting

livery uniform

loafing offside of a player: caught inside the opposing blueline when the puck is shot out of that end

loan send a player to another team temporarily (usu. in minor leagues and early days of NHL)

lob lift the puck out of the defensive end or into the offensive end, in a high, lazy arc

lobby 1. public area at front of hotel where players often congregated 2. try to influence league ("Smythe is lobbying for stricter penalties")

local 1. player from nearby 2. ~ **fans** home fans 3. ~ **ice** home ice 4. ~**s** home team

lock 1. sure thing ("he's a lock to win the Calder Trophy this year") 2. ~ **up** clinch a specific position in the standings

locker boxing closed-door, dressing room fights between two teammates in gloves and helmets, usu. until one loses consciousness (also ***bucket fighting*** and ***helmet and gloves***)

lockout disagreement between players and owners whereby the latter refuse to let the former into their buildings to play

loft see *lie*

log accumulate, usu. ice time ("Degray has logged a ton of ice time tonight")

logjam multi-player or –team tie in any statistical category

logo team emblem

lone 1. ~ **assist** the only assist awarded on a goal 2. ~ **dash** one-man rush up ice 3. ~ **goal** the only goal of a game or period 4. ~ **marker** var. of ***lone goal***

Long Beach Sports Arena arena in

southern California that hosted several Los Angeles Kings home games during their first NHL season (1967-68)

long 1. ~ **5-on-3** two-man advantage for an extended period (i.e., more than one minute) 2. ~ **game** game stopped frequently by whistles or fights, extending its duration well past the standard of about two and a half hours 3. ~ **grind** gruelling part of schedule 4. ~ **memory** ability to remember a slight (such as a dirty hit) by a particular opponent, so as to seek revenge later 5. ~ **night** situation in which a goalie or team are being beaten badly ("the Bruins are down 3-0 and we haven't even played five minutes — it's going to be a long night for Boston") 6. ~ **one** shot from far away from goalie 7. ~ **pass** pass from one player to another that covers half the ice or more 8. ~ **range** shot from far out 9. ~**-range plans** strategy, usu. in terms of player personnel decisions, over the next several years 10. ~ **reach** attribute that enables a player to retrieve a puck or pokecheck an opponent from some distance away 11. ~ **shift** shift that extends beyond the usual 45 seconds or so 12. ~ **shot** shot from far away from the goalie 13. ~**-suffering fans** supporters of a team that has been losing or missing the playoffs for many years in succession 14. ~**-term** many years into the future 15. ~**-term contract** contract for a player or other team personnel which extends several years 16. ~**-term deal** var. of *long-term contract*

longshot player or team not likely to succeed

look 1. tryout ("we'll give him a look and see how he does") 2. ~ **at** give a player a look 3. ~ **for blood** seek revenge 4. ~ **good** play impressively 5. ~ **for a loose puck** go after a puck that is not in anyone's clear possession 6. ~ **lost** player who isn't playing well ("he looks lost out there") 7. ~ **for the man** puck carrier who looks for a teammate to pass to 8. ~ **out** expression that anticipates a big hit 9. ~ **for a pass** get into the clear to accept a pass 10. ~ **for the puck** try to locate and gain possession of the puck among a crowd of players 11. ~ **for a rebound** move toward goal after a shot in hopes of getting to a loose puck 12. ~**-see** tryout 13. ~ **sharp** play particularly well in a game (usu. of a goalie) 14. ~ **for trouble** play an agitating or physical game in order to start a fight or inspire his team

loop 1. league 2. to skate ("loop around the goal")

loose 1. relaxed 2. ~ **cannon** player who has a short fuse, usu. resulting in penalties or physical play 3. ~ **play** play marked by sloppy passing and few sustained attacks 4. ~ **puck** puck in possession of neither team

lopsided of a game or final score: one-sided; not close

Lord Kilcoursie aide-de-camp to Lord Stanley, who read the governor general's famous letter to Ottawa players in 1892 announcing the creation of a championship trophy for hockey, later called the Stanley Cup

Lord Stanley of Preston Canada's governor general, 1888-1893, and donor of the trophy that came to be known as the Stanley Cup

Lord Stanley 1. ~**'s bowl** nickname for Stanley Cup 2. ~**'s chalice** nickname for Stanley Cup 3. ~**'s goblet** nickname for Stanley Cup 4. ~**'s mug** nickname for Stanley Cup 5. ~**'s**

silverware nickname for Stanley Cup

Los Angeles Kings NHL member team since 1967

Los Angeles Kings Illustrated Los Angeles' game-night program

Los Angeles Sports Arena part-time home rink of Los Angeles Kings in 1967-68; also home of WHA Los Angeles Sharks, 1972-74

lose 1. ~ **the battle** fail to gain possession of the puck from an opponent 2. ~ **a draw** fail to win a faceoff 3. ~ **an edge** fall awkwardly because of dull skates 4. ~ **the game** fail to score as many goals as the other team in a given game 5. ~ **the handle** fan on a shot 6. ~ **one's balance** fall unexpectedly 7. ~ **one's cool** retaliate or initiate a fight 8. ~ **one's feet** fall to the ice 9. ~ **one's helmet** fail to maintain helmet on head, usu. as a result of a big hit 10. ~ **one's stick** drop one's stick or have it knocked from one's hands 11. ~ **one's temper** retaliate or initiate a fight 12. ~ **one's wind** suffer loss of breath because of a big hit to the stomach, a long shift, or general unfitness 13. ~ **a player** of a team: be without the services of a player, during the course of a game because of injury or after a game because of suspension 14. ~ **possession** fail to maintain control of the puck 15. ~ **the puck** lose possession 16. ~ **sight of the puck** a. of a goalie: have one's view of the puck obstructed, often causing him to allow a goal b. of a referee: lose track of the puck's whereabouts, necessitating a whistle to stop play 17. ~ **ugly** lose a game marked by very poor play

loser 1. losing team in a game 2. player plagued by bad luck

losing cause defeat (usu. in connection with a valiant effort—"Brodeur made

43 saves in a losing cause")

loss failure to win a game

lost ~ **to injury** of a player: absent from lineup due to injury

Louis, Joe, Arena see *Joe Louis Arena*

Louisville Slugger model of stick made under the Wally model by the Ingersoll Hockey Stick Company

Love & Bennett sporting goods store in Toronto in 1930s and 1940s

love tap slash

love tap

low 1. corners of the rink, near the goal ("they like to cycle the puck down low") 2. ~ **hit** dirty hit, or one that attempts to injure the knees of the puck carrier 3. ~-**percentage shot** shot with little chance of going in (because it is from too far out or from a bad angle) 4. ~ **shot** shot along the ice or just a few inches off the ice

lower 1. ~ **berth** the bottom (and more preferable) bunk on the sleeper car of a train 2. ~-**body injury** injury below the waist (vague, to obscure the true nature of the injury, esp. from opponents) 3. ~-**body strength** strength in the legs 4. ~ **the boom** line up a hit, hit hard

lows negative emotions (opposite of *highs*)

lug 1. big fellow 2. ~ **the puck** carry the puck up ice, often slowly

lumber 1. stick 2. move slowly and gracelessly

lumps bruises, etc., from being checked ("he's taking his lumps out there tonight")

lunchbucket player player who lacks skill but plays with heart and determination

lunchpail player var. of *lunchbucket player*

Lunn (late 19th C.) brand of skates (called style makers) in Montreal

Luxembourg IIHF member nation since 1912

luxury suites private or corporate boxes which feature high-quality amenities

Luzhniki Sports Palace Moscow arena made famous for hosting the final four games of the Summit Series in September 1972

Mm

M & NW Association Manitoba & Northwest Association

MAAA Montreal Amateur Athletic Association

MAC official IIHF abbreviation for Macau

MADC Medical Anti-Doping Controls

MADCC Medical Anti-Doping Controls Committee

MCI Center name of Washington Capitals' home arena, 1997-2006 (renamed Verizon Center)

MCL medial collateral ligament—ligament along the inner part of the knee that connects the femur to the fibula

MEX official IIHF abbreviation for Mexico

MIN international abbreviation for minutes played by a goalie

Mins abbreviation for minutes, referring either to penalties in minutes or minutes played by a goaltender

MLG abbreviation for Maple Leaf Gardens

MON official IIHF abbreviation for Mongolia

MTHL Metropolitan Toronto Hockey League (now Greater Toronto Hockey League)

MRI magnetic resonance imaging—medical technique for creating images of internal tissues, used in sports to determine the extent of injuries

MVP most valuable player, usu. at international tournaments

Macau IIHF member nation since 2006

madcaps offensive, high-scoring team

Madison Square Garden home arena of New York Rangers

magic feet skates with long blades used mostly for speed skating

magnetic hockey 1930s table hockey game

Magnetic Hockey Instructional Board designed by Herb Carnegie in 1961 as a variation to Xs and Os on a chalkboard

magnetized blackboard blackboard used to demonstrate plays and strategies in Xs and Os

maim hurt badly

Main Street 1. play centre 2. centre lane of ice

mainstay NHL-calibre player

maintenance 1. minor ice repairs performed, usu. by on-ice officials, during stoppage in play—e.g., filling in a small hole in the ice 2. ~ **crew** group of people who look after the ice, Zamboni, benches, and penalty box area

major 1. short for major penalty 2. ~ **foul** infraction that warrants five-minute penalty 3. ~ **league** league of the highest calibre (e.g., NHL) 4. ~ **penalty** five-minute penalty, assessed for a severe act such as boarding, intent to injure, etc., which requires penalized team to play short-handed for the duration 5. ~ **penalty shot** (archaic) between 1941 and 1945, penalty shot awarded after certain infractions by skaters; shooter was allowed to skate in on goal and try to score (as opposed to *minor penalty shot*) 6. ~ **ranks** NHL 7. ~**s** var. of *major league*

make 1. ~ **a change** of a coach: send a new forward line onto the ice 2. ~ **changes** a. alter a team's roster b.

put a new line on the ice 3. ~ **contact** a. check b. touch puck slightly, usu. with a high stick or slight deflection on a goal 4. ~ **a dash** rush up ice with the puck 5. ~ **a goal** score 6. ~ **good** perform as expected, or take full advantage of opportunity to play 7. ~ **a good impression** play well 8. ~ **headlines** do something that puts oneself or one's team in the spotlight (and, therefore, attracts media coverage) 9. ~ **a living** area in front of net which is toughest to fight for position ("he makes his living by screening goalies and knocking in the rebound") 10. ~ **no mistake** take advantage of an opportunity ("he had the open side and he made no mistake") 11. ~ **a save** of a goalie: prevent a shot from entering the net 12. ~ **a shot** take a shot 13. ~ **the team** win a spot on a roster 14. ~ **things interesting** do something (such as score a timely goal) that makes a game thought to be won into one that is potentially very close

Maki-Green incident vicious stick fight between Wayne Maki (of the St. Louis Blues) and Ted Green (of the Boston Bruins) during an exhibition game in Ottawa on September 20, 1969, in which Maki came close to killing Green with his stick; Green required brain surgery and a plate inserted in his head

man 1. player ("Vancouver is playing down a man for the next two minutes") 2. ~ **advantage** power play (i.e., when one team has one more player on the ice than its opponent) 3. ~ **at the mike** play-by-play announcer 4. ~ **down** short-handed 5. ~ **games** aggregate number of games played by members of a team (i.e., each game played by a team equals 20 man games) 5. ~ **games lost** statistic designed to measure impact of injuries on a team ("Montreal has had seven injuries this season for a total of 147 man games lost") 6. ~ **in front** player stationed in the slot 7. ~ **on** player who is

make a save

closely watched by another or who is about to be hit by an opponent or stripped of the puck, usu. by surprise 8. ~ **short** short-handed 9. ~ **shy** var. of *man short*

manager short for general manager

managing director (archaic) general manager

Manger Hotel Boston hotel where visiting teams stayed during "Original Six" era

manhandle overpower

manila goal net ("he swayed the manila with that shot")

manoeuvre 1. deke or other move to avoid an opponent 2. **room to** ~ open ice (esp. during four-on-four overtime)

manoeuvre

manpower 1. number of players available to play ("Toronto's manpower has been weakened by the loss of Sundin") 2. ~ **shortage** situation when a team must play short-handed

manufacture create (usu. a scoring chance)

Maple Leaf Gardens home arena for the Toronto Maple Leafs, 1931-1999, and WHA Toronto Toros, 1974-76

Maple Leaf Gardens Official Sport Magazine former name of Toronto Maple Leafs' game-night program

Maple Leafs nickname of Toronto's NHL team, 1927-present

maple white ash kind of wood used to make hockey sticks

Mapleos journalistic slang for Maple Leafs

Marathon brand of hockey stick

marathon 1. long overtime game 2. (pejorative) long NHL season

march to the Cup Stanley Cup playoffs (usu. in reference to winning team)

margin 1. goal differential ("Sudbury has a three-goal margin heading into the third period") 2. difference between teams in the standings 3. ~ **of victory** a. number of goals by which winning team outscores opponent b. goal that ensures a win ("Henderson's goal proved to be the margin of victory")

Marine Midland Bank Arena name of Buffalo Sabres' home arena, 1996-99 (renamed HSBC Arena)

Mario Jr. anagram for Jaromir (Jagr), younger teammate of Mario Lemieux in Pittsburgh in the 1990s

mark 1. record ("his 802nd goal sets a new all-time goal scoring mark") 2. specific time of play during a game ("he scored near the six-minute mark") 3. shadow (an opponent) 4. plateau, milestone ("they've reached the 50-shot mark, and it's still early in the third)

marked man player who is the target of retribution by opposing team, usu. after trying to injure a player

market 1. team conditions which encourage trades 2. **buyer's** ~ situation in which supply for certain players exceeds demand 3. **free-agent** ~ period after July 1 when players' contracts expires and those who are eligible for free agency are available to all teams 4. **in the** ~ in need of ("the Flames are in the market for another defenceman") 5. **on the** ~ a. of a team: available for purchase b. of a player: available for trade 6. **seller's ~** situation in which demand for certain types of players exceeds supply

marketing means of promoting a team or league

marketplace var. of *market*

markings designated areas on the ice to denote faceoff circles, red and blue lines, etc.

marksman goal scorer

marksmanship accurate shot

Maroons nickname of Montreal's second NHL team, 1924-38

marred spoiled, usu. by an ugly incident ("the game was marred by a vicious spear on Neil")

mascot 1. performer who appears in costume at games and roams the seats and corridors of arena, entertaining fans 2. (archaic) young boy, usu. relative of someone associated with the team, who acted as stick boy, dressing-room helper, and good-luck charm 3. (archaic) animal, usu. a dog, that served as a team's good-luck charm and often appeared in team photos

mask face-protecting equipment, worn by goalies and (in the form of a wire cage) by junior players and younger

massage therapist person skilled in the manipulation of muscles and other tissues to relieve pain and inflammation

masseur team employee who gives massages to players

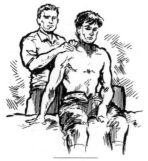

masseur

masterful alert; inspired (of coaching or play on ice)

Masterton, Bill, Memorial Trophy see *Bill Masterton Memorial Trophy*

match 1. game 2. offer a player a contract that equals in salary a competitor's offer 3. respond in kind ("the teams are matching each other hit for hit") 4. **~ foul** (archaic) game misconduct 5. **~ lines** make strategic use of forward units (such as putting a defensive line on the ice to check a scoring line) 6. **~ misconduct penalty** penalty assessed against a player who has, in the opinion of the referee, deliberately tried to injure an opponent; the player is ejected from the game, and his team plays short-handed for five minutes 7. **~ penalty** var. of *match misconduct penalty*

matchup face-to-face or head-to-head meeting, between lines, teams, or players

material top prospect ("he's NHL material")

mates linemates or teammates

matinee afternoon game

matters any specific situation or game ("with the Oilers trailing by two goals, Gretzky took matters into his own hands and tied the score," "if the league doesn't crack down on the abuse against Crosby, the Penguins might have to take matters into their own hands")

mature 1. develop and grow in skill 2. having developed and grown in skill

maturity state of being capable of mature play during game (i.e., poised, doesn't make bad mistakes, etc.)

maze 1. chaotic grouping of players, usu. in front of the net 2. **through a ~** of a shot: through a pile-up in front of the net

McCullough & Boswell Winnipeg manufacturers famous for making hockey skates from reachers by shortening the blades

McGill Redmen intermural hockey team of McGill University in Montreal; oldest continuously active hockey team in the world

McGill Rules first published rules of hockey, developed in 1877 by students at McGill University

McNichols Sports Arena home rink of Colorado Rockies, 1976-82, and Colorado Avalanche, 1995-99

McNiece-Orchard (late 19th C.) Ottawa skatemakers

McVeans hockey stick manufacturer in Dresden, Ontario

mean streak capacity for dirty play or ornery intensity

measure up pass the test

medal hunt pursuit of one of the top three places in an international tournament

medallion award

meddle interfere (usu. an owner, with the general manager's player-personnel decisions)

media 1. employees of newspapers or radio or television stations; reporters, columnists, announcers 2. ⁓ **access** privileges extended to members of media to interview players, coaches, etc. 3. ⁓ **guide** book produced by a team or organization containing historical facts, statistics, and other pertinent information

mediator person who resolves disputes between players and teams

medical 1. ⁓ **attention** care given to an injured player by team doctors ("he seems to be in quite some pain and requires medical attention") 2. ⁓ **report** assessment of any injury by qualified doctor

medicals examinations of players' physical condition during first days of training camp

Medicine Hat Tigers Memorial Cup champions in 1987 and 1988

medico (archaic) team doctor

medico

meeting 1. official get-together 2. game ("these two teams have another meeting this Saturday") 3. on-ice discussion between players or officials

megg-nets goal nets held in place by magnets rather than steel pegs, thus enabling them to give way when a player falls or skates into them with some degree of force (thus preventing injuries)

melee scrum or fight involving more than two players

Mellon Arena name of Pittsburgh Penguins' home arena, 1999-present (formerly Civic Arena)

melon head, usu. goalie ("he took that shot right off the melon")

member 1. ⁓ **of a league** club or team ("Toronto is an original member of the NHL") 2. ⁓ **of a team** player of a team

member nation country that belongs to IIHF

Memorial Auditorium home arena of Buffalo Sabres, 1970-96

Mem Cup short for *Memorial Cup*

Memorial Cup trophy emblematic of Canadian major junior championship, donated in 1919

memorial game (archaic) game played to honour a player who recently died

mend on the ⁓ recuperating (from injury)

meniscus also called cartilage, there are two—medial and lateral—in the knee that help absorb weight and pressure to the joint

menace scoring threat

men's league league for recreational players

mentor coach

mercy at his ⁓ of a goalie: state of being badly out of position when an opponent has control of the puck near the net

merger consolidation of two teams or leagues into one

message physical actions, usu. early in a game, to let the opposition team or a specific player know that this will not be an easy game ("by putting Probert out there to start, he's sending a message they won't be intimidated tonight")

mesh netting used to enclose goal net

Met Center short for *Metropolitan Sports Center* in Bloomington, Minnesota

metacarpals five long bones that connect the fingers to the wrist

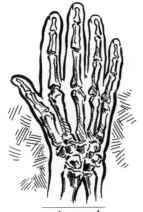

metacarpals

metal shaft shaft (usu. hollow) of a stick made of aluminum or some other metal

metal support stanchion or bracket to keep pieces of Plexiglas together

metatarsals the five long bones that connect the toes to the ankle

Metro Atlantic Athletic Conference defunct NCAA Division I hockey league (1997-2003), replaced by *Atlantic Hockey*

metropolis hockey city

Metropolitan Sports Center home arena of Minnesota North Stars

Metropolitan Toronto Hockey League see *Greater Toronto Hockey League*

Mets short for Seattle Metropolitans

Mexican standoff (archaic) game in which very little happens

Mexico IIHF member nation since 1985

mezzanine intermediate tier of seats between upper and lower levels

Miami Arena home arena of Florida Panthers, 1993-99

Michel Brière Memorial Trophy award for Pittsburgh Penguins' rookie of the year

Micron brand of skates

mid-ice 1. centre-ice area 2. ⁓ **collision** two or more players involved in contact near centre ice

midseason 1. middle part of the regular schedule 2. ⁓ **form** top or peak form 3. ⁓ **report cards** analysis of players and teams halfway through the season, usu. conducted by local media 4. ⁓ **trade** trade completed during the season (as opposed to summer)

middle centre-ice area

middle period second period

midget level of hockey for players age 15-17

midsection stomach (usu. goalie)

Mighty Ducks 1. Disney movie which gave NHL team its nickname 2.

former nickname of Anaheim team in NHL

Mighty Ducks of Anaheim former name of Anaheim team in NHL (changed to Anaheim Ducks in 2006)

Mi'kma'q Native people who played an early form of hockey on frozen waters, mostly in Nova Scotia

mill about push and shove

Millionaires' Row worst seats in the house at any arena

million-dollar prospect 1. Conn Smythe term for top prospect 2. (derogatory) player who is anything but a top prospect

mind the nets play goal

mingle 1. play game 2. push and shove after whistle

Miniature a model of hockey stick produced by Doolittles of St. Marys, Ontario

miniature Cup replica of Stanley Cup, approximately one foot high, given to players or executives after their team wins the Cup

miniature gold puck small gold puck given out, usu. to honour an outstanding achievement

mini-camp short training camp

Minnesota North Stars NHL member team, 1967-93 (moved and renamed Dallas Stars)

Minnesota North Stars Magazine North Stars' game-night program

Minnesota Wild NHL member team, 2000-present

minor 1. two-minute penalty, assessed for routine infractions such as tripping or hooking 2. ~ **atom** level of hockey for players age 9-10 3. ~ **foul** non-violent foul or one that does not warrant a penalty 4. ~ **hockey** amateur hockey played by youngsters (midget age and younger) 5. ~ **league** North American pro league of

lower calibre than NHL (also minor leagues) 6. ~ **leaguer** player who plays in the minor leagues or whose skill level is inadequate for NHL 7. ~ **midget** level of hockey for players age 15-16 8. ~ **offence** var. of *minor foul* 9. ~ **official** any off-ice official (i.e., not a referee or linesman) 10. ~ **peewee** level of hockey for players age 11-12 11. ~ **penalty** two-minute penalty 12. ~ **penalty shot** (archaic) between 1941 and 1945, penalty shot awarded after certain infractions committed by goaltender, and taken from a line painted 30 feet from the goal line (contrast with *major penalty shot*) 13. ~ **pro** minor league 14. ~ **procedure** small operation

minors short for minor league ("Anderson was sent to the minors yesterday")

minus 1. without ("the Flames are minus Hull, who is nursing an injury") 2. a. a negative number credited to a player in the plus-minus statistical column when he is on the ice for an even-strength goal against b. player who has a negative rating in plus-minus statistics; a poor defensive player 3. ~ **player** player who is weak defensively, one who has a negative number in the plus-minus statistics

minute book official record of meetings (e.g., of the NHL Board of Governors)

minutes 1. NHL executive business records 2. amount of time played in a period or game ("he plays a lot of minutes for this team every night") 3. ~ **played** amount of time a player spends on ice, usu. recorded as a seasonal total for goalies and a per-game average for skaters

Miracle 1. short for *Miracle on Ice* 2. movie based on events of 1980 USA Olympic hockey team

Miracle on Ice game in which USA defeated the heavily-favoured Soviets 4-3, en route to a gold medal at 1980 Olympic Winter Games in Lake Placid, New York

Miracle on Manchester upset victory by Los Angeles Kings over Edmonton Oilers in first round of 1982 Stanley Cup playoffs; Kings overcame a 5-0 deficit to win 6-5 and eliminate Edmonton

Mirakel Swedish for "miracle," made famous when women's team at 2006 Olympic Winter Games defeated USA in a shootout in semi-finals; for the first time, Canada and USA did not meet in the finals of a world-class women's tournament

mirror-image benches player benches identical for both teams (length, height, etc.)

misconduct 1. ten-minute penalty 2. ~ **penalty** ten-minute penalty assessed against a player who argues a call vociferously, refuses to go to the penalty box, or commits an offence above and beyond routine infractions

miscue mistake which often leads to good scoring chance or goal

misfire mishit the puck, shoot wide, or otherwise miss good scoring opportunity

mishandle 1. of a goalie: bobble the puck or give it away 2. of an organization: make error in developing the talents of a young player

mishap 1. accident that leads to injury 2. fight

misplay error in judgement by player

missile hard shot

missing 1. injured player ("she's missing tonight because of her wonky knee") 2. ~ **in action** (pejorative) player who plays poorly, disappears, esp. in playoffs 3. ~ **ingredient** player who

comes to a new team and helps it excel, notably in the playoffs

Mission 16W slogan coined by Colorado Avalanche in 2001, referring to number of games the team would need to win Stanley Cup

mistake error

mitt goalie glove

mitts players' gloves

mix 1. ~ **freely** game full of scrums 2. ~ **it up** fight 3. ~ **lines** change composition of forward lines throughout a game

mix-up 1. fight 2. confusion 3. error

mixed zone interview area for reporters at international hockey games

mob surround a player after goal, save, or win

mobile of a defenceman: gifted at skating and handling the puck

moguls executives or owners

molest interfere with or assault an official or opponent

Molson Centre see *Centre Molson*

Molson Cup trophy sponsored by that brewery, presented to the member of each Canadian-based team who has been named one of the Three Stars of a game most frequently during the season

momentum force that enables a successful team to continue succeeding

Monarch hockey stick manufacturer in New Hamburg, Ontario

Moncton Hawks Allan Cup champions in 1933 and 1934

Moncton Victorias Stanley Cup challengers in March 1912

money 1. ~ **game** important game 2. ~ **goalie** goalie who plays particularly well during important games, notably Stanley Cup playoffs 3. **put one's ~ on** a. bet ("my money's on the Generals tonight") b. put one's trust in

moneyed ranks professional leagues, usu. NHL ("he's left junior hockey to join the moneyed ranks")

money runs playoffs

Mongolia IIHF member nation since 1999

moniker nickname

monogram NHL shield

monopoly 1. exclusive control over a business ("the Leafs have a monopoly on hockey in Toronto") 2. apparent first call on talent ("Montreal has a monopoly on the good Quebeçois players in the league")

Montreal brand of hockey stick

Montreal AAA see *Montreal Amateur Athletic Association*

Montreal Amateur Athletic Association umbrella organization for various Montreal sports groups whose affiliated hockey team, the Montreal Hockey Club (also known as Montreal AAA), was the first winner of the Stanley Cup, in 1893, and won the Allan Cup in 1930

Montreal Arena home arena of Montreal Canadiens and Wanderers for part of 1917-18 season; burned down January 2, 1918

Montreal Canadiens charter member of NHL (1917-present); originally founded in 1909

Montrealers teams or players from Montreal

Montreal Junior Canadiens junior team affiliated with Montreal Canadiens; Memorial Cup champions in 1950, 1969, and 1970

Montreal Maroons NHL member team, 1924-38

Montreal Royals Allan Cup champions in 1947 and Memorial Cup champions in 1949

Montreal Rules see *McGill Rules*

Montreal Shamrocks Stanley Cup champions in 1900

Montreal style rules which placed the goal posts side by side facing the goal posts at the other end (i.e., conventional hockey rules), as opposed to *Halifax style*

Montreal Surprise brand of hockey stick

Montreal Victorias Stanley Cup champions, 1895-99

Montreal Wanderers team founded in 1903 and Stanley Cup champions in 1906, 1907, 1908, and 1910; charter member of NHL in 1917, but withdrew when arena burned down after the team had played just four games

Montreal Winter Carnival annual festival started in 1883, at which first-ever hockey tournament was played

moorings 1. small posts, one end of which slips into the ice, the other into the underside of goal posts, to ensure that goal nets remain firmly in place 2. **off its ~** of a goal net: dislodged

moorings

Moreale slang for Montreal

Morenz, Howie, Memorial Game see *Howie Morenz Memorial Game*

morning skate brief on-ice workout held the morning of game (opposed to practice, which occurs on non-game days)

Moscow International Tournament
name of the former *Izvestia tournament* in 2003

mosquito level of hockey for player age 4-6

most valuable player player deemed the best of any game, series, or season

motivation drive to perform well

motor skate quickly

mount 1. ~ **an attack** begin an offensive charge 2. ~ **a comeback** score a goal that draws the team to within striking distance of tying or winning a game that was earlier thought to be out of reach 3. ~**ing injuries** accumulation of injured players at about the same time

Mount Royal Arena home arena of Montreal Canadiens, 1919-26

Mount Royal Hotel hotel in Montreal where Amateur Drafts were conducted, 1960s to late 1970s

mouthguard plastic protective covering for the teeth

mouth guard

move 1. deke or feint 2. trade a player 3. transaction 4. ~ **player from in front of the net** push player away from the area immediately in front of the goal 5. ~ **in** close in on opposing goalie, usu. with the puck 6. ~ **in alone** go on a breakaway 7. ~ **it!** command issued by referee to force

players fighting for the puck along the boards to free it up and continue playing rather than freezing the puck for a whistle 8. **make a** ~ trade a player 9. ~ **out** start a breakout play 10. ~ **a player off the puck** check the puck carrier so that he loses possession 11. ~ **up ice** skate forward or pass the puck forward to a teammate 12. ~ **up in the standings** win game or series of games to advance in the standings

movies (archaic) video; game films

Mowbray brand of hockey stick

much-needed important ("that was a much-needed goal")

muck in the corners dig or fight for a puck in the corner with one or several opponents

mucker 1. player who is particularly adept at going into the corner to fight for the puck and successfully obtaining it 2. less-talented player

mucking style of play characterized by play in the corners and fighting for the puck in the corners

muff miss badly

muff

mug 1. colloquial for the Stanley Cup 2. knock down or knock off puck 3. strip opponent of the puck unexpectedly

mugging knocking an opponent down or stripping him of the puck

Murderers' Row back row seats of arena in Ottawa in 1917, where fans were vocal against refs and opponents

muscle 1. strength 2. ~ **a man off the puck** use physical play to strip an opponent of the puck 3. **use ~** play physically in order to create scoring chances or intimidate opponents

Muskoka brand of hockey stick

Mustang brand of hockey stick under the Canadian Husky model produced by EL-WIG in Durham, Ontario

mustard 1. spice—as in hard shot ("he had a little mustard on that shot and it stung Healy") 2. that which cannot be cut by a second-rate player or team

muster organize (usu. generating offence—"they're trying to muster an attack late in the game")

Mutual Street Arena home arena for Toronto NHL teams, 1917-31 (also known as Arena Gardens)

myositis inflamed muscle

mysterious ailment euphemism for injury, used during playoffs so as not to tip off opponents as to the nature of any particular injury to a player

Nn

NAHL *North American Hockey League*

NAM official IIHF abbreviation for Namibia

NBC Game of the Week weekly telecast on national TV in the U.S. in the 1970s, usu. on Saturday or Sunday afternoons

NCAA *National Collegiate Athletic Association*

NED official IIHF abbreviation for the Netherlands

NHA *National Hockey Association*

NHL *National Hockey League*

NHL Breakout street hockey tournament organized by the NHL and staged in various cities in North America and Europe during the summer

NHL Enterprises NHL's licensing branch

NHLer short for NHL player

NHL FANtasy interactive aspect of NHL's website which allows fans to participate in NHL games and events

NHL Images branch of the NHL that oversees licensing of photographs and video of players in game action

NHLOA NHL Officials' Association

NHLPA NHL Players' Association

NHL shield famous black and orange trademark (changed in 2005 to black and silver)

NJ Devil New Jersey Devils' mascot since 1993

NOHA Northern Ontario Hockey Association

NOHL Northern Ontario Hockey League

NOR official IIHF abbreviation for Norway

NTDP (U.S.) National Team Development Program

NWHL National Women's Hockey League

NZL official IIHF abbreviation for New Zealand

nab penalize

Nagano Japanese city that hosted hockey at the 1998 Olympic Winter Games

Nagano Cup tournament held annually in Japan for the unofficial senior amateur championship of the world

nagging injury injury that, although healed, continues to hamper a player from playing at an optimal level

nail 1. hit (an opponent) hard 2. ~ed to the end of the bench not playing; benched ("coach Kasper has Neely nailed to the end of the bench")

nail-biter close, exciting game

name announce ("they'll be naming the team this Friday")

name plate small piece of rectangular plastic with player's name engraved on it which hangs above his stall in the dressing room

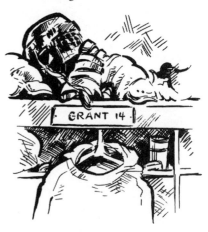

name plate

name player well-known player

Namibia IIHF member nation since 1998

narrow 1. ~ **the gap** goal that draws the trailing team closer to tying the game 2. ~ **miss** shot that barely goes wide of the net 3. ~ **the score** var. of *narrow the gap* 4. ~ **victory** victory by a close margin

Nassau Veterans' Memorial Coliseum home arena of New York Islanders

nasty 1. dirty or ugly (of a play or incident) 2. ~ **cut** deep or large cut 3. ~ **game** game marked by dirty play 4. ~ **gash** var. of *nasty cut*

National hockey stick manufacturer in Durham, Ontario

National Car Rental Center former name (1998-2002) of Florida Panthers' home arena (renamed Office Depot Center)

National Collegiate Athletic Association governing body for intercollegiate sports in U.S.

national game var. of *national telecast*

National Hockey Association forerunner to NHL (1909-17)

National Hockey League established 1917, the world's pre-eminent pro hockey league

National Hockey League Alumni Association group that represents retired NHL players

National Hockey League Awards Night ceremony held each June to honour the NHL's trophy winners for the past season

National Hockey League All-Star Game game pitting two teams of NHL stars in a loosely played game

National Hockey League All-Star Weekend weekend during which the NHL All-Star Game, Skills Competition, and other events occur

National Hockey League Entry Draft process by which all teams have equal chance to claim rights to the best 18-year-old players in the world

National Hockey League Official Guide and Record Book NHL publication that contains statistical information on current players as well as historic facts

National Hockey League supervisor league employee who oversees the production and running of a game, from officials' performance to video review

National Hockey League Writers' Association former name (prior to 1971) of *Professional Hockey Writers' Association*; donors of the Bill Masterton Memorial Trophy

National Hockey League Officials' Association collective bargaining unit that represents the NHL's on-ice officials

National Hockey League Pension Society organization founded in 1947 to establish and administer players' pension funds

National Hockey League Players' Association collective bargaining unit that represents the NHL's players

national team team made up of players who are deemed to be the best in the country and represent a cross-section of the country

national telecast game which is seen from coast to coast (as opposed to a regional or local telecast)

National Women's Hockey League top women's pro league in North America

Nationalliga top division of Swiss league

Nationwide Arena home rink of Columbus Blue Jackets

native person born in a particular place ("the Caledonia native has been playing hockey since he was three years old")

nats short for national team, esp. in Canada (also *young nats*)

natural 1. player who has been blessed with an abundance of skill 2. ~ **centre** player who may play on the wing but whose greatest contributions occur when he plays centre 3. ~ **hat trick** three consecutive goals by the same player 4. ~ **ice** ice made by Mother Nature (as opposed to artificial ice) 5. ~ **winger** player who may play centre but whose greatest contributions occur when he plays on the wing

near 1. ~ **boards** boards closest to where play-by-play announcer is situated 2. ~ **post** post closest to where the puck is 3. ~ **riot** melee or fight that comes close to erupting into a full-scale brawl but does not 4. ~ **side** side of the ice closest to where the puck is

neat pass skilful, tricky pass

neck brace protective support for the neck, usu. worn en route to the hospital after on-ice injury or in days following a neck injury

neck brace

needle 1. bother an opponent 2. an injection

needless penalty penalty for a foul that occurs far away from the play or has no bearing on the possibility of being scored upon

Neeld Shield mask designed by Guardian Sports Equipment that prevents any stick or puck from making contact with the face, so designed to protect Greg Neeld, who lost an eye in a hockey injury in 1976-77

negate 1. ~ **an icing** hustle into the offensive end to touch the puck on an icing call before the defenceman gets to it, thereby cancelling the icing call 2. ~ **a penalty** draw a penalty to offset a penalty recently incurred

negotiate 1. get by 2. discuss terms of a contract 3. **fail to** ~ unable to make a play ("he failed to negotiate the pass and the puck skimmed harmlessly away")

negotiation list (archaic) list of unsigned players whom a team reserves the exclusive right to sign

net 1. goal mesh 2. score a goal ("she netted the game's third goal") 3. ~ **carrier** instrument used to carry a net on and off ice 4. ~ **tie bar** cord that holds the net to the iron posts

netcam small camera affixed inside the goal net

nets in the ~ playing goal ("Favell is in the nets again tonight")

Netherlands IIHF member nation since 1935

netman goalie

netminder goalie

netminding 1. playing goal ("his netminding has been flawless tonight") 2. ~ **chores** var. of *netminding*

netting screen suspended above Plexiglas at ends of rink to prevent fans from being hit by pucks

neutral-site game game played in neither team's home city

neutral zone 1. (U.S.) area between the two blue lines (i.e., centre-ice area) 2. ~ **trap** stifling defensive system whereby all members of the defending team position themselves between the blue-lines to prevent the opposition from penetrating their defensive end

new face 1. recent addition to a team 2. ~ **in the lineup** var. of *new face*

New Glasgow Stanley Cup challengers in December 1906

New Jersey Devils NHL member team, 1982-present (formerly Colorado Rockies)

new lease on life 1. opportunity for a player to revive his career through a change of team 2. opportunity for a team to revive its hopes of winning a playoff series after a fortunate turn of events

new material new player

New NHL term coined to capture spirit of NHL after salary cap agreement in 2005 which also saw a crackdown on restraining fouls to open the game and generate more exciting hockey

New Westminster Bruins Memorial Cup champions in 1977 and 1978

New Year's Eve game game of December 31, 1975, between Montreal Canadiens and Central Red Army, a 3-3 tie considered one of the finest games ever played

New York usu. pejorative, referring either to the commissioner or other league executives working out of the NHL's New York offices

New York Americans NHL member team, 1925-41 (renamed Brooklyn Americans)

New York Islanders NHL member team, 1972-present

New York Rangers NHL member team, 1926-present

New York Rovers farm team of New York Rangers in "Original Six" era

newcomer rookie or recent addition to a team

New Zealand IIHF member nation since 1977

Newmarket Reds Memorial Cup champions in 1933

next level improvement over current play ("he's got to take things to the next level once the playoffs start")

Niagara Falls Flyers Memorial Cup champions in 1965 and 1968

nice pass skilful, elegant pass

nick 1. small cut 2. rut in skate blade 3. ~ **one** score a goal

nickname 1. affectionate or familiar name 2. the name a city's franchise goes by

nifty 1. skilful 2. ~ **pass** skilful playing of the puck to a teammate 3. ~ **play** smart or skilful play, with or without the puck, that helps team maintain possession of the puck or yields a good scoring chance 4. ~ **player** player who has skills beyond the basic skills needed to play in the NHL

night special honour for a player bestowed upon him prior to a home game

night in, night out consistent ("he's a scoring threat night in, night out")

night off lethargic effort in a game ("they decided to take a night off and wound up losing 5-0")

Nike equipment maker and owner of the Bauer brand

Nilsson feint breakaway deke on the goalie invented by Kent Nilsson and made famous by Peter Forsberg; the shooter moves to one side of the goalie and, with just one hand, shifts the puck back to the open side of the net and slides it into the net

nine-man hockey hockey as played in its infancy, with nine players a side

Ninety-Nine All-Stars team assembled by Wayne Gretzky during the NHL lockout of 1994-95 which toured Europe as a goodwill gesture

nip defeat narrowly

nip and tuck close

Nissan Cup held annually in Switzerland since 1988 featuring top four European national teams

no 1. ~ **chance** goal scored which the goalie hadn't a hope to stop 2. ~ **goal** call by a referee to nullify a disputed goal 3. ~ **Hit League** cynical acronym for NHL under new rules which penalize physical play more than previously 4. ~ **icing** expression used by linesmen to wave off an icing call 5. ~ **letting up** relentless (of a team's attack or pressure) 6. ~-**look pass** play in which the puck carrier looks in one direction while passing the puck in another direction to a teammate 7. ~ **penalties** phrase used in game summaries to indicate absence of penalties in a period 8. ~ **score** of a period or game: no goals scored 9. ~ **scoring** phrase used in game summaries to denote a goalless period 10. ~ **tomorrow** no alternative but to win, usu. toward the end of a playoff series 11. ~-**touch icing** rule whereby an icing call is made immediately after the puck crosses the end red line, whether or not a defending player touches the puck (opposed to touch icing) 12. ~-**trade clause** stipulation in a player's contract that forbids a team from trading him without his consent

nobody 1. player of little skill or repute 2. ~ **home** pass that lands in open ice ("he made a pass to the middle but there was nobody home")

noggin head

nomination suggestion to give a player an award

non-call decision by a referee not to call a penalty on a play that might have warranted a call (the non-call being the better decision)

non-contact hockey type of hockey in which bodychecking is not permitted (usu. house league or recreation hockey)

nonchalant 1. overly casual with the puck 2. lax (regarding checking)

noodle head ("he took a puck off the noodle in the first period")

noodle

Nordiques nickname of Quebec's team in WHA, 1972-79, and NHL, 1979-95

Nords short for Quebec Nordiques

Norris Division one of four NHL divisions, 1974-93

Norris, James, Memorial Trophy see *James Norris Memorial Trophy*

Norris Trophy annual award given to the best defenceman in the NHL

Norrismen Detroit Red Wings, during the years the team was owned by the Norris family

North America one of two teams that played in the NHL All-Star Game for five years, 1998-2002 (the other being Team Europe)

North American Hockey League 1. minor pro league, 1973-77, that inspired the movie *Slap Shot* 2. U.S. junior league 3. English name for *Ligue Nord-Americaine de Hockey*

Northeast Division one of six NHL divisions, 1993-present

Northern model of hockey stick produced by Clarks in Breslau, Ontario

Northern Ontario Hockey Association governing body for amateur hockey in Northern Ontario

North Korea IIHF member nation since 1964

north-south direction from opponent's goal to own goal (as opposed to east-west, or side to side—"he goes north-south as fast as any player in the league")

Northern Fusiliers hockey team admitted to the NHA in 1916-17, also called the 228th Battalion, made up of Canadian soldiers

Northland Professional brand of hockey stick

Northlands Coliseum former name (1974-95) of Edmonton Oilers' home arena (renamed Edmonton Coliseum)

North Stars nickname of Minnesota's former NHL team

Northwest Hockey League minor pro league, 1933-36 (formerly the Western Canada Hockey League, continued as Pacific Coast Hockey League in 1936)

Norway IIHF member nation since 1937

nosedive tailspin

nose out win by a narrow margin (i.e., a game or a roster spot)

not out of it not yet defeated or eliminated, although all indications point strongly in that direction ("even though it's 3-0, they're not out of it just yet")

notable 1. star player 2. important news

nothing goalless ("they lost three-nothing again last night")

notch 1. score (a goal) 2. record ("they notched their fifth win in a row tonight")

notes written thoughts or stories by coach, reporter, scout, etc., about a game or player

noteworthy excellent

Notre Dame Roman Catholic boarding school (full name the Athol Murray College of Notre Dame) in Wilcox, Saskatchewan, founded by Athol Pere Murray, noted for its hockey program, which has sent dozens of boys on to the NHL

novice 1. level of hockey for players age 7-8 2. **pre-~** level of hockey for players under 6 years old

nudge 1. defeat narrowly 2. check ("Young nudged his man off the puck and made a perfect pass")

nuisance 1. pesky player 2. European word for unsportsmanlike behaviour

nullify cancel or offset, usu. an icing call or a penalty

number-one goalie goalie who starts most of his team's games

Number Four Bobby Orr (after his sweater number)

numbers game situation in which a player is scratched, traded, or demoted from a team ("he got caught in a numbers game and couldn't get into the lineup on a regular basis")

nurse 1. **~ an injury** play despite an injury which prevents a player from performing at an optimal level 2. **~ a lead** play cautiously and defensively while trying to maintain the advantage in a game 3. **~ the puck** maintain careful control of the puck

Nystrom, Bob, Award see *Bob Nystrom Award*

Oo

OHA *Ontario Hockey Association*

OHL *Ontario Hockey League*

OPHL Ontario Professional Hockey League

OT abbreviation for overtime

OTL abbreviation for overtime loss during the regular season

OUA Ontario University Athletics, governing body for interuniversity sport in Ontario

"O Canada" Canadian national anthem played or sung prior to home games in Canadian cities

Oakland/Alameda County Arena home rink of Oakland Seals/California Golden Seals

Oakland Seals NHL member team, 1967-70 (renamed California Golden Seals for 1970-71 season)

O'Brien Trophy award presented to league champions of NHA, 1910-17, then to NHL Canadian Division champions (1928-39), and runner-up in Stanley Cup finals, 1939-50

obscene language abusive language toward an official, punishable by a gross misconduct penalty, fine, or both

obscurity play in ~ of a player: perform better than his reputation or be a skilled player in a lesser league

obstruction impeding the progress of an opponent through hooking, holding, or interfering

obtain 1. acquire (a player) 2. score (a goal)

occasion 1. moment 2. **rise to the ~** make a great play or save at a critical point in a game

octopus eight-armed cephalopod thrown onto the ice by Detroit Red Wings fans to celebrate a goal during the playoffs (orig. because a team needed eight wins to capture the Stanley Cup in "Original Six" days)

odd goal 1. occasional goal 2. weird goal

odd-man 1. **~ advantage** situation in which a team has one or more players on ice than the opposition 2. **~ rush** offensive foray in which attackers outnumber defenders on a rush

odd-man rush

off 1. **~ the boards** puck played out of harm's way by banking it off the boards 2. **~ the crossbar** shot that hits the crossbar 3. **~ game** poor game 4. **~ the glass** puck played out of harm's way by banking it off the Plexiglas 5. **~ the mark** of a shot: missing the net 6. **~ night** var. of *off game* 7. **~ the post** shot that hits the post 8. **~ the record** comments by player, coach, or manager to a reporter that are explicitly not for publication or public consumption 9. **~ the rush** of a goal, scoring chance, or other play: result of the puck being carried from the defensive end to the offensive in a fluid motion 10. ~ **season** a. poor year b. interval of several weeks between seasons (i.e., the summer) 11. ~**-target** var. of *off the mark* 12. ~ **the wall** var. of *off the boards* 13. ~ **wing** opposite wing to the side a player shoots from (i.e., a left-hand shot playing the right wing) 14. ~ **year** poor season

offence team's ability to generate scoring chances and score goals ("their offence is the most potent in the league")

offender 1. player who makes a mistake 2. player who commits a foul; penalized player

offensive 1. ~ **defenceman** defenceman who has the skills and ability to rush the puck up ice, join the attack, and generate goals as much as prevent them 2. ~ **power** ability to generate scoring chances and score goals 3. ~ **zone** area inside the defensive team's blueline

Office Depot Center former name (2002-05) of Florida Panthers' home arena (formerly National Car Rental Center; renamed BankAtlantic Center)

officer executive or representative of a team

official 1. any employee of league or governing body that oversees the operations of a game 2. ~ **report of match** documentation compiled by league officials, including goals, penalties, lineups, and game comments 3. ~ **rules** formal rules agreed to by all parties which govern the adjudication and interpretation of a game 4. ~**'s timeout** a. timeout called by an on-ice official, usu. to allow for television commercials b. timeout called by off-ice official, usu.

to review a possible goal 5. ~ **score** true result of games as certified by the league 6. ~ **scorer** league employee who records all goals, assists, and penalties 7. ~ **scoresheet** part of the official report that records goals and assists, and times these plays occurred 8. **off-ice** ~ member of the officiating staff who oversees a game but is not on the ice during the game (timekeeper, goal judge, etc.) 9. **on-ice** ~ referee or linesman

officiating 1. adjudication of game by referees and linesmen 2. the quality of work by the on-ice officials (i.e., "the officiating has been great tonight") 3. ~ **supervisor** league representative who evaluates performance of on-ice officials

offsetting minors minor penalties equally distributed between two teams such that, no matter how many are assessed, neither team is left with a power play

offsetting penalties any combination of minor and major penalties between two teams such that, no matter how many are assessed, neither team is left with a power play

off side early spelling of offside

offside 1. status of an offensive player who crosses the blueline ahead of the puck; the puck re-enters the offensive end while a player is still inside the

offside

blueline; or (formerly), a pass that crosses any two lines on the ice 2. ~ **interference** infraction whereby a defending player forces an offensive player to go offside by deliberately pushing him over the blueline before the puck has crossed it 3. ~ **pass** pass that results in play being blown dead because of offside 4. ~s (archaic) var. of *offside* 5. **a mile** ~ play that is offside by several feet

OHA Senior level of play above OHA Junior and OHA Intermediate

Oil, The alternative nickname for Edmonton Oilers ("the Oil are on the road for a game tonight")

Oilers nickname of Edmonton's NHL team

Oilers, The Edmonton Oilers' game-night program

Oilers Zone Edmonton Oilers' game-night program

oilman (archaic) trainer

old 1. unkind epithet for veteran player who is slowing down or not as skilled as he once was 2. ~ **days** glorious years of previous hockey experiences 3. ~ **fox** veteran 4. ~ **mug** nickname for Stanley Cup 5. ~ **rivals** two teams that have been competing against each other for decades 6. ~ **self** top form, returned to after a slump, injury, or any other period when a player's productivity or effectiveness has been lacking

Old Country hockey hockey in England

oldsters old-timers

old-time 1. of days gone by 2. ~ **hockey** a. hockey marked by entertaining stretches without whistles, plenty of goals and scoring chances, or little obstruction b. game marked by many fights

old-timer 1. retired player 2. veteran player well beyond his prime 3.

~s team made up of retired or older players

Olympia 1. Detroit Red Wings' home arena, 1927-79 2. ice-cleaning machines made by Resurfice Corporation of Elmira, Ontario

Olympia gates var. of *Zamboni entrance*, for Olympia ice-cleaning machines

Olympia Review Detroit Red Wings' game-night program

Olympic 1. model of hockey stick produced by the Monarch Hockey Stick Company of New Hamburg, Ontario 2. brand of hockey stick of the Wally model produced by the Ingersoll Hockey Stick Company

Olympic Arena arena used for hockey games at Olympic Winter Games in Lake Placid in 1932

Olympic break pause in league schedule to allow players to participate in Olympic Winter Games (1998-present)

Olympic qualification series of tournaments that determine which teams (beyond those that automatically receive berths based on world rankings) earn the right to play in Olympic Winter Games

Olympic qualifier var. of *Olympic qualification*

Olympic Saddledome former name (1983-96) of Calgary Flames' home arena (renamed Canadian Airlines Saddledome)

Olympic-size rink rink (used in European and international hockey) of wider dimensions than a Canadian rink (200 feet by 100 feet vs. 200 feet by 85 feet)

Olympic Sporting Goods Company retailer of sticks in Detroit

Olympic Winter Games quadrennial even which is the embodiment of world superiority in a variety of winter sports

Omni, The Atlanta Flames' home arena

on 1. checking a man ("he's on him like glue") 2. ~ **the attack** mounting an offensive charge 3. ~ **the beam** (archaic) in fine form 4. ~ **the bench** not playing, usu. goalie ("Potvin is on the bench for a sixth attacker") 5. ~ **the block** of a player: available to be traded 6. ~ **the boards** play along the boards 7. ~ **the brink** of a team: perilously close to losing a game or being eliminated from a series 8. ~ **the bubble** of a player in training camp: among the least likely to make the team, but not yet cut 9. ~ **the doorstep** directly in front of the goal crease 10. ~ **the fence** in the penalty box 11. ~ **fire** performing well, usu. uncannily so 12. ~ **the fly** of a line change: while play continues 13. ~ **hand** in attendance ("there are 21,273 fans on hand for the game tonight") 14. ~ **him** checking an opponent closely 15. ~**-ice ad** advertisement painted into the ice surface 16. ~**-ice logos** emblems (usu. promotional) painted into the ice 17. ~**-ice official** referee and linesman 18. ~**-ice portrait** team picture taken on ice after a victory, usu. Stanley Cup win 19. ~ **the line** describes a puck that has reached the goal line but does not cross it before the goalie makes a save 20. ~ **loan** playing with a team on a temporary basis only 21. ~ **the mend** recovering from injury 22. ~ **net** of a shot: shot on goal 23. ~ **the phone** (colloquial) of a referee: consulting with video-replay officials (via telephone) over a possible goal 24. ~ **a roll** enjoying a great deal of success; on a winning streak 25. ~ **the rush** mounting an offensive 26. ~ **the shelf** injured 27. ~ **the tape** of a pass: perfectly accurate, received by the intended target with ease 28. ~ **their heels** of a defending team: reeling from opponents' offensive flurry 29. ~ **top** leading 30. **play** ~ **a line** with be a member of a forward unit ("Woods will play on a line with Jones and Daly tonight")

on the doorstep

one 1. a shot ("Harris lets one go before heading off") 2. **~-against-one** var. of *one-on-one* 3. **~-handed** pass, shot or slash attempted with only one hand on the stick 4. **~-handed pass** pass made with just one hand on the stick 5. **~-handed shot** shot taken with just one hand on the stick 6. **~-knee slide** a. goalie exercise designed to improve mobility b. early shot-blocking method introduced by Lionel Conacher 7. **~ man back** situation in which only one skater occupies the defensive team's end to face an offensive rush 8. **~-on-one** situation in which puck carrier needs to beat only one defender to reach the goal 9. **~-on-one battle** fight for the puck between one player and one opponent 10. **~-on-two** situation in which puck carrier must beat two defending players to reach the goal 11. **~ piece** kind of stick produced so that shaft and blade are a single unit, rather than an assembly of two parts 12. **~ point** credit a team earns in the standings as a result of a tie game (or, more recently, a loss in overtime or a shootout) 13. **~-sided** lop-sided (of a game or trade) 15. **~-timer** shot that a player takes as soon as the puck reaches the player's stick without taking the time to control it 16. **~-touch** of a pass: made quickly, without stickhandling or skating any distance with the puck

110% all-out effort

onlookers fans

only assist goal in which only one player is credited with an assist ("Ouellette gets the only assist on James's goal")

onside 1. play at the blueline which is allowed to continue because the puck has crossed the line before any offensive player 2. **~ hockey** any game during which very few offsides occur

onslaught attack

Ontario Hockey Association governing body for amateur hockey in Ontario, with the exception of major junior

Ontario Hockey League one of Canada's three major junior hockey leagues

oochamkunutk Mi'kmaq for bat or ball stick in 1880s

O-Pee-Chee primary producer of NHL trading cards for many years

open 1. free, available 2. **in the ~** unchecked (of a player) 3. **~ corner** area of the net not guarded by the goalie 4. **~ hand** legal play of the puck using a glove 5. **~ hostilities** undisguised contempt between teams 6. **~ ice** areas of the ice where no players are situated 7. **~-ice check** hit by a player away from the boards 8. **~-ice hit** var. of *open-ice check* 9. **~ it up** attempt to make the game more offensive or create more scoring chances 10. **~ man** unguarded player available to receive a pass 11. **~ net** net undefended by goalie (who is out of position or has been pulled) 12. **~ the scoring** score first goal of the game ("Nattrass opened the scoring at 1:06 of the first) 13. **~ side of ice** area of ice where no players

one-timer

open side of the net

are situated 14. ⁓ **side of net** part of the net to the rear of the goalie 15. ⁓ **wing** side of rink where no players are situated 16. **wide** ⁓ in the clear with no opponent nearby

Open Ice Summit meeting staged by Hockey Canada in Toronto in 1999 to reassess the way the game is organized, from grassroots level to the pro ranks

opening 1. open ice 2. unguarded part of the net ("he saw the opening and fired quickly") 3. ⁓ **ceremony** any on-ice event that occurs immediately before a game to honour or remember a player, executive, or other dignitary 4. ⁓ **goal** first goal of the game 5. ⁓ **period** first period 6. ⁓ **round** first round of playoffs

operation 1. organization 2. surgery

operating on all cylinders of a team: playing at peak form (also "firing on all cylinders")

opponent team or player whom one must play against

opportunity 1. chance to make a team or impress the coach 2. **scoring** ⁓ chance to score

oppose play against ("Kamloops will oppose Red Deer tomorrow night")

opposite wing off wing (i.e., opposite to the side a player shoots)

opposition var. of **opponent**

optic related to the eye (e.g., optic nerve)

option 1. right of a player (or coach) or team to choose to extend the term of a contract 2. ⁓ **year** extension to a player's contract, made when either the player or team exercises right to do so 3. **pick up his** ⁓ of a team: choose to extend a player or coach's contract by a year

optional practice practice that players may choose not to attend (as opposed to a mandatory practice)

oral report verbal assessment of players or teams by scouts (rather than a written report)

ordeal (archaic) game

ordinary average; not exceptional ("they are a great team five-on-five but they have a very ordinary power play")

ordinary time (archaic) regulation time

organ musical instrument commonly found in arenas until 1990s, used to whip fans into a frenzy

organist musician who plays the organ during games

organize set up or direct (the power play)

organized hockey hockey played by teams in leagues (as opposed to shinny or rec hockey)

original 1. ⁓ **penalty** first penalty of what turned out to be several called after a scrum, melee, or fight 2. ⁓ **save** first save by a goalie from among a flurry of shots 3. ⁓ **shot** first shot of a flurry

"Original Six" NHL from 1942-67, when it comprised six teams

Orillia Terriers Allan Cup champions in 1973

Oshawa Generals Memorial Cup champions in 1939, 1940, 1944, and 1990

Osterreichischer Eishockeyverband (OEHV) governing body of hockey in Austria; created in 1912

Ottawa Capitals Stanley Cup challengers in 1897

Ottawa Civic Centre home arena of Ottawa Senators, 1992-96, as well as WHA Ottawa Nationals, 1972-73, and Ottawa Civics, 1976

Ottawa Cliffsides Allan Cup champions in 1908

Ottawa Commandos Allan Cup champions in 1943

Ottawa-Hull Canadiens Memorial Cup champions in 1958

Ottawa RCAF Allan Cup champions in 1942

Ottawas (archaic) journalistic nickname for Ottawa Senators

Ottawa Senators 1. charter member of NHL which moved to St. Louis in 1934 2. NHL expansion franchise that began play for the 1992-93 season 3. Allan Cup champions in 1949

Ottawa Silver Seven alternate nickname of Ottawa Senators during Stanley Cup dynasty of 1902-06

Ottawa 67's Memorial Cup champions in 1984 and 1999

O2 Arena arena in London, England, which hosted two NHL regular-season games in September 2007

oust eliminate (from the playoffs)

out 1. not playing ("he's out of the lineup with a groin injury") 2. over the blue-line ("the puck goes out and they make a line change") 3. ⁓ **indefinitely** status of an injured player whose condition is uncertain 4. ⁓ **of action** injured 5. ⁓ **of bounds** of a puck: over the glass or boards 6. ⁓ **of the box** describes a player who leaves the

out of bounds

penalty box after the expiration of his penalty time 7. ⁓ **of danger** of a puck: cleared out of the defensive end 8. ⁓ **of harm's way** var. of *out of danger* 9. ⁓ **of the lineup** not playing 10. ⁓ **of the net** of a goalie: caught out of position 11. ⁓ **of play** var. of *out of bounds* 12. ⁓ **of position** of a player: not where he should be on the ice 13. ⁓ **of shape** not physically prepared to play 14. ⁓ **of-town-game(s)** game(s) played in cities other than the one being watched or televised 15. ⁓ **of-town scoreboard** list of games and scores in other cities being played the same night as the one being watched or televised 16. ⁓ **on the ice** in the game ("Williams is out on the ice now, so the Flyers had better keep their heads up") 17. **play** ⁓ play as a position player opposed to a goalie ("I used to play goal, but now I play out")

outbreak fight

outburst 1. flurry of goals 2. verbal tirade, usu. by a coach

outchance of a team: get more scoring chances than the opposition

outcheck of a team: do the majority of the bodychecking ("they're outchecking their opponents in every corner of the rink")

outclass play better than opposition

outcome result; score of game

outdoor 1. ⁓arena arena, usu. with natural ice, neither enclosed by walls nor covered by a roof 2. ⁓ **game** any game played outside; more specifically, the NHL game played November 20, 2003, between Montreal and Edmonton in Edmonton's Commonwealth Stadium

outfit team

outflank get by or pass (an opponent)

outguess of a goalie: stops a shot from close range

outhit var. of *outcheck*

outhustle work harder than the opposition

outing game

outlaw hockey (archaic) use of professionals in an amateur game

outlaw league league that is not affiliated with or recognized by a sanctioning body

outlet 1. open player up ice 2. ⁓ **pass** forward pass to open player outside of defensive end, which enables team to make the transition to offense

outmuscle play more physically than opponent

outplay play better than opposition

outright release team decision to cut a player with no chance of him

returning under the current contract

outscore score more goals than opposition

outshoot take more shots than opposition

outside 1. away from the middle of the ice 2. ⁓ **edge** part of the skate blade closer to the boards than to the other skate blade 3. ⁓-**inside** fancy deke whereby the puck carrier fakes skating to the outside (towards the boards) and instead cuts inside, towards the goal 4. ⁓ **of the post** part of the post that sends the puck into the corner after a shot 5. ⁓ **speed** ability to skate extremely quickly down the wing 6. ⁓ **the line** beyond the blueline

outskate a. skate faster than opponent b. defeat or outplay

outsmart gain the puck or advantage through wily manoeuvring

outstanding excellent

outwit var. of *outsmart*

ovation prolonged applause, often accompanied by fans rising to their feet (i.e., "standing ovation")

ovation

over 1. finished ("and the game is over!") 2. ⁓-**ager** 20-year-old playing major junior hockey in Canada 3. ⁓ **the boards** a. player who comes onto the ice b. puck that goes out of bounds 4. ⁓ **the glass** of a puck: over the protective glass and out of bounds 5. ⁓ **the line** a. of a puck: across the goal line b. of a puck carrier: across the blueline into the offensive end

"Over-the-Hill Gang" nickname for coach Punch Imlach's team of Toronto Maple Leafs that won the Stanley Cup in 1966-67

overcome recover from a setback ("Can Ottawa overcome its bad start to win? We'll see in the third period.")

Overdrive skate blade extra blade on a goalie's skate (illegal in pro leagues) to help him get up more quickly after going down

overlapping penalties at least two penalties to one team that occur at different times within two minutes, forcing team to play short-handed by two men for a brief period of time

overload send more than one player to a particular part of the ice to force the opposition into making a turnover or error

overlook ignored; unnoticed ("he was overlooked in the draft, but this guy is loaded with skill")

overrated having a reputation that exceeds actual performance

overskate

overrule of a referee: have the final say; prevail over coaches' or players' objections

overskate unintentionally skate past the puck without gaining possession

overtime 1. of the NHL: additional period(s) of play, for the purpose of breaking a tie (limited to five minutes during the regular season; unlimited during the playoffs) 2. in international hockey: sudden-death period of play, limited to five minutes in rounds prior to the playoffs, 10 minutes in playoff games leading up to the gold-medal game, and 20 minutes in the gold-medal game, used to determine winner of game tied after regulation time 3. ~ **loss** loss which occurs during overtime 4. ~ **winner** game-winning goal scored in overtime

Overtime magazine about women's hockey

Owen Sound Greys Memorial Cup champions in 1924 and 1927

Owen Sound Mercurys Allan Cup champions in 1951

own goal (British) goal scored into a player's own net

owner group or individual who owns the team and who has the power to hire and fire whomever he pleases

owners' lockout cessation of NHL play in 1994-95 and 2004-05 as a result of the owners' inability to agree to a new collective bargaining agreement with the players

oxygen compressed gas in a tank, used as a breathing aid at the player's bench by the Detroit Red Wings on April 16, 1949, in game 4 of the team's playoff series against the Toronto Maple Leafs

Pp

P abbreviation for points

PA short for Players' Association (contraction of NHLPA)

PCL (posterior cruciate ligament) the ligament that prevents the tibia from moving

PCHA *Pacific Coast Hockey Association*

PCHL *Pacific Coast Hockey League*

pim 1. abbreviation for penalties in minutes 2. ~s (archaic) var. of *pim*

PK 1. short for penalty killing 2. ~ **unit** short for penalty-killing unit

PMI model of hockey stick

PMS 298 Pantone colour specification for blue paint applied to ice to demarcate the goal crease

POL official IIHF abbreviation for Poland

POR official IIHF abbreviation for Portugal

PP 1. abbreviation for *power play* 2. ~ **unit** short for *power-play unit*

PPG abbreviation for *power-play goal*

PRK official IIHF abbreviation for North Korea

Pts abbreviation for points, usu. as a header for columns of statistics

pace 1. lead the attack ("he paced the attack with two goals") 2. speed of a game ("they're playing at a terrific pace") 3. lead to victory

pacemakers leaders of a division or league

pacesetters var. of *pacemakers*

Pacific Coast Hockey Association major pro league, 1911-24, founded by Frank and Lester Patrick, which competed with the NHA and NHL for the country's top players

Pacific Coast Hockey League minor pro league, 1945-52, forerunner to *Western Hockey League*

Pacific Coliseum former home arena of the Vancouver Canucks, 1970-95 and WHA Vancouver Blazers, 1973-75

Pacific Division one of four divisions in NHL, 1993-98, and one of six divisions in NHL, 1998-present

Pacific Rim Tournament international women's tournament, held in 1995 and 1996, between Canada, USA, China, and Japan

pacifist player who prevents fights or who eschews fighting as part of the game

pack all teams not in first place ("the Canucks have pulled away from the pack, opening a 12-point lead on second-place Calgary")

package trade involving several players (also "package deal")

pact contract

pad sheet of ice in a multi-rink facility ("there are four pads at this arena")

pad save save made by goalie using one or both of his pads

pad save

padding protective apparatus used by skaters and goalies to prevent injury

paddle goalie stick, esp. its shaft

pads protective equipment worn by goalies to prevent injuries to their legs, shins, and calves

paid attendance number of seats that have been paid for at any game (differing from the number of people in the arena because the former figure includes all no-shows)

painted mask goalie mask embellished with some graphic design element

pair 1. two goals 2. two seats 3. defence unit 4. ~ **off** fight

pairing any two players who have played together, esp. on defence

Palestra arena in Laurium, Michigan, considered the first in U.S. to be built specifically for hockey

palm 1. leather or other form of covering for the inside of the hand on gloves 2. ~**less gloves** introduced by Carl Brewer, early 1960s; hockey gloves with the palms cut out, which enabled a player to hold an opponent without being detected by the referee (illegal) 3. ~ **the puck** cover the puck with the glove (usu. illegal)

panic 1. make a rash or unwise play because of lack of experience or inability to cope with a particularly pressure-filled situation 2. **push the ~ button** usu. of a general manager: make changes to a team rashly when it is playing below expectations

Panthers nickname of Florida team in NHL

pants part of equipment that includes protection for hips and upper legs

paper wrap coloured bands on shaft of a hockey stick to identify model and style

parade 1. apotheosis of Stanley Cup celebrations 2. series of penalty calls ("there's been a steady parade to the penalty box all period")

parade

paraphernalia goalie equipment (term often used by Danny Gallivan: "and the puck is caught up in Larocque's paraphernalia")

parent club senior partner in any player-development agreement, but usu. NHL team as it relates to a farm team

parity general equality among all teams in a league, such that the separation in the standings between the best team and the worst (or the difference in on-ice quality) is negligible

park establish position, generally in front of the net or crease

partial breakaway situation in which puck carrier has a clear path to the goal, but an opposing player is racing to get back and check him

partially screened shot on goal taken when the goalie's view of the puck is obscured slightly (usu. by another player)

partisan crowd fans who overwhelmingly support one team

partisanship enthusiastic support for a favourite team, to exclusion of all others

partner player who plays frequently with another, usu. on defence ("they've been partners on the blueline for the better part of two years now")

part of the defence goalie whose puck-handling abilities enhance and facilitate the efforts of the team's defence

part with trade (a player)

pass 1. move the puck to a teammate using one's stick 2. **bank ~** pass that caroms off boards to intended recipient 3. **hard ~** sharply struck pass 4. **~ out** a. retire from the game ("he passed out of the league last season") b. lose consciousness 5. **saucer ~** pass that travels above the ice with a consistent spinning motion, so that it lands flat on the ice and is easily controlled by a teammate 6. **soft ~** careful pass made using finesse rather than force to propel it 7. **take a ~** a. receive a pass b. decide not to sign or draft a player ("every team but one took a pass on Schriner until the Oilers drafted him")

passenger player who contributes less than his teammates or doesn't give full effort

passing 1. movement of the puck between teammates 2. **~ ability** skill at moving the puck to teammates 3. **~ drills** practice plays designed to improve one's ability to pass the puck 4. **~ lane** gap between players through which the puck carrier can pass the

passing

puck freely to a teammate 5. **~ play** set play in which the puck is moved effectively between two or more players, generally creating a scoring chance

paste 1. hit hard 2. beat badly on the scoreboard

pat 1. **~ on the back** support, usu. offered by coach to player

patch special crest worn on team sweaters, usu. to acknowledge an important event in team history or a player (or any other team member) who is badly injured, ill, or has recently passed away

patella kneecap

patented of a play or skill: unique to a single player ("he scored with that patented slapshot of his")

patience ability to remain calm under pressure, usu. while handling the puck

Patrick Division one of four NHL divisions, 1974-93

Patrick, Lester, Trophy see *Lester Patrick Trophy*

Patricks brothers, Lester and Frank, founders of the Pacific Coast Hockey Association, the most influential league in the early days of professional hockey

patrol cover an assigned area, usu. the wing or blueline

patronage fan support

pattern personal stick design for a player

Patty Kazmaier Award annual honour bestowed upon the MVP of women's hockey in NCAA since 1998, in memory of the player from Princeton University who succumbed to a rare blood disease in 1990 at age 28

Paul Goodman High-Scoring Trophy trophy awarded in the late 1920s to the player who scored the most goals in an NHL season (early incarnation of Rocket Richard Trophy)

pay 1. salary 2. ~ **a visit** play a road game ("Toronto will pay a visit to Calgary this Saturday") 2. ~ **the price** be willing to absorb a hit to make a good play or move the puck

payback retaliation or retribution

paying customers fans

peace bond (archaic) sum of money a player pays to a league, usu. after a violent game, as promise of no further violence against a particular player or team

peacemaker player who tries to prevent a fight between two players

peak form height of one's playing abilities

peak performance var. of *peak form*

peanut division of kids' hockey, below *pee wee*

peanuts common snack food sold at arenas

peanuts

Pearson, Lester B., Award see *Lester B. Pearson Award*

pedal back skate backwards, backcheck

peddle trade, or offer for trade

pee wee level of hockey for players age 11-12

peel 1. turn 2. ~ **away** skate away from puck carrier to go into checking mode or to turn lazily away from the play 3. ~ **a banana** deke a goalie one

way, then the other, and slip the puck between his legs

peg one placing (i.e., drop a peg in the standings)

'Pegs short for Winnipeg Victorias

pegged targeted for; intended for

pelican player who, in a defensive position, lifts one leg so as to avoid being hit by a shot—cowardly move that often results in his goalie being screened or fooled and a goal being scored

pelvic protector protective equipment for a woman's crotch, hips, and lower back

penalized player player who is punished for committing a foul

penalized team team whose player has received a penalty

penalty 1. a. infraction b. punishment imposed on a player for committing an infraction 2. **bad** ~ infraction caused by laziness or being out of position rather than aggressive play 3. ~ **bench** (archaic) area where penalized players from both teams would sit side by side (replaced by two penalty boxes, one for each team) 4. ~ **box** area of the rink where players must go to serve penalties 5. ~ **clock** timepiece on the scoreboard that keeps fans and players informed of time remaining in penalties 6. ~ **faceoff** (archaic) faceoff directly in front of the goalie, usu. because he held the puck too long 7. ~**-filled** of a game: marked by many fights or chippy play, resulting in many players being penalized 8. ~**-free** describes a game or period in which no penalties were assessed 9. **good** ~ infraction which is worth the two minutes' punishment because it prevented a sure goal or great scoring chance 10. ~ **kill** short for penalty killing 11. ~ **killer** player who plays frequently (or specializes in situations) when his team is short-handed 12. ~ **killing** process of playing short-handed, when penalized team's primary concern is to keep the other team from scoring 13. ~-**killing efficiency** statistic that expresses a team's success in preventing goals while it plays short-handed 14. ~-**killing percentage** var. of *penalty-killing efficiency* 15. ~-**killing unit** group of players assigned to play together while team is short-handed 16. ~ **king** fighter or goon who leads the league in penalty minutes 17. ~ **list** complete list of penalties from a given period or game 18. ~ **minutes** short for penalties in minutes— amount of time a player or team has spent in the penalty box or played short-handed 19. ~ **record** a. official statistics for penalties in a game or period b. new standard set for penalties or penalties in minutes 20. ~ **shot** a. free shot on goal, awarded by the referee when a player is tripped on a breakaway, when a defenceman covers the puck in the crease, or the net is dislodged intentionally with less than two minutes to play in a period b. **major ~ shot** introduced in 1941-42: penalty shot in which the shooter is permitted to skate in on goal and try to deke the goalie c. **minor ~ shot** penalty shot awarded after certain infractions by a goaltender; shooter took the shot standing behind a line 30 feet from the goal line (1941-45) 21. ~-**shot circle** (archaic) circle in front of the goal from which penalty shots were taken 22. ~-**shot line** (archaic) line painted on ice, 30 feet from goal line (1941-45) 23. ~ **time-keeper** off-ice official who sits in the penalty box and keeps track of start and finish times of all penalties 24. ~ **timer** official timepiece held by penalty timekeeper as backup to scoreclock for the purpose of timing the start and finish of all penalties

penalty bench

penetrate establish puck possession and apply pressure inside opponent's blue-line

Penguins nickname of Pittsburgh team in NHL

Penguins Magazine Pittsburgh Penguins' game-night program

Pens short for Penguins

pension fund fund established by NHL and players in 1947 to provide post-retirement benefits for players

Penticton Vees Allan Cup champions in 1954

pep 1. energy 2. ~ **talk** inspirational speech, given usu. by coach or team captain, to inspire a team

pepper take many shots at a goalie within a short time

pepper-pot rambunctious, never-stopping skater

Pepsi Center home rink of Colorado Avalanche, 1999-present

perch seat

Percival, Lloyd Canadian athlete and coach (1913-74) who pioneered concepts of nutrition and fitness as ways to improve on-ice play

perform play

performer player

performance display of skill by any player

perimeter on the ~ a. not at the centre of play (often used euphemistically for ineffective play) b. offensive play on the outside of the defensive box, on a power play

period 1. 20-minute span of playing time, three of which constitute a regulation-length game 2. any span of time within a game

perpetual motion skating non-stop or with constant energy; first used by Foster Hewitt to describe the play of Dave Keon

perpetual rookie a player who is called up for five or six games a year for a number of years

personnel players

pesky describes a player who checks and annoys opponents

pest player, usually a forward, who checks diligently to the point of aggravating opponents with pushes after the whistle, jabs with the stick, and other marginally unsportsman-like play

pester be a pest

Pete name of the Pittsburgh Penguins' mascot in 1968 (a penguin), one of the first mascots in pro sports

Peterborough Petes Memorial Cup champions in 1979

Peter Puck

Peter Puck cartoon character, created by Hanna-Barbera and developed by Brain McFarlane, who explained hockey strategy and rules in intermission features that aired in the 1970s

Petrolia Squires Allan Cup champions in 1979 and 1981

pets (archaic) players, usu. in ref to a GM or coach

pew seat

phenom young sensation

Philadelphia Arena early arena in Philadelphia, home of the NHL's Quakers (1930-31)

Philadelphia Flyer, The Philadelphia Flyers' game-night program

Philadelphia Flyers NHL member team, 1967-present

Philadelphia flu phantom illness, sometimes cited as an excuse to avoid playing the Flyers during their brawling days in mid-1970s

Philadelphia Quakers NHL member team, 1930-31 (formerly Pittsburgh Pirates)

Philips Arena Atlanta Thrashers' home arena

Philly nickname for Philadelphia

philosophical differences disagreement between players and coach or coach and GM, often cited to explain one's dismissal

phiz face

Phoenix Coyotes NHL member team, 1996-present (formerly Winnipeg Jets)

phone booth metaphoric confined space inside which the greatest puckhandlers are skilled enough to manoeuvre

Phone Booth unofficial nickname for the Bell Centre, Montreal

physical 1. style of play marked by heavy checking ("it's been a physical game so far tonight") 2. ~ **abuse of**

officials any contact made by player or coach with on-ice official which results in game misconduct and further disciplinary action 3. ~ **play** play marked by frequent hitting and contact

physician doctor

physiotherapist accredited individual who aids an injured player's recovery through physiotherapy

physiotherapy series of exercises geared specifically to the rehabilitation of an injury

Piccadilly Hotel hotel where visiting teams usually stayed when playing the New York Rangers in Manhattan during "Original Six" days

pick 1. term derived from basketball whereby a player without the puck runs into an opponent, blocking an area of the ice so that a teammate with the puck can skate to open ice or see an open lane to make a play 2. ~ **a corner** score with an accurate shot to one of the four corners of the net 3. **draft** ~ a. player selected in a draft b. team's right to choose a player in a draft 4. ~ **a fight** look purposefully to start a fight with an opponent 5. ~ **a spot** a. see an open part of the net to shoot at b. select a time to do something unusual or special 6. ~ **off** intercept, usu. a pass 7. ~ **his pocket** strip an opponent cleanly of the puck

pick up 1. a. acquire; claim (as on waivers) b. receive credit for ("she picked up her third assist of the night on that goal") 2. ~ **a loose puck** beat all other players to the puck and gain control of it 3. ~ **a man** check a player who was previously unchecked 4. ~ **a pass** collect a pass, whether one is the intended recipient or not 5. ~ **the slack** a. increase the tempo b. play more effectively, esp. in the absence of a star player

pickup 1. var. of *pickup hockey* 2. ~ **hockey** informal game of hockey; shinny 3. ~ **team** casually assembled group of shinny players

picture goal beautiful goal

picture of health in excellent condition (esp. after recovering from injury)

pierce get past opposition defence

pierce

pig selfish player

Pike's peak increase in quality of play at important points during a game (after coach Alf Pike)

pile into skate into a goalie or group of players intentionally to create a ruckus

pileup tangled heap of players from both teams, usu. in one team's goal area

pill puck

pillows goalie pads

pilot 1. coach or manager of a team 2. to coach or manage a team

pin 1. knee 2. ~ **their hopes** on rely heavily upon, usu. a team on its star player 3. ~s knees 4. ~ **him to the boards** check an opponent against boards and keep him there, immobile

pinch of an offensive defenceman: maintain position at the blueline as the defensive team tries to clear the puck out of its own end or as the offensive team applies pressure

pine 1. players' bench 2. **ride the** ~ of a player: sit idle on the bench during a game

ping descriptive word for sound puck makes as it hits the goalpost

pink of condition (archaic) healthy

pink stick stick used by NHL players in 2005-06 and 2006-07 for one game to raise funds and awareness for breast cancer

Pink *Tely* sports section of the *Toronto Telegram* the pages of which were pink

pinned blade stick blade nailed into the shaft

pinpoint accuracy extreme precision

pinpoint passing very accurate passing

pipe 1. goalpost ("that shot hit the pipe straight on") 2. ~s goalnet ("Lafrenière is between the pipes for Oshawa tonight")

pipe

pipe-and-hemp man goalie

Pirates nickname of Pittsburgh NHL team, 1925-30

pit match up against ("the game pits Edmonton against Calgary")

pitch heel higher than toes in skate boot

pitchfork spear

Pittsburgh Penguins NHL member team, 1967-present

Pittsburgh Pirates NHL member team, 1925-30

pivot 1. the centre position, centreman 2. spin quickly

plagued by injuries of a team or player: afflicted with a series of injuries in a short period of time

Plan B name Pittsburgh city officials gave to alternate plan for a new arena in 2006 if proposed builders did not receive a casino licence their project hinged upon

plant 1. station (oneself in front of the net) 2. establish footing before shooting or turning

plaster 1. hard check or shot 2. used in the treatment of cuts (archaic)

plastic 1. ~ **blade** (1970s) replacement blade (often used in road hockey) that attaches to shaft of stick 2. ~ **heel tip** (1960s) white, protective cap that covered back end of skate blades 3. ~ **ice** synthetic skating surface used as a replacement for frozen water

platinum highest-priced section of seats at Air Canada Centre, Toronto

plaudits words of praise

play 1. game action 2. compete against 3. (19th C.) referee's command as he faced the puck 4. **blow the** ~ **dead** of referee or linesman: blow whistle to stop game action 5. ~ **ahead** pass the puck forward 6. ~ **along the wall** cycle or move puck along the boards 7. ~ **the body** ignore the puck and check the puck carrier 8. ~ **for keeps** play with as much determination as possible 9. ~ **has been whistled dead** var. of *play is called* 10. ~ **is called** referee or linesman has stopped game 11. ~ **is stopped** var. of *play is called* 12. ~ **the man** var. of *play the body* 13. ~ **the point** position oneself at the opposition blueline on a power play 14. ~ **the puck** go after the puck directly instead of checking a man off the puck with physical play 15. ~ **the puck ahead** move the puck up ice to a teammate 16. ~ **their hearts out** of a team: make an all-out effort 17. ~ **together** play on a line or as a defence pair ("Scott is playing together with Johnson on the blueline tonight") 18. ~ **with** var. of *play together*

play-by-play broadcast description of a game's events as they occur (contrast with *colour commentary*)

play-by-play

playdowns (archaic) playoffs

player 1. any member of a team 2. jargon for talented player 3. ~ **agent** person who represents a player mostly for the purpose of negotiating contracts 4. ~ **bonus** extra money paid to a player for reaching statistical or achievement levels, such as scoring 50 goals or winning a major award 5. ~ **contract** written agreement between player and team 6. ~ **development** system that promotes the advancement of players' skills and performance, through farm system and coaching staffs 7. ~ **of the game** in international hockey, selection of one player on each side to be honoured for superior play in a game 8. ~ **of the month** award for top player in any month during the season 9. ~ **of the**

week award for top player in any week during the season 10. ~ **of the year** award for top player in any season 11. ~ **portrait** usu. photograph taken of a player for promotional use 12. ~ **rep** player chosen to speak on behalf of his teammates at players' association or management meetings 13. ~ **to be named later** last and usu. most insignificant part of a trade (now called future considerations)

players' bench area adjacent to the boards where players who are not on the ice are seated

Players category category for induction into Hockey Hall of Fame

players-only meeting private discussion by players, without coach or manager, usu. to address recent poor play

players' strike 1. dispute during first two weeks of April 1992, causing NHL games to be cancelled for the first time in league history 2. refusal by players to play games, usu. because of a contract dispute between their union and the league

playing 1. ~ **coach** person who both plays for a team and coaches it as well (no longer permitted in NHL) 2. ~ **code** unwritten standards of conduct among players 3. ~ **days** career 4. ~ **lineup** roster 5. ~ **manager** person who both plays for and manages a team 6. ~ **owner** player who owns the team for which he plays 7. ~ **surface** ice 8. ~ **time** minutes allotted to the running of a game (i.e., 20 minutes for a period, five minutes for regular-season overtime) 9. ~ **togs** (archaic) uniform

playing with 1. ~ **a broken stick** infraction punishable by a two-minute penalty 2. ~ **an illegal stick** use of a stick with a blade curved beyond the acceptable limit, or, in the case of a skater, use also of a goalie's stick, either of which is punishable by two-minute penalty

playing with a broken stick

playmaker player whose forte is passing rather than scoring

playoff 1. game or series held after the regular season that helps advance one team toward the championship while eliminating the losing team 2. ~ **beard** facial hair grown at the beginning of the playoffs which is not shaved off until the end of the playoffs—ideally, after Stanley Cup victory 3. ~ **berth** place in the playoffs 4. ~ **dates** nights when playoff games are scheduled 5. ~ **fever** excitement within a team or among its fans during the playoffs or as the playoffs approach 6. ~ **game** contest played after the regular season as part of process of determining a champion 7. ~ **hockey** style of hockey marked by added intensity or excitement 8. ~ **hopes** team's aspirations to qualify for the playoffs 9. ~ **hunt** pursuit of a spot in the playoffs, which grows increasingly intense as the regular season winds

down ("the Senators must continue winning if they hope to remain in the playoff hunt") 10. ~ **picture** overview of teams likely to qualify for playoffs 11. ~ **pool** contest in which participants stage a mock draft of players on playoff teams and are credited with points those players record in playoff games 12. ~ **race** var. of *playoff hunt* 13. ~ **run** length of time a team survives in the playoffs 14. ~ **spot** position in the playoffs 15. ~ **stretch** var. of *playoff run* 16. ~ **team** team that qualifies for the playoffs or is of sufficient calibre to do so

playoffs series of games played after the regular season, in which the league's best teams compete for league championship

pleasant surprise player who performs above the team's expectations

pleasure skate pejorative for lack of effort made by a lazy or indifferent player ("he's out there on a pleasure skate tonight")

Plexiglas see-through, virtually unbreakable acrylic sheets that shield fans from play on ice

pluck 1. bravery; competitiveness 2. ~ **it out of mid-air** of a goalie: catch the puck after making an initial save or corralling a loose puck

plug jam an area of the ice

plugger less-talented player who gives his all in every game

plumber var. of *plugger*

plus-minus difference between the number of even-strength goals a player's team scores and allows while he is on the ice 2. ~ **rating** statistic that represents plus-minus for every player

plus player player who has a positive plus-minus rating (and therefore, theoretically, is not a defensive liability)

plyometrics exercise regimen consisting of stretching, maximum effort, and minimal ground contact

poach sign a player who was expected to sign with another club

pocket 1. score a goal 2. ~ **the puck** physically pick the puck up after a milestone goal 3. ~ **the whistle** stop calling penalties, usu. late in a close game or playoff game

point 1. position in seven-man hockey, akin to today's defenceman 2. the area inside the opponent's blueline where the defencemen station themselves 3. goal or assist 4. ~ **blank** from directly in front of the goalie (also "from point-blank range") 5. ~ **derby** scoring race 6. ~**-getter** a. player who is awarded a point on a particular play b. consistent scorer 7. ~ **king** a. scoring champion b. in NHL: Art Ross Trophy winner 8. ~ **man** player (usu. defenceman) who stations himself inside the blueline, usu. on a power play 9. ~ **of release** moment at which the blade of the stick meets the puck during the motion of taking a shot 10. ~ **producer** player who is offensively gifted 11. ~ **production** rate at which points are accumulated by any player or team 12. ~**-scoring streak** run of consecutive games during which a player or team earns at least one point 13. ~ **shot** shot taken by a player stationed just inside the blueline on any offensive foray 14. ~ **the finger** blame; accuse 15. ~ **title** scoring championship

points 1. credit a team receives in the standings for winning or tying games 2. aggregate number of goals and assists accumulated by a team 3. number of goals and assists recorded by a player 4. ~ **race** a. for players: scoring race b. for teams: standings

poise ability to maintain one's composure in pressure-filled situations

poke 1. jab with stick at the puck or an opponent 2. punch 3. ~ **away** jab repetitively and insistently 4. ~ **it in** score by quickly pushing puck over the goal line

poke check method of stripping puck from an opponent by jabbing at it with the stick, usually covertly and quickly to catch that opponent by surprise

poke check

pokey jail (i.e., penalty box)

Poland IIHF member nation since 1926

pole 1. post 2. ~s goal net

Pole Nord first artificial ice rink opened in Paris, in 1892

policeman player whose prime job is to protect his team's star players from vicious checks, dirty work, and physical play on the part of the other team

Pollock Amendment arrangement (named after Montreal Canadiens GM Sam Pollock) that gave Montreal the option to choose two French-Canadian players with the first- and second-overall selections in the Amateur Draft in 1968 and 1969

pond 1. colloquial for hockey rink 2. ~ **hockey** a. casual hockey game in which players come and go throughout the day and play a sporting, non-contact game b. free-wheeling game between two NHL teams, from which defence and physical play are mostly absent

pooh-bah high-ranking individual, usu. owner, GM, or league official

pool in international hockey, a grouping used to determine schedules

poolies devotees of fantasy hockey or playoff pools

poor decision play made by a player which results in a good scoring chance by opposition

poor exhibition 1. dull game 2. absence of skill or effort on part of player or team

pop 1. slang for beer 2. hit hard 3. ~ **home** score 4. ~ **out** of a puck: enter and exit the net in an instant

popcorn snack commonly sold at arena concession stands

populace fans

porous defence weak defensive play that allows opponents to score often or generate frequent scoring chances

portable skate sharpener device which can be transported easily, used to hone edges of skate blades

portable skate sharpener

portable X-ray machine equipment which can be transported easily, used to produce X-ray photographs

Portage la Prairie Terriers Memorial Cup champions in 1942

Port Arthur Allan Cup champions in 1925, 1926, 1929, and 1939

Port Arthur Bearcats 1. Stanley Cup challengers in March 1911 2. silver-medal team at 1936 Olympics representing Canada

Port Arthur West End Bruins Memorial Cup champions in 1948

Portland Rosebuds Stanley Cup challengers in 1916

Portland Winter Hawks Memorial Cup champions in 1983 and 1998

port side left side of goal or ice

portsider left winger

Portugal IIHF member nation since 1999

position 1. station (oneself) 2. one of three set roles on a hockey team (goal, defence, and forward) 3. ~ **in standings** ranking of a team in the standings 4. **play one's** ~ fully carry out responsibilities of one's position (whether goal, defence, or forward)

positional play carrying out of responsibilities of any specific position

positioning stationing oneself at appropriate points on ice

possession control (of the puck)

post 1. short for goalpost 2. record ("they posted their second win of the week last night") 3. ~ **a shutout** record a shutout 4. **off the** ~ **and in** of a shot: caroming off the goalpost and into the net 5. ~**s** goal net ("Crozier is between the posts for tonight's game") 6. ~ **to post** from one side of the goal to the other with speed ("he goes post to post as fast as anyone in this league")

post-concussion syndrome lingering effects of a concussion, usu. in the form of dizziness after light exercise or loss of strength or memory

postmortem discussion after any game, series or season (esp. after a loss)

postseason 1. playoffs   2. summer months

postpone put off a game until a later date, usu. due to weather conditions during the winter months

pot 1. score (a goal)   2. ~ **shot** shot on goal that has little chance of going in but is taken in desperation

potent offence of a team: skilled at scoring

potential promise, based on raw skill, that a young player may develop into an elite player

pounce on 1. check a man quickly   2. control a rebound quickly   3. recover a loose puck quickly

pound 1. defeat (another team) soundly   2. strike an opponent with one's fists   3. ~ **the puck out**   clear puck emphatically from defensive end off boards

pour 1. ~ **down the wing** skate hard   2. ~ **in goals**   score several goals in a short period of time   3. ~ **it on** apply pressure   4. ~ **onto the ice** jump over the boards en masse

powder 1. defeat an opponent badly in a fight   2. hard shot

Powell River Regals Allan Cup champions in 1997 and 2000

power 1. physical strength   2. ~ **forward** forward who combines scoring ability with physical play

powerhouse team that possesses all elements of a champion

power play 1. situation in which a team has more skaters on the ice than its opponent because of penalties   2. **abbreviated** ~ power play that is less than two minutes long as a result of overlapping penalties assessed against each team   3. **extended** ~ power play that is longer than two minutes as a

result of more than one minor penalty being assessed (not simultaneously) against the other team   4. ~ **efficiency** statistic (expressed as percentage) that indicates a team's success scoring on power plays   5. ~ **goal** goal scored while scoring team has a man advantage   6. ~ **percentage** var. of *power-play efficiency*   7. ~ **point** goal or assist recorded while one's team is on the power play   8. ~ **quarterback** player, usu. defenceman, who is able to make passes to set up scoring chances and who also has an excellent shot and, therefore, directs his team's power-play unit from the point

Power Play official magazine of the NHL Players' Association

power skating intense drills designed to improve players' skating ability

Pow-R-Puck (1960s) heavier-weight puck used in practice to improve shooting strength

practical joker player who plays pranks on teammates, usu. in the dressing room or on road trips

practice 1. time period on non-game days during which team members run through drills intended to improve various aspects of play   2. ~ **facility** small community or private arena where an NHL team practices, often some distance from game-night arena   3. ~ **goalie** (archaic) in days when teams dressed only one goalie for games, goalie who didn't play in games but was available for practice   4. ~ **rink** var. of *practice facility*   5. ~ **session** time spent on ice in practice

Practise 1. model of Hilborn stick produced by Salyerds in Preston, Ontario   2. model of hockey stick produced by McVeans in Dresden, Ontario

practitioner expert ("he's a rare practitioner of the hip check")

Pragobanka Cup annual tournament (1994-97) staged in the Czech Republic and featuring Europe's top national teams (renamed Ceska Pojistovna Cup in 1998)

prairie champs (archaic) champions of the Western Hockey League

prank harmless, albeit slightly humiliating, joke intended to keep a team's spirits high

prankster player who executes a prank

preach of a coach: emphasize or repeatedly urge players to perfect some aspect of their play ("coach Davidson has preached defence from the first day of training camp")

precaution measure taken to avoid further injury or damage to a player or team (also "precautionary measure")

Precision model of hockey stick

Predators nickname of Nashville's NHL team

Preds short for Predators

pre-game 1. prior to the opening faceoff 2. ~ **ceremony** on-ice celebration or presentation prior to the start of a game, usu. to honour a player for special and specific achievement 3. ~ **meal** food consumed on the day of a game day, usu. early afternoon 4. ~ **nap** rest period, usu. lasting several hours, after pre-game meal and before leaving home or hotel to go to the arena to play a game 5. ~ **ritual** any tasks habitually performed by a player or team prior to a game 6. ~ **skate** skate that takes place about half an hour before a game and consists of limbering up and taking light shots to prepare for the game itself 7. ~ **warmup** var. of *pre-game skate*

pre-season 1. taking place before the start of the regular season 2. ~ **game** exhibition game played prior to the start of the regular season

preliminary round 1. first playoff round (esp. in NHL, 1975-79) 2. in international competitions, round of games prior to medal round

preliminary warmup any exercise performed prior to a game

premature substitution infraction committed when a sixth attacker, replacing a pulled goalie, plays the puck before the goalie is within five feet of the players' bench; no penalty is called, but play is whistled dead and there is a faceoff at centre ice

prep school (U.S.) private high school, often one that emphasizes sports such as hockey

Presentation Cup the official Stanley Cup given to the champion at the end of the NHL playoffs (contrast with the *Replica Cup*)

preserve keep intact a tie or lead late in a game

president topmost leader of any club, league, or organization

Presidents' Trophy award given to the NHL team that finishes first overall at the end of the regular season

press 1. media 2. attack or apply pressure 3. ~ **box** a. area from which media watch the game, usu. high above the ice surface b. area from which scratched or injured players watch game ("if he keeps playing like that, he'll be watching the next game from the press box") 4. ~ **conference** any meeting between members of a team and members of the media 5. ~ **corps** media, reporters 6. ~ **hard** a. forecheck b. try to score, usu. a tying goal

presser short for *press conference*

pressing trying too hard and lacking in success as a result

pressure forecheck and attack the goal or the puck carrier

Preston Rivulettes hockey team based in southwestern Ontario that was the predominant women's team of the 1930s

pretender team that believes it can win a championship but really doesn't stand a chance

pretty 1. of a play: successful, imaginative, and visually pleasing 2. ~ **to watch** of a player: gifted with great skill

pretzel mask early goal mask made of Fibreglas twisted into shape

prevail win

prevent defend successfully against (an attempt to enter the zone, score a goal, win a game, etc.)

prexy (archaic) slang for league president

price tag salary demand ("he can be signed, but he carries a hefty price tag")

pride intangible attribute that makes a player perform better than his mere skills might normally permit

Prince Albert Raiders Memorial Cup champions in 1985

Prince of Wales Conference one of two conferences in NHL, 1974-93, the other being the Clarence Campbell Conference

Prince of Wales Trophy award presented (since 1994) to the winners of the NHL's Eastern Conference finals; awarded to first-place team in American Division, 1928-38; first-place team overall, 1939-67; first-place team in East Division, 1968-74; first-place team in Prince of Wales Conference, 1975-81; winner of Prince of Wales Conference final, 1982-93

Priority Selection Ontario Hockey League's annual draft of midget-age players

pro 1. short for professional 2. ~ **bow** NHL debut 3. ~ **company** (archaic)

NHL 4. ~ **puck chaser** professional player 5. ~ **puckster** NHL player 6. ~ **ranks** slang for NHL 7. ~ **scout** employee of NHL team whose job it is to assess the skills and qualities only of other players in the NHL 8. ~ **shop** store inside an arena which sells skates, sticks, and other necessary hockey equipment

pro shop

Pro model of hockey stick produced by EL-WIG in Durham, Ontario

Pro Goal model of hockey stick produced by EL-WIG in Durham, Ontario

pro tem short for *pro tempore*, for the time being; used in context of rule whereby each team has a player who acts as captain on the ice at all times, even if that player doesn't wear the "C"

proceed go, usu. to penalty box

proceedings events of a game

procure acquire (a player)

product (of) 1. native of ("he's a product of the Soo") 2. graduate of, usu. junior or minor pro team ("he's a product of the Kitchener Rangers")

production offensive output of player or team

Production Line 1. (1950s) Detroit Red Wings forward unit of Ted Lindsay, Gordie Howe, and Sid Abel 2. (late 1960s) Detroit Red Wings unit of Gordie Howe, Frank Mahovlich and

Alex Delvecchio (a.k.a. Production Line II)

professional 1. any player who receives a salary 2. player who demonstrates skill and maturity on ice and off

Professional 1. model of hockey stick produced by McVeans in Dresden, Ontario 2. model of hockey stick produced by Clark's in Breslau, Ontario

Professional Hockey Writers' Association organization made up of print and broadcast journalists, responsible for naming end-of-season all-star teams as well as winners of Lady Byng, Calder, Elmer Ferguson, Hart, Norris, and Selke awards

professionalism 1. conduct becoming of a professional 2. (early 20th C.) movement to lure players to teams through money ("professionalism is tearing the heart out of the amateur game")

proficient adept; successful

profile biography or portrait of player or team

prognosticator 1. writer; member of media 2. bettor

program 1. publication sold at arenas on game night, containing player profiles, game lineups, and other stories on the team and league 2. ~ **additions** lineup changes announced by public-address announcer just before the start of a game

Progress brand of stick produced by Doolittles of St. Marys, Ontario

prolific consistently productive

Pro-Line Canadian sports-related lottery whose players try to predict outcomes of league games

promenade (archaic) standing room area

prominent well-known; easily recognized (of a player or team)

promise indication of future greatness (or, at least, improvement)

promote 1. cause to advance to another level or league 2. recall (a player) from minors

proper fit player whose skills and effort mesh well with a team's style of play

property player whose rights are owned by a team ("he's the property of the Toronto Maple Leafs")

proposition (archaic) contract offer

prospect player who shows great promise to become a regular player in the NHL

prostrate of a goalie: prone

protect 1. defend a teammate by fighting with or standing up to an opponent 2. omit a player's name from a list of those eligible to be selected in an Expansion Draft 3. ~ **the goalie** ensure the safety of the goalie (through on-ice actions or by amending the rules) 4. ~ **a lead** play defensively late in a game to hold onto a lead 5. ~ **the puck** use one's body to shield the puck from opponents

protected list list submitted by teams prior to certain drafts (Expansion Draft, Intra-League Draft) which names players who are not eligible to be selected by other teams

protection goon player ("he's going to need protection if the team wants him to score 50 goals this year")

protective 1. ~ **cup** jock 2. ~ **equipment** any equipment used to prevent injury

protective cup

to a player 3. ~ **glass** Plexiglas or other similar shield used to enhance the safety of spectators

protest 1. official objection to a ruling, filed during a game 2. objection to any call or ruling during a game

Proulx, H.A. see *H.A. Proulx*

Provost model of hockey stick produced by Rettie's Landing Wood Production in Coboconk, Ontario

prowess skill ("his prowess around the net is indisputable")

pry ~ **the puck loose** free the puck from a scrum of players or from under goalie's glove

psychologist doctor who is employed by players or teams to help better prepare them for games

public 1. ~-**address announcer** person who informs spectators of goals, assists, penalties, lineup changes, etc. 2. ~-**address system** amplification system which enables spectators to hear announcements about the game 3. ~-**relations department** team staff responsible for distributing information to the media and public, and for facilitating meetings between players, coaches, etc., and the media

puck 1. black disc made of vulcanized rubber that must enter the net for a goal to be scored 2. slang for a goal, usu. in context of betting ("if you take Montreal, I'll give you two pucks") 3. ~ **bunny** teenage girl who hangs around junior hockey players, usu. with sexual connotations 4. ~ **carrier** player who is in possession of the puck 5. ~ **chaser** player 6. ~-**chasing sport** hockey 7. ~ **control** ability of player or team to maintain possession of the puck for extended periods of time 8. ~-**control relay** skills demonstration in which a player or team must maintain control of the puck for the longest

while performing other tasks such as skating and turning 9. ~ **drop** opening faceoff 10. ~ **foils** illegal additions to goalie pads, made of plastic and attached to the bottom of the pads 11. ~ **game** slang for hockey 12. ~ **handler** var. of *puck carrier* 13. ~ **hog** player who rarely passes the puck and prefers to try to score single-handed 14. ~ **juggler** skilled stick-handler 15. ~ **movement** advancement of puck towards opposition goal 16. ~ **on end** of the puck: rolling on its rounded edge instead of the flat side, making it more difficult to control 17. ~ **possession** in control of the puck 18. ~ **pressure** heavy forechecking whereby two or more players try to wrest the puck from an opponent 19. ~ **pursuit** a. chasing a loose puck b. slang for hockey game 20. ~ **ragger** player who skilfully holds onto the puck without losing possession, usu. to kill time during a short-handed situation 21. ~ **scramble** hockey game 22. ~ **sense** ability to anticipate the play 23. ~ **shy** a. of a goalie: nervous, jittery, or ineffective b. of a skater: resistant of physical play as a means of gaining possession of the puck 24. ~ **smarts** var. of *puck sense* 25. ~ **star** top-notch player 26. ~ **stop** on a goalie's skate, extra section of blade between top of skate blade and boot, which prevents the puck from slipping through this gap; invented by Starr Skate Company as an alternative to traditional boots (illegal in most league and tournament competitions) 27. ~ **stopper** goalie 28. ~ **support** positional play by other members of the team for the player who is in possession of the puck, usu. to ensure continued possession

Puck Stop skate (late 19th C.) goalie skate developed by Starr Manufacturing whose boots were equipped with *puck stops*

puckey player

puckhead person obsessed with hockey

puckist player

Puckomat (1970s) Swedish-invented machine that fires pucks at goalies

puckster player

pugilism element of fighting in a game

pull 1. ~ **ahead** take the lead in a game 2. ~ **the goalie** a. remove goalie from the game for an extra attacker in the dying moments of a game b. remove goalie from the game, usu. because of inferior play 3. ~ **one's man down** hook, hold, or foul an opposing player 4. ~ **out all the stops** make a desperate attempt to score, usu. late in a game to try to tie the score 5. ~ **the reins in** order a defenceman to stop rushing the puck so much 6. ~ **the trigger** a. shoot b. make a trade 7. ~ **a Wayner** fall easily to the ice to draw a penalty

punch 1. hit with fist 2. high level of energy 3. ~ **it home** score 4. ~ **it in** var. of *punch it home*

Punch Line Montreal Canadiens' forward line in the 1940s, consisting of Elmer Lach, Toe Blake, and Maurice Richard

punch-up brawl; fight

punchless weak; lacking in spirit or offensive ability

punish penalize

punishing check hard, clean check

pupil young player

purchase acquire a player for cash

pure hat trick three consecutive, uninterrupted goals by the same player

purple language swearing

purples seats farthest from the ice at Air Canada Centre, Toronto

pursue 1. chase opponent, usu. the puck carrier 2. try to sign player ("Edmonton is pursuing Smyth in the off-season")

pursuit slang for hockey game

push 1. force teammates or players to try even harder 2. final, great effort 3. ~ **ahead** move puck up ice with quick, often awkward pass 4. ~ **a man** check an opponent 5. ~ **him off the puck** strip opponent of the puck through physical means 6. ~ **the puck** stickhandle

pushing and shoving jostling, usu. after a whistle, but not fighting

put 1. ~ **away his whistle** of a referee: stop calling penalties, usu. late in a close, exciting game, to let players, not officials, decide a game's outcome 2. ~ **the game on ice** score a decisive goal 3. ~ **on a clinic** demonstrate excellent hockey skills, usu. stickhandling, during the course of a game 4. ~ **on the brakes** stop suddenly, usu. to avoid a big hit 5. ~ **the play offside** make a move or play that results in an offside call 6. ~ **the puck in the net** score 7. ~ **the puck home** var. of *put the puck in the net*

pylon player who is weak defensively and is easy to skate around with the puck

pylon

pyramid power (mid-1970s) belief that pyramids have supernatural properties, leading Toronto coach Red Kelly to place them in the dressing room and under the bench during the 1976 playoffs

Qq

QHL *Quebec Hockey League*

QMJHL *Quebec Major Junior Hockey League*

QSHL *Quebec Senior Hockey League*

QSSF *Quebec Student Sports Federation*

QUAA *Quebec University Athletic Association*

quadriceps group of four muscles at the front of the thigh that run from the hip to the patella, where they meet, and allow for knee extension

qualifying offer contract offer a team may make to a restricted free agent to prevent him from signing with another team

qualifying round series of round-robin games during IIHF World Championship, held between preliminary round and playoff elimination rounds

quality scoring chance good chance to score

quarterback player (usu. defenceman) who directs his team's power-play

quarter-finals playoff round in which eight teams pair off in four elimination series

Quebec Aces Allan Cup champions in 1944

Quebec Arena home rink of the Quebec Bulldogs

Quebec Bulldogs NHL member team, 1917-1920; Stanley Cup champions, 1912 and 1913

Quebec Hockey League 1. name given to top junior league in Quebec, later known as Quebec Major Junior Hockey League 2. name taken by Quebec Senior Hockey League after 1953

Quebec Major Junior Hockey League one of Canada's three major junior leagues

Quebec Nordiques WHA member team, 1972-1979, and NHL member team, 1979-1995 (moved to Colorado and renamed Avalanche)

Quebec Remparts Memorial Cup champions in 1971 and 2006

Quebec Senior Hockey League senior amateur league (1944-53) that became the semi-pro Quebec Hockey League in 1953

Quebec Student Sports Federation governing body for intercollegiate athletics in Quebec since 1989

Quebec University Athletic Association governing body for intercollegiate athletics in Quebec, 1971-89

Queen City nickname for Toronto and for Buffalo

Queen Elizabeth Hotel Montreal hotel which often hosted visiting NHL teams during "Original Six" era and which frequently hosted NHL Amateur Draft between 1963 and 1979

Queen's University university in Kingston, Ontario; Stanley Cup challengers in 1895, 1899, and 1906; Allan Cup champions in 1909

quest mission; attempt (usu. to win the Stanley Cup)

question dispute (an official's call)

question mark 1. player whose participation in a game is doubtful 2. young player whose development is inconsistent

questionable 1. ~ **call** ruling by an official that might not be the correct one 2. ~ **tactics** unsportsmanlike conduct by a player or team

quick 1. speedy, fast (of a skater) 2. ~ **exit** early elimination from playoffs 3. ~ **release** ability to shoot the puck in little time ("he has a quick release") 4. ~ **shift** short burst of energy by a player who goes onto the ice and comes off just a short time later 5. ~ **start** impressive beginning to a game or season 6. ~ **whistle** decision by official to blow play dead suddenly, perhaps before the puck has been frozen, or been lost sight of, or play has drawn to a full conclusion

quiet leader captain or other important member of a team who shows leadership ability more through actions than words

Quikblade disposable skate blade designed by former NHLer Rick Hampton

quintella scoring of a goal in each of five possible ways: even-strength, power-play, short-handed, penalty shot, and empty net; only Mario Lemieux, on December 31, 1988, has ever accomplished this feat in a single NHL game

quit leave a team

quitter player who lacks integrity or competitive spirit and gives up easily

quick release

Rr

R to indicate a player shoots right

RBC Center Carolina Hurricanes' home arena

RCAF Flyers team composed largely of current and former military men who won a gold medal for Canada at the 1948 Olympics

RD right defence

RICE mnemonic device for method of treatment for common injuries (R=rest; I=ice; C=compress; E=elevate)

ROM official IIHF abbreviation for Romania

RSA official IIHF abbreviation for Republic of South Africa

RT regulation tie

RUS official IIHF abbreviation for Russia

RW right wing

rabble rouser player who is a disruptive force on ice

race 1. short for playoff race or points race 2. ~ **back** backcheck quickly to help prevent scoring chance 3. ~ **for the (loose) puck** skate hard with the sole purpose of obtaining possession of puck

rack up 1. accumulate, usu. points or penalty minutes

radius bone in the forearm that runs from the elbow to the wrist toward the thumb

rafters 1. name given to uppermost seats in arena ("we're sitting in the rafters tonight") 2. beams that support arena roof, from which championship banners and retired player sweater numbers are usually suspended

rag flood method of cleaning the ice which adds water but doesn't scrape ice

rag the puck skate with the puck only with the intention of maintaining control, so as to kill time off the clock as a penalty winds down or the game nears completion

ragged haphazard (usu. of a team's play marked by incomplete passes and lack of flow)

rail 1. winger 2. row of seats adjacent to boards ("we have great seats, right along the rails") 3. ~ **bird** fan who is privileged enough to have a front-row seat

raiser children's term for shot that leaves the ice en route to the goal

rally come back to tie or win game after trailing

ram 1. hit from behind 2. ~ **it in** score 3. ~ **the disc** score

rampage 1. violent episode 2. **scoring** ~ brief period during which many goals are scored

Rangers nickname for New York team in NHL

"Rangers' Victory Song" song popular in "Original Six" days, written to honour and celebrate that team

ranking order in which teams are listed in standings, from best to worst

ranks 1. team ("he's the finest player in their ranks") 2. level of play (e.g., the amateur ranks) 3. **junior** ~ var. of *junior hockey*

rap 1. hit 2. slash 3. heavy criticism 4. ~ **it home** score 5. ~ **it in** var. of *rap it home*

rapid-fire of a series of shots: taken quickly, one after the other (also "rapid-fire succession")

rapid succession var. of **_rapid-fire_**

Rare Jewel name of the horse that Leafs owner Conn Smythe bet on, then used the huge winnings to buy King Clancy from Ottawa

rash spate, usu. of injuries

rate rank

Rat Portage Thistles Stanley Cup challengers in March 1903 and March 1905

rats plastic rodents thrown onto the ice by Florida Panthers fans

Rats diminutive for Rat Portage Thistles

rattle 1. hit an opponent hard 2. score ("rattle the cage") 3. ~ **it in** score 4. ~ **it off the glass** shoot puck hard off glass, usu. to clear defensive area 5. ~ **it off the post** hit the post with a hard shot

rattled unnerved

rave reviews praise in the media (or by a coach) for an excellent performance

Ravina Gardens Toronto Maple Leafs' practice rink in 1930s

Rawlings sporting goods manufacturer (no longer active in hockey)

Raymond's Hardware retail store in Montreal that sponsored the Canadiens' hockey sticks

razor-sharp of a goalie: playing extremely well

reach back of a goalie: reach desperately behind oneself to make a save

reach back

reach terms agree to a contract

reachers (archaic) skates with long blades (banned by NHL in 1927)

read the play anticipate how play is unfolding and react accordingly

read the riot act scream at players (usu. a coach, to his team)

real beaut beautiful (of a pass, goal, or save)

realignment redistribution of teams into new structure of divisions or conferences

Real Time system of tracking and updating a game's events and statistics as they occur, and published instantly on NHL's website

rearguard defenceman

rebound of a puck: bounce off goalie's equipment so that it remains in play

rebuild reorganize a team's roster (usu. one that has played below expectations)

rebuilding program mandate by a team to rebuild

recall promote a player from the minors or junior

recallable waivers form of waivers that enables a team to take a player back if another team claims him; often used to determine whether the player has trade value

receipts proceeds from sale of tickets to a game

receive take (usu. of a pass)

reclamation project player whose skills or production has declined, whether through age or injury or lack of motivation, acquired in faint hope that he might return to form

reconstructive surgery rebuilding of a joint (often knee, shoulder, or elbow)

record 1. body of statistics amassed by a player ("Sundin's career record speaks for itself") 2. summary of results of games played by a team or goalie ("with the win, Edmonton's record improves to 17-12-4") 3. superlative (i.e., unmatched) statistical accomplishment 4. register, usu. a shutout by a goalie 5. **off the ~** remarks to a reporter not intended for publication or broadcast 6. **on ~** having expressed an opinion ("coach Sutter is on record as saying he is happy with his team's play") 7. **~-breaking** setting a new standard ("Gretzky's 92 goals in a season is a record that might never be broken")

recover 1. regain position (usu. of the goalie) 2. **~ one's balance** regain one's footing on one's skates 3. **~ from injury** complete one's rehabilitation 4. **~ a loose puck** gain possession of a puck that is up for grabs

recruit newly arrived player

recurring injury injury that continues to hamper a player over the course of a season or career

Red popular nickname for red-haired players

Red Beavers fans of Team Norway in international hockey

red caps ushers

Red Deer Rebels Memorial Cup champions in 2001

red hot playing extremely well (usu. a goalie)

Red Knights fans of Team Denmark in international hockey

red light goal indicator affixed to the top of the Plexiglas directly behind goal net

red line 1. lines painted on ice at either end of the rink that act as goal lines and icing lines 2. **centre ~** line that divides the ice into two equal halves 3. **end ~** line that designates the outside of the net from the inside (i.e., to determine goals) but that extends the full width of the ice to demarcate line for icing calls as well

red line

Red Line Report guide to North American top prospects

red tape complications that hinder acquisition of a player, usu. from Europe

Red Wing Magazine Detroit Red Wings' game-night program

Red Wings nickname of Detroit's NHL team

Redbands alternative nickname for Montreal Wanderers

Redbirds alternative nickname for Detroit Red Wings

redhead player who has red hair

redirect deflect

Reds (archaic) alternative nickname for Detroit Red Wings

Redshirts (archaic) alternative nickname for Detroit Red Wings

reel period of play

reeling of a team: having been scored upon frequently in a short period of time

re-enter of a drafted player who has not signed a contract within two years: become eligible to be selected again

ref short for referee

re-face (archaic) drop puck again

referee 1. on-ice official who adjudicates play during a game and has the final word on infractions and rule interpretations 2. **~-in-chief** league executive who oversees on-ice officials

referee's bell (archaic) bell used to start and stop play

referee's crease red half-moon painted on ice at penalty box area, which players are not allowed to enter during disputes, discussions, or assessment of penalties

referee's whistle wind instrument used by referee to signal start and stop of play

reflex save quick save by goalie who instinctively thrusts out an arm or pad in hopes of stopping puck

regain form recover from stretch of poor play

regime lengthy period when a team is under control of a particular coach or manager ("the Habs won eight Cups under the Toe Blake regime")

Regina Monarchs Memorial Cup champions in 1928

Regina Pats Memorial Cup champions in 1925, 1930, and 1974

Regina Rangers Allan Cup champions in 1941

Regina Victorias Allan Cup champions in 1914

register 1. score 2. A-Z list of players in the league 3. apply for membership in a league

regroup rally after a bad stretch of play to perform well again

regular 1. player who is in the lineup every night ("he's become a regular this year after several seasons of part-time play") 2. ~ **season** schedule of games succeeding the exhibition season and preceding the playoffs during which eligibility for and seeding in playoffs are determined 3. ~ **shift** player who is on the ice every third or fourth shift all night, every night 4. ~ **turn** var. of *regular shift*

regulation 1. rule 2. regularly scheduled 60 minutes of play, divided into three equal periods, that constitute a standard game ("the game is tied after regulation and we'll go to overtime") 3. conforming to league standards ("those goalie pads are not regulation") 4. ~ **tie** game tied after regulation time (i.e., 60 minutes)

rehab short for rehabilitate, the process by which a player recovers from an injury

Reijo Rule NHL By-Law 28, which prohibited players from joining the NHL for the playoff run after finishing their season in a European league, as Reijo Ruotsalainen did in 1986-87

reinforced heel base of stick blade which has additional Fiberglas coating to increase durability

reinforcements call-ups (usu. because of injuries)

re-injure sustain injury to a body part that has been injured recently

reins the job of coaching

reinstate (archaic) restore amateur standing to a player who has turned pro

reject 1. of a player: a failure 2. player cut by a team 3. ~ **an offer** refuse to sign a contract under terms put forth by management

rejoin come back to a team, after injury or after having played for another team

release 1. cut (a player from a team) 2. shooting motion ("she's got such a quick release that goalies have a tough time stopping her shots") 3. ~ **a shot** shoot the puck

relegate 1. demote (a team) to a lower level of play in IIHF competition 2. ~ **to the minors** demote a player to the minor leagues 3. ~ **to the press box** scratch a healthy player from the lineup

relegation game game in IIHF competition that helps determine which teams will be relegated for the next season's tournament

relentless without easing up, usu. heavy pressure on opposition defence or commitment to physical play

reliable consistent; worry-free ("the Habs are looking for a reliable backup to Penney")

relief man backup goalie or other substitute player

relieve 1. come on in place of; substitute for 2. ⁓ **pressure** get puck out of defensive end

relinquish give up, usu. a lead

remain intact of a roster: stay the same after bad loss or bad season

remove 1. pull goalie from game 2. take player out of lineup 3. cut player from roster

Rendez-vous '87 two-game series in Quebec City in 1987 between NHL all-stars and Soviet Union all-stars which replaced the NHL's All-Star Game

renegotiate redefine terms of a contract while it is still valid

renew acquaintances play ("the teams renew acquaintances next week")

renew hostilities var. of *renew acquaintances*

Renfrew Creamery Kings founding team in the National Hockey Association (NHA)

rent-a-goalie 1. goalie for hire, called upon to play shinny, which requires two goalies for an ideal game 2. TV show (broadcast on the Showcase channel in Canada) about a goalie-rental service run out of a coffee shop

rental 1. slang for rented goalie (shinny) 2. ⁓ **player** player acquired at trade deadline whose intended contribution to the team will last only until season's end (usu. because he is due to become an unrestricted free agent)

rep hockey short for "representative hockey"; level of youth hockey that emphasizes competition, assigns players ice time according to skill, and entails out-of-town travel for regular-season games (contrast with *house league*)

repairs medical treatment, usu. stitches ("he's gone off for repairs but should be back shortly")

repairs

repel thwart; successfully defend ("the Canucks repelled Calgary's top line all night long")

replace 1. substitute for 2. ⁓ **in goal** change goalies

replacement officials officials of lesser calibre than those usually employed by a league, hired to substitute for striking officials

replay playback of videotape of a play (also *instant replay*)

Replica Cup copy of Stanley Cup that is displayed at the Hockey Hall of Fame on days when the Presentation Cup (i.e., the original) is on the road

reply score a goal soon after allowing a goal

report 1. attend training camp 2. performance assessment

reporter 1. writer who covers the players and league for newspapers, magazines, or other publications 2. broadcaster who does the same for radio or television

represent 1. play on behalf of 2. usu. of player agent: negotiate on behalf of

repulse 1. hold off an attack 2. defeat

reputation history of using dirty tactics or playing in an unsportsmanlike manner

reservation ~ of French-Canadian players (archaic) privilege extended to Montreal Canadiens briefly in 1930s, giving them first call on all players born in Quebec, requiring teams wishing to sign a French-Canadian player to give the Canadiens a 14-day window in which to exercise their right of first refusal

reserve 1. substitute or spare player 2. **~ clause** prior to free agency, clause in every player's contract that gave a team the option to unilaterally renew the contract at its completion (i.e., "pick up his option"), a process that could be repeated indefinitely, preventing a player from moving to another team or leveraging a salary increase 3. **~ list** prior to free agency, list submitted by each team to the league office, naming those players who were property of the team

reserved seats assigned seating in any arena

resident 1. **~ clown** team prankster 2. **~ tough guy** team goon or fighter

resign leave a team of one's own volition

re-sign sign a new contract with the same team ("the Leafs re-signed Tucker for four more years")

respond 1. answer a goal with a goal 2. **~ to pressure** play well at a critical times

responsibility on-ice assignment ("it's his responsibility to shut down their top line")

rest 1. time off 2. **~ an injury** avoid playing, so as to recover fully from an injury

restore 1. regain, usu. lead in a game 2. **~ order** after a melee or brawl, return the players' focus to playing hockey

restrain hinder (an opponent's progress)

restraining foul illegal act that prevents opponent from skating freely—usu. hooking, holding, or interference—punishable by a two-minute penalty

restraining foul

restraining lines var. of *hash marks*

restricted free agent player whose contract has expired, but whose former team may retain exclusive negotiating rights by making a qualifying offer

result 1. score ("here are the results from last night's games") 2. decision (win, loss, tie, overtime or shootout win or loss)

resume hostilities play ("Toronto and Ottawa will resume hostilities Saturday night at the ACC")

resume play 1. start play during a game after a stoppage 2. playoff series which continues after a layoff

retain 1. **~ the Cup** win Stanley Cup for a second straight year 2. **~ his rights** maintain ownership of exclusive right to a player's services 3. **~ the lead** maintain superior score in a game 4. **~ possession** hold onto the puck

retaliate hit back; match foul for foul

retaliation act of retaliating

retaliatory penalty penalty incurred by the player who fouls an opponent, even though the initial foul by that opponent has gone unpunished

retire 1. leave the ice, usu. because of injury 2. quit the game

retired number sweater number taken out of circulation by a team to honour its last wearer for a remarkable career

retreat play defence

return 1. come back to play for a team again 2. ~ **engagement** second game of a home-and-home series 3. ~ **pass** pass to a teammate from whom the puck carrier previously received a pass 4. ~ **to action** rejoin team after having recovered from an injury 5. ~ **to form** play well after several games marked by poor play 6. ~ **to the ice** a. step onto the ice after serving a penalty b. step onto ice after intermission 7. ~ **to the fold** rejoin team after having played elsewhere 8. ~ **to the lineup** var. of *return to action*

Reunion Arena home arena of Dallas Stars

reunite bring linemates together, after a period of time of not playing together

revamp alter lineup in hope of improving team's performance

revenge retaliation

Reverse Draft draft in which minor pro teams were entitled to claim players from rosters of NHL teams

reverse 1. go against flow 2. ~ **pass** pass made against the flow of play 3. ~ **the flow** send the puck in the direction opposite to where play had been

reverse sweater night game in which the home team wears the opposite colour sweater to the one it usually wears

Rexall Place name (since 2003) of Edmonton Oilers' home arena

rhubarb (archaic) fight or melee

Richard Riot aftermath of game of March 17, 1955, between Detroit and Montreal at the Forum, which was suspended after the first period when a fan protest over Maurice Richard's suspension turned violent

Richfield Coliseum home arena of WHA's Cleveland Crusaders (1974-76) and NHL's Cleveland Barons (1976-78)

ricket form of shinny first played in Canada in Nova Scotia

rickets (19th C.) stones used to mark goals for pond hockey

ricochet carom; deflect

riddled with injuries of a team: suffering from multiple loss of players to injury

ride 1. steer (opponent into boards) 2. harass (usu. a teammate) in a friendly manner 3. ~ **the bike** exercise on stationary bike, usu. after a game to relieve body of lactic acids 4. ~ **the buses** play in the minors, where teams travel by bus rather than by plane 5. ~ **the pine** sit on the end of the bench, dressed but not playing

ride the bike

Rideau Hall governor general's residence, where hockey was played during Lord Stanley's term (1888-93), inspiring his donation of the Stanley Cup

Rideau Hall Rebels team composed of members of Lord Stanley's family, entourage, and circle of friends

rifle 1. shoot the puck hard 2. a hard shot ("he's got a rifle for a shot")

rigging goal net

right 1. ~ **defence** defenceman who guards right side of the rink, esp. inside his own blueline 2. ~**-hand shot** player who places the stick on the ice to the right of his body 3. ~ **point** player who stations himself to the goalie's left on the power play 4. ~ **side** that side of the ice ("he likes to carry the puck down the right side and cut in on goal on his off wing") 5. ~ **wing** forward who plays predominantly to the right side of the centreman (also *right winger* or *right wing man*)

right defence

rim send puck around the boards

Rimouski Oceanic Memorial Cup champions in 2000

ring 1. sound a gong to indicate the end of a period or game 2. short for Stanley Cup ring 3. score (a goal) 4. ~ **a gong** (archaic) announce end of play of a game or period 5. ~ **ceremony** party during which players receive their Stanley Cup rings 6. ~ **the puck around the boards** shoot puck fully around boards in defensive end from one side to the other 7. ~ **a shot off the post** hit the post with a shot

ringer excellent player added at the last minute to a low-level team to boost its chances of winning

ringette form of hockey (formerly for young girls) played with just the shaft of the stick and a round, soft, oversize puck with a hole in the middle for stickhandling

ringette

rink 1. sheet of ice, enclosed by boards, on which hockey is played 2. ~ **advertising** advertising affixed to the boards 3. ~ **board** white chalkboard affixed to the Plexiglas, used by coaches during practices to draw up plays 4. ~**-length dash** var. of *end-to-end rush* 5. ~ **management** personnel who oversee the operations of an arena 6. ~ **rage** parents at youth hockey games who become angered at anything that negatively affects their child 7. ~ **rat** kid who spends all his free time at the local arena

rinkside area just off the ice (e.g., Zamboni area)

Rinkside magazine produced by the NHL for season-ticket holders in all cities

rinkwide pass pass that travels from one side of the ice to the other

riot melee or brawl

rip 1. criticize 2. beat badly 3. shoot hard

ritual action performed by a player every game which, in his mind, helps him play better

rivalry longstanding animosity between two teams or players

river hockey 1. hockey played on a frozen river in winter 2. hockey played by casual rules

rivet bolt that attaches skate holder to skate boot

Rivs short for Preston Rivulettes

road 1. ~ **apple** piece of frozen dung used as a puck 2. ~ **hockey** hockey played on a road, in summer or winter 3. ~ **game** game played in opponent's arena 4. ~ **team** visiting team 5. ~ **trip** string of several games away from team's home arena, requiring team to travel 6. ~ **uniforms** sweaters worn for road games (in the NHL, white sweaters) 7. ~ **warrior** player who excels at playing in opponent's arena 8. ~ **win** victory achieved in opponents' arena

roar 1. ~ **back** a. backcheck while skating as fast as possible b. rally to tie or win a game 2. ~ **down the wing** skate hard down the wing 3. ~ **in on goal** skate with determination to the net with the puck 4. ~ **to the net** skate hard to the goal

rob 1. make a great save 2. get the better of a trade 3. ~ **blind** var. of *rob*

Robertson, John Ross, Cup see *John Ross Robertson Cup*

rock 1. extremely reliable player, usually a defenceman ("he's a rock out there on the blueline") 2. hit hard ("he rocked Kaiser coming in over the line")

rock elm kind of wood used in the making of hockey sticks

rock 'em, sock 'em hard-hitting, fistic brand of hockey

rocker 1. curvature in a skate blade from toe to heel 2. ~ **blade** skate blade featuring a curve from back to front 3. ~ **skates** skates featuring a rocker blade (as opposed to a perfectly linear blade)

rocker

rocket hard shot

Rocket Richard Trophy annual trophy given to the NHL's leading goal scorer

Rockies nickname of Colorado's NHL team (1976-82)

Rocky hockey style of hockey played by the Colorado Rockies

role player player who sees limited ice time and is used only for specific purposes such as killing penalties or checking

roll 1. on a ~ of a team or player: play well over a number of games 2. ~ **away** of a puck: leave the stick of the player in possession 3. ~ **four lines** assign roughly the same amount of ice time to all four forward units, rather than concentrating ice time among three best lines (coaching strategy) 4. ~ **in front of the net** of a puck: move dangerously into the crease 5. ~ **off a man** turn away from a check, spinning 360-degrees to get past the opponent 6. ~ **off a stick** var. of *roll* *away* 7. ⁓ **out** a. of a puck: just barely make it out of the defensive area ("and the puck rolls out over the blueline") b. of a puck: skitter out of the defensive area toward the middle of the ice ("and the puck rolls out to centre") 8. ⁓ **to the line** of a puck: travel toward the goal line or blueline without crossing it

roller hockey hockey played on inline skates

roller polo (U.S., 1880s) var. of *ice polo*

rolling puck puck that travels on end (often unpredictably), rather than sliding smoothly in a straight line

Romania IIHF member nation since 1924

romp win by a wide margin

rondelle Fr., puck

rondelle

ronkram indigenous form of hockey played in Brazil using sticks and coconuts

roof 1. score into the top of the net 2. top of the goal 3. ⁓ **it** score into top of net

rook short for rookie

rookie 1. first-year player 2. ⁓ **camp** training camp intended specifically to evaluate and train young players 3. ⁓ **dinner** team dinner, usu. on the road, in which the rookie players pay the bill for the entire team 4. ⁓ **mistake** a. error made by first-year player b. fundamental error made by experienced player 5. ⁓ **of the year** league's

best first-year player 6. ⁓ **salary cap** limitation on how much players entering the league may be paid

room 1. open space on the ice 2. portion of the net that a goalie leaves unprotected ("she left a lot of room on the short side and Chu fired it home") 3. short for dressing room 4. board with, usu. on road trips, when players must share hotel rooms 5. ⁓ **to move** ample open space in which to mount an attack 6. **all kinds of** ⁓ wide open to receive a pass

roommate player who shares hotel room with teammate during road trips

rooter fan

Rose City (archaic) Portland

Rosno Cup successor (in name) to Baltica Cup, 2004-05

Ross, Art see *Art Ross*

Rossmen alternative nickname for Boston Bruins during the days when Art Ross was the team's general manager

roster 1. list of players on a team 2. ⁓ **decision** alteration to a team's roster (releasing, demoting, promoting, trading, signing, etc., a player) 3. ⁓ **freeze** periods during the season when teams may not alter their roster in any way 4. ⁓ **limit** maximum number of players a team is allowed to carry 5. ⁓ **report** information provided by teams and the league indicating the health and status of all players 6. ⁓ **sheet** official document filled out by a coach prior to a game which identifies all players in the lineup by name and sweater number

rotator cuff group of four muscles in the shoulder that allow the joint to move smoothly and which can be seriously aggravated by overuse

Rotomatic Sportstimer mid-1940s state-of-the-art time clock, designed by Devenish Display Products

rough 1. overly physical 2. ~ **customer** player who relies heavily on physical tactics 3. ~ **game** game marked by heavy hitting 4. ~ **going** var. of *rough game* 5. ~**-house tactics** deliberately physical play to throw a player or team off its game 6. ~ **it up** deliberate attempt to start a fight 7. ~ **play** stretch when there is much hitting 8. ~ **ride** physical play given a particular player in an attempt to reduce his effectiveness 9. ~ **stuff** var. of *rough play*

roughing two-minute penalty for excessively physical play

round 1. ~ **into condition** work one's way into top physical shape, usu. after injury 2. ~ **into form** play one's way to peak performance 3. ~ **out** finish off, usu. the scoring

roundup league summary of games

rout 1. lopsided score 2. defeat badly

routine 1. any action performed regularly out of habit or good training 2. ~ **play** basic play that should be executed with ease every time 3. ~ **save** easy stop of the puck by a goalie

rover (archaic) position in seven-man hockey; rover lined up between the three forwards and two defencemen and became either an extra attacker or an extra defender, depending on the situation

roving usu. of a goalie: wandering

roving

row 1. line of seats 2. fight

rowdyism brawling

Royal Bank Cup national tournament to determine Canada's Junior A champion

Royal York Hotel hotel in downtown Toronto where visiting teams stayed during "Original Six" era

R system (1950s) four clubs that comprised the New York Rangers' system: Rangers (NHL), New York Rovers (Eastern Hockey League), Philadelphia Ramblers (Can-Am League), and Lake Placid Roamers

rubdown body massage

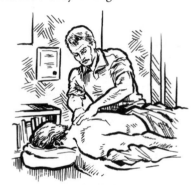

rubdown

rub out eliminate from play

rubber 1. puck 2. material used on floors in arena corridors for safe passage in skates between dressing rooms and ice 3. **see a lot of** ~ of a goalie: face many shots

ruckus pushing and shoving; fighting

rude awakening shock; sudden realization of true nature of a situation

Rude Pravo Cup international tournament, played in Czechoslovakia beginning in 1977, usu. featuring the best four European teams

rugged 1. physical (usu. of a defenceman) 2. ~ **play** physical play

rule 1. written regulation 2. ~ **book** publication containing the complete code of conduct for a league 3. ~ **change** alteration or amendment to rule book 4. ~ **off** penalize (a player)

rules 1. collection of regulations by which a game is played 2. ~ **committee** body of people who discuss rule changes or implement various changes to the rule book 3. ~ **of play** var. of *rules*

ruling any interpretation of the rules, usu. made by the referee

rumbles melee

rumour mill source of gossip (usu. in the media) about trades or controversies involving league's players

rumpus rough play

run 1. **great** ~ usu. in playoffs: extended winning streak 2. ~ **around** turn in a sloppy defensive effort ("they're running around in their own end") 3. ~ **the goalie** charge at a goalie before hitting him 4. ~ **interference** get between an opponent and a teammate who has the puck, thus preventing the teammate from being checked 5. ~ **into** check; hit 6. ~ **a man** charge at a player before hitting him 7. ~ **out of gas** lack energy in the latter stages of a shift or game 8. ~ **over** check hard 9. ~ **the power play** a. coach that aspect of a team's play b. take charge of a team during man advantage, usu. defenceman (see *quarterback*) 10. ~ **a practice** take charge of a team during practice 11. ~ **a team** manage a team's operations 12. ~ **up the score** continue to score goals long after the game is out of reach (often

considered unsportsmanlike) 13. **take a** ~ **at** charge opponent with the intent of hurting him

runners 1. figure skates 2. skates with long blades used in hockey until the 1920s

runner-up 1. second-place team 2. team that loses championship game or series

running 1. ~ **around** defensive play marked by lack of cohesion and inability to stop offensive surge by opposition ("the Jets are running around in their own end right now") 2. ~ **time** timing method under which clock does not stop when the whistle is blown to stop play (as opposed to *stop time*)

rush carry the puck up ice

rush back 1. return (usu. too soon) from an injury, resulting in a recurrence of the injury 2. backcheck

rushing defenceman defenceman skilled at carrying the puck from his own end deep into the opposition end

Russia IIHF member nation since 1992, when *perestroika* triggered the breakup of the Soviet Union

rut 1. depression in the ice 2. slump

rut

Ss

"S" Line (1930s) Montreal Maroons threesome of Babe Siebert, Nels Stewart, and Hooley Smith

SAP Arena principal arena in Mannheim, Germany

SH abbreviation for short-handed

SHG abbreviation for short-handed goal

SIHR *Society for International Hockey Research*

SIN official IIHF abbreviation for Singapore

SJHL Saskatchewan Junior Hockey League

SLO official IIHF abbreviation for Slovenia

SOG international abbreviation for shots on goal

S.P.A. Sportsmen's Patriotic Association

SRO standing room only

SUI official IIHF abbreviation for Switzerland

SVK official IIHF abbreviation for Slovakia

SV % abbreviation for save percentage

SVS international abbreviation for saves

SWE official IIHF abbreviation for Sweden

Sabre-Tooth Buffalo Sabres' mascot

Sabres nickname of the Buffalo franchise in the NHL

Sabres Magazine Buffalo Sabres' game-night program

sacrifice subject self to physical punishment, usu. to block a shot ("he'll sacrifice his body all night if it means preventing a shot on goal")

sacroiliac the area where the pelvis and the lower back meet

sacrum five lower vertebrae that comprise part of the pelvis

sag 1. let down 2. ~ the net score

sail 1. descriptive term for inaccurate shot 2. ~ in of a high shot: beat the goalie 3. ~ in alone of a player: create a breakaway through his great speed 4. ~ into hit hard

St. Boniface Seals Memorial Cup champions in 1938

St. Catharines Tee Pees Memorial Cup champions in 1954 and 1960

Saint John Vitos Allan Cup champions in 1992

St. Lawrence Starch Company Mississauga, Ontario-based company which produced Bee Hive photos between 1934 and 1967

St. Liedwi (of Scheidam) patron saint of skating since A.D. 1396

St. Louis Arena home of the St. Louis Eagles, 1934-35, and St. Louis Blues, 1967-94

St. Louis Blues NHL member team since 1967

St. Louis Eagles NHL member team, 1934-35 (formerly Ottawa Senators)

St. Mary's mask welder's mask worn by Johnny Bower during practice in 1960s to prevent facial injury

St. Michael's Allan Cup champions in 1910

St. Michael's Majors Junior A team sponsored by Toronto Maple Leafs prior to 1962 and affiliated with St. Michael's College School in Toronto; Memorial Cup champions in 1934, 1945, 1947, and 1961

St. Mike's short for St. Michael's Majors

St. Nicholas Rink pre-eminent arena in New York City that hosted many amateur and college games, 1896-1914

St. Pats short for Toronto St. Patricks

St. Petersburg Grand Prix tournament held since 1975, featuring Europe's national B teams

St. Petersburg Times Forum home arena of Tampa Bay Lightning

salary 1. sum of money paid by a team to a player 2. ~ **arbitration** process by which a player and team that cannot agree to terms agree to put the dispute before a neutral third party to be resolved 3. ~ **cap** limit on how much a team may pay its players (imposed by league) 4. ~ **demands** level of compensation sought by a player (generally higher than what a team is prepared to pay) 5. ~ **disclosure** publication of player salaries by players' association, so that others may gauge their own comparative value 6. ~ **dispute** disagreement between player and team over how much the player ought to be paid 7. ~ **dump** trading of a quality player simply to reduce the team's payroll 8. ~ **increase** raise in a player's pay 9. ~ **terms** details of a contract related to a player's compensation

salt the game away ensure victory, usu. said of a goal or penalty that virtually ensures one team will win the game

Salt Lake City host city of 2002 Olympic Winter Games

salvage rally for a tie ("the Leafs came back from 4-2 down in the third period to salvage a 4-4 tie")

Salyerds hockey stick manufacturer of Hilborn models in Preston, Ontario

sample phial of urine used to test for drugs in a player's system

sandpaper grit (i.e., willingness to hit or fight for the puck in the corner, check, and do the myriad unpleasant little things in a game that lead to victory)

San Jose Arena name of San Jose Sharks' home arena, 1993-2001 (renamed Compaq Center)

San Jose Sharks NHL member team since 1991

San Jose Sharks Magazine San Jose Sharks' game-night program

Sani Sport cabinet-like device that eliminates odours and bacteria from hockey equipment

Saskatchewan Junior Hockey League provincial Junior A league made of Saskatchewan-based teams

satellites (archaic) minor leagues

saucer pass pass that travels above the ice with a consistent spinning motion (like a Frisbee), so that it lands flat on the ice and is easily controlled by a teammate

Sault Ste. Marie Greyhounds Allan Cup champions in 1924 and Memorial Cup champions in 1993

savage 1. fierce 2. ~ **attack** vicious use of stick on opponent 3. ~ **blow** a. fierce hit b. bad loss 4. ~ **butchery** var. of *savage attack*

save 1. move made by a goalie to prevent puck from entering his net 2. ~ **from** (archaic) var. of *save* 3. ~ **percentage** ratio of saves made by a goalie to the total shots faced

Savvis Center name of St. Louis Blues' home arena, 2000-05

sawbones (archaic) doctor

saw-off tie

Sazka Arena principal arena in Prague, Czech Republic

scalp 1. hit an opponent over head with stick 2. sell tickets at a premium to face value

scalper person who sells tickets at a premium to face value, usu. right outside arena

scamper 1. rush with puck 2. ~ **back** backcheck furiously 3. ~ **to the bench**

hurry to skate off to complete a line change

scalper

Scandinavium principal arena in Gothenburg, Sweden

scar visible residual effects of a cut

scarlet blood

schedule 1. year 2. season 3. slate of games to be played

schedule-maker 1. (archaic) person— usu. Phil Scheuer—responsible for crafting the NHL schedule of all teams, formerly a manual task but more recently performed by computer 2. personification of computer-generated schedule ("the schedule-maker has not been kind to Vancouver, sending the Canucks on a seven-game road trip to start the year")

scholarship 1. financial incentive offered by U.S. college to attract hockey players to study and play there, usu. including free tuition and room and board

school 1. short for hockey school 2. teach 3. make a fool of ("Smithson schooled the defenceman on the faceoff")

sciatic nerve one of a pair of nerves (the largest in the body) that connect the lower back with the legs

sciatica pain caused by irritation of the sciatic nerve; also, any pain in power back or buttocks

scintillating save outstanding save by goalie

scoop 1. reporter's exclusive story 2. ~ **in the rebound** lift puck into net from close range in a scramble 3. ~ **shot** (1880s) wrist shot 4. ~ **up a loose puck** take possession of a puck that is up for grabs

scoot skate quickly (esp. when describing a smaller player)

scorching shot hard shot

score 1. tally of goals registered by each team 2. put the puck in the net 3. ~ **in bunches** score several goals in a short period of time 4. ~ **on the rush** score a goal as a result of quick movement up ice, as opposed to a set play on the power play or after long possession in offensive end

scoreboard electronic device suspended above centre ice that informs fans of score, time remaining in period and penalties, and other salient information (also scoreclock)

scoreless period or game in which no goals have been scored

scorer official at penalty bench or above ice who assigns credit to players who have scored or assisted on goals

scorer's table (archaic) area between penalty benches where scorer records statistical information as game progresses

scores var. of *goals* ("their three scores in the second period blew the game wide open")

scoresheet official document on which the game's statistical events are recorded

scoring 1. summary of goals in period or game 2. ~ **chance** good opportunity to score 3. ~ **leadership** first place in a league (or on a team) in goals or total points 4. ~ **opportunity** var. of *scoring chance* 5. ~ **punch** offensive power (on a team) 6. ~ **race** var. of *scoring leadership* 7. ~ **slump** prolonged period during which a top player does not score 8. ~ **spree** a. numerous goals in a short period of time during game b. over course of several games in succession 9. ~ **streak** period of several games in succession in which a player scores at least one goal 10. ~ **summary** statistical table listing goals, assists, penalties, and goaltending information about a game 11. ~ **threat** player who scores consistently 12. ~ **touch** skill around the opposition goal 13. ~ **unit** a. top forward line b. any five-man unit used specifically on power plays

Scotiabank Place name of Ottawa Senators' home arena since 2005 (formerly known as Corel Centre)

Scottrade Center name of St. Louis Blues' home arena since 2005 (formerly known as Savvis Center)

scout 1. person who watches games to assess player talent 2. attend games to assess player talent 3. **amateur** ~ scout who assesses talent at the pre-professional levels 4. **pro** ~ scout who assesses talent among professional teams and leagues

Scouts nickname of Kansas City team in NHL, 1974-76

scrag lose

scramble 1. loosely played game 2. hurry 3. ~ **back** backcheck expeditiously

scrambly play play marked by lack of flow, incomplete passes, and few scoring chances

scrap fight

scrape 1. **dry** ~ partial resurfacing of rink by shaving off a layer of old ice without laying down a sheet of water

to create a new surface (performed prior to a shootout) 2. ~ **by** defeat narrowly, as much through luck as skill 2. ~ **the ice** part of resurfacing process: shave away old ice before applying a sheet of water to create a new surface

scrapper player (usu. a smaller one) who struggles to be in the lineup every night and plays with feisty energy

scrapping fighting

scrappy play game marked by pushing, shoving, and other minor rough tactics

scratch remove from lineup ("Fukufuji has been scratched from the game tonight")

screamer hard shot

screen 1. block the view of goalie so that a shot, usu. from the point, cannot be seen by him 2. ~ **shot** shot directed at the goal while one or more players is between the shooter and the goalie, making it difficult for the goalie to see the shot

screened cage (archaic) enclosure for goal judges in front row of seats behind net

scribbler journalist

scribe journalist

scrimmage 1. informal game 2. battle for the loose puck in which numerous players are involved

scrub amateur or lower-level player

scrum jostling between several players on both teams

scuffle pushing and shoving, without fisticuffs

scuttlebutt gossip; rumours

seal ensure, usu. victory

Seals nickname of Oakland team in NHL, 1967-70; also, short for Golden Seals, nickname of California team in NHL, 1970-76

seal up tighten up on defence

seam 1. scar 2. small space between panes of Plexiglas 3. narrow opening between players; passing lane

seamless glass type of protective glass between ice surface and fans that does not require metal supports to hold panes together

season 1. period of time when hockey is played, from the first day of training camp to the last day of play-offs 2. ~ **opener** team's first game of the season 3. ~ **series** all games played between two specific teams during a given season 4. ~-**ticket holder** person who has pre-purchased tickets for every home game of a given season 5. ~ **tickets** tickets for every home game of a given season

seasoned veteran player who has been in the league several years

seasoning experience ("they've sent Williams to the minors for seasoning")

seat 1. players' bench 2. ticket to a game

Seattle Metropolitans Stanley Cup champions in 1917

second 1. one-sixtieth of a minute; one tick on the scoreclock 2. next-to-highest rank in standings 3. ~ **assist** point awarded to the player who passed the puck to the player who passed it to the goal scorer 4. ~ **chance** second shot at goal after goalie stops first shot 5. ~ **effort** renewed attempt to score or gain possession of puck after first attempt failed 6. ~-**guessers** people who question a trade, roster move, or coaching decision 7. ~ **half** a. (archaic) latter of two 30-minute periods (when games consisted of two equal halves) b. from 1917-20, latter portion of NHL season c. part of a season after the midpoint ("his play improved in the second half of the

year") 8. ~ **intermission** break in play between second and third periods 9. ~ **line** forward unit with scoring ability and some defensive savvy as well 10. ~ **period** middle 20 minutes of game 11. ~ **power-play unit** five men who play as a group on the power play after the first unit has tired and come off the ice 12. ~ **season** the playoffs 13. ~ **star** second-best player of a given game, as voted on usu. by a member of the media 14. ~ **string** player slightly less than top calibre 15. ~-**string goalie** backup goalie 16. ~ **unit** any group of players—forward line, defensive pairing—that plays after the first unit has come off the ice

Second All-Star Team year-end selection of second-best players in league at every position

Second Team All-Star member of Second All-Star Team

section 1. (archaic) division 2. area of an arena

secure 1. score (a goal) 2. acquire 3. safe 4. gain control (of puck) 5. acquire rights to 6. ~ **victory** win game or series

security knowledge that one's job is safe—enjoyed by a player who signs a long-term contract

see the ice be aware of where all players are on ice at all times

seeing-eye 1. ~ **shot** goal scored on a shot taken blindly through maze of players 2. ~ **pass** pass completed blindly through maze of players

segment portion of game or season (e.g., a ten-game segment)

selection process steps taken during the consideration of which player to draft

selfish of a player: prone to putting himself before his teammates

sellout 1. game for which there are no unsold seats 2. player who leaves a team for another for an increase in salary or opportunity to win a championship

semi-finals penultimate playoff round

semi-pro level of hockey where players are paid, but not enough to make it a full-time career

Senators nickname of both Ottawa teams to play in the NHL

send 1. ~ **him away** trade 2. ~ **him in alone** pass to a teammate who immediately goes on a breakaway 3. ~ **him into the clear** var. of *send him in alone* 4. ~ **him off** penalize 5. ~ **him packing** trade, cut, or demote a player 6. ~ **him to the fence** (archaic) penalize 7. ~ **him to the minors** demote a player 8. ~ **him to the penalty box** penalize 9. ~ **a man flying** hit a man in colourful fashion

send a man flying

10. ~ **a message** hit a player or start a fight in retaliation for earlier incident or to establish an aggressive, confident tone early in a game or series 11. ~ **out feelers** gauge the desirability of a player a team is considering trading 12. ~ **a pass** make a pass 13. ~ **the puck down the ice** ice the puck 14. ~ **a shot on goal** shoot the puck at the net 15. ~ **a team ahead** score a go-ahead goal 16. ~ **them packing** eliminate an opponent from playoffs

senior 1. elder; veteran 2. ~ **hockey** amateur hockey for players age 20 and up 3. ~ **league** league populated by older players 4. ~ **ranks** senior hockey

Senior A level of senior hockey below Senior AAA

Senior AAA level of senior hockey whose teams are eligible to compete for Allan Cup

Senior Intercollegiate early university designation

Sens short for Senators

sentence penalty

sentiment 1. soft feelings 2. opinion

septet (archaic) team—used in days when rules allowed seven players a side

sequence period of time

series 1. (archaic) league schedule 2. string of games played between two teams as part of playoffs 3. **long ~** best-of-seven playoff matchup that requires six or seven games to decide a winner 4. **short ~** best-of-seven playoff matchup that ends after just four or five games 5. **home-and-home ~** back-to-back games between the same two teams, one played in each team's arena

Series of the Century name for Canada-Soviet Union Summit Series of September 1972

serve 1. ~ **a penalty** spend time in penalty box as a result of an infraction

services player's commitment to a team ("they've acquired the services of Wilson for the coming season")

session period

set 1. series ("they play a home-and home set this weekend against Calgary") 2. ~ **for a faceoff** with one's stick on the ice, ready for the official to drop the puck 3. ~ **lines** forward lines that feature the same three members all game or season long 4. ~ **play** carefully planned and rehearsed strategy 5. ~ **position** body posture in which a goalie squares himself to the shooter to maximize his ability to make the save 6. ~ **the tone** make a play early in a game that establishes the team's desired style of play 7. ~**-to** fight 8. ~ **to go** ready to play 9. ~ **up** a. create a good scoring chance for a teammate b. gain control of the puck on the power play 10. ~ **ice** newly resurfaced ice that has been allowed to freeze properly

setback 1. loss of a game 2. hindrance to progress ("this loss is a real setback to the team's playoff hopes")

settle 1. agree to a contract 2. ~ **down** calm one's nerves in pressure game or situation 3. ~ **the puck down** get the puck to lie flat on the ice and under control 4. ~ **the question** score goal (or do anything else) that decides game's outcome 5. ~ **a score** get even 6. ~ **their differences** a. fight b. resolve dispute

set-up man player who is more skilled as a passer than as a shooter

seven (archaic) team ("the Renfrew seven play Ottawa tonight")

seven-man hockey (early 20th C.) version of the game in which seven players played on each side

seven-man rules Western rules that allowed for seven men a side while Eastern rules allowed for only six

seventh defenceman spare defenceman, rarely used in a game

sextet (archaic) team of six players ("the Winnipeg sextet will next play on Saturday")

shade win by a narrow margin

shadow check a specific man closely for the course of a game

shaft long, straight part of the stick between the butt end and the blade

shaft

shaibu Russian for puck, usu. used to cheer the team on to score a goal

shake off a check move speedily or craftily away from checker to get the puck or get into scoring position

shaken up slightly injured

shake up a lineup alter roster to jolt players into playing better

shaking hands 1. gesture of sportsmanship engaged in at the conclusion of a playoff series 2. expression used in describing imminent end of a playoff series ("if the Nordiques don't win tonight, they'll be shaking hands with the Canadiens")

shaky 1. unreliable 2. nervous 2. ~ **start** unreliable beginning to a game or season

shamateur players who claim to be amateur but are, in fact, being paid (as in Eastern bloc countries in 1950s through to 1980s or in eastern Canada, c. 1902-10)

Shams short for Montreal Shamrocks

shared shutout shutout in which both of a team's goalies play in the game, neither getting credit for it in their personal statistics

Sharks nickname of San Jose's NHL team

sharp 1. focused, usu. in reference to play of a hot goalie 2. ~ **angle** position close to the end red line, from which scoring is least likely 3. ~-**angle shot** shot taken from close to the end red line with little likelihood of scoring

sharp angle

sharpen skates hone the edges of skate blades

sharpshooter gifted scorer

shatter 1. ~ **glass** break Plexiglas 2. ~ **record** break existing statistical standard

shatter glass

sheep's shank bones material used to make skate blades in Europe up to 1650

shelf 1. **on the** ~ injured ("he'll start the season on the shelf until doctors clear him to play") 2. **top** ~ uppermost part of the inside of the net

shell-shocked of a goalie: confused or exhausted after allowing many goals or facing many shots in a game

shellack beat soundly

shelled of a goalie: having allowed many goals or faced many shots in a game

shelved sidelined by injury

sheet ice surface

Sherbrooke Beavers Allan Cup champions in 1965

Sher-Wood long-time hockey stick manufacturer

shield 1. NHL logo 2. hold onto puck by putting the body between it and an opponent

shift 1. period of time spent on ice 2. change positions ("he shifted from left wing to centre this past season") 3. ~ **disturber** player whose prime role is to disrupt and irritate opponents 4. ~ **gears** a. quickly step up one's level of play b. accelerate quickly

shifty of a stickhandler: skilled; difficult to hit or check

shine star; play well

shin 1. ~ **guard** protection for front of lower leg 2. ~ **pad** var. of *shin guard* 3. ~ **splint** inflammation of the muscles or connective tissue in the lower leg

shining light big star

shinney var. of *shinny (1)*

shinnie var. of *shinny (2)*

shinning 1. kicking the puck with the shin (illegal in early days) 2. slashing at an opponent's shins

shinny 1. informal game 2. early type of hockey stick made from a peeled sapling that had crooked roots

shiner 1. bruise 2. black eye

shinty early Scottish word for hockey

ship trade

shocker surprising trade or game result

shoe skates skates whose blades attached to the underside of street shoes

shoo-in 1. sure winner 2. something that is sure to happen

shoot 1. fire puck towards goal 2. ~ **a goal** (archaic) score a goal 3. ~ **a pass** (archaic) make a pass 4. ~ **against the grain** take a shot while skating in one direction while aiming the puck towards the other (i.e., moving to the right of the goalie but shooting to one's left) 5. ~ **their bolt** go all out

shooter player who takes a shot at the goal

shoot-in strategic play whereby the puck carrier shoots the puck to the end of the ice as soon as he crosses the centre red line

shooting 1. ~ **accuracy** statistic calculated by dividing total goals scored into total shots taken 2. ~ **drills** practice exercises intended to improve velocity and accuracy of a player's shot 3. ~ **lane** clear path between the puck carrier and the goalie 4. ~ **percentage** var. of *shooting accuracy* 4. ~ **star** top player

shootout 1. method of deciding a tie game, whereby teams take a series of penalty shots to determine a winner 2. game that ends in a high score

shoots left player who holds the stick so that the blade is to his left side

shoots right player who holds the stick so that the blade is to his right side

shop 1. try to trade a player ("the team is shopping Young around in hope of landing a scorer") 2. try to acquire a player ("the team is shopping for an experienced defenceman")

shore up 1. add strength or depth at a position ("the Flames are looking to shore up their scoring") 2. ~ **the blueline** improve the overall quality of the defensive corps

short 1. ~**-handed** situation in which one team has one or two fewer skaters on the ice because of penalties 2. ~**-handed goal** goal scored while team has fewer players on the ice than its opponents 3. ~**-handed 2-on-1** odd-man rush mounted by team with fewer men on the ice 4. ~ **a man** short-handed 5. ~ **pants** hockey pants 6. ~ **pass** pass to a nearby teammate 7. ~ **series** a. playoff matchup b. playoff matchup that is likely to be decided in fewest games ("if they keep playing this poorly, it's going to be a short series") c. of a playoff series: comprising fewer than seven games (i.e., best-of-three or best-of-five) 8. ~ **shift** a. brief turn on ice b. coaching strategy of rotating lines quickly to keep players fresh 9. ~ **side** side of the goalie on the same side as the puck carrier 10. ~ **term** anything to do with the immediate, as opposed to long range, future 11. ~**-term deal** contract or agreement of a lesser rather than greater duration 12. ~**-term solution** roster move designed to improve the team immediately, but not necessarily for a long time

shortcomings weaknesses

shorten the bench of a coach: decide to concentrate ice time among fewer players (i.e., go with three lines or four defencemen), leaving some to sit on the bench for extended periods

shorty slang for *short-handed goal*

shot 1. propelling of the puck towards the goal 2. hit or check ("Lindsay will give him a shot every chance he can") 3. ~ **at goal** shot directed towards the net but not actually on the goal 4. ~ **blocker** a. glove worn by the goalie on his stick hand b. player other than goalie who places himself in the path of a shot as a defensive move 5. ~ **clock** electronic display, installed in an arena, that tracks number of shots on goal by each team 6. ~ **for goal** (archaic) var. of *shot on goal* 7. ~ **its bolt** of a team: lacking energy or effort, having spent it completely before end of a game or series 8. ~ **nerves** nervousness or inexperience, usu. by a goalie, resulting in ineffective play 9. ~ **on goal** shot taken from inside centre ice that would have entered the net had the goalie not made a save 10. ~ **wide** of a player: having taken a shot that misses the net 11. ~ **wild** (archaic) var. of *shot wide* 12. **taking ~s** pre-game drill that entails shooting pucks at goal, to warm up the two goalies and give skaters some practice shots ("take a few shots on him before the game")

shoulder 1. check man off puck with one's upper body 2. ~ **cap protector** piece of equipment worn by a goalie as part of shoulder pads, which specifically covers the top of the shoulder and must conform to a specific size and shape to be considered legal 3. ~ **check** (U.S.) bodycheck 4. ~ **clavicle protector** piece of equipment worn by the goalie as part of shoulder pads which specifically protects that part of the body and must conform to a specific size and shape to be considered legal 5. ~ **drop** tactic by which a player (usu. a defenceman) lowers his shoulder to make forceful contact with an opponent in a legal manner 6. ~ **pads** equipment worn to protect shoulders and shoulder blades 7. ~ **patch** a. emblem sewn on sweater shoulder to commemorate passing of a player or team VIP b. emblem sewn on sweater shoulder to promote special event (such as Stanley Cup finals) or team anniversary c. alternate team logo sewn on sweater shoulder

shove 1. push, either player or puck 2. ~ **it in** push puck over goal line

shove

shovel 1. push pass 2. **~ the puck into the net** pick up a rebound near the crease and push it over the goal line 3. **~ shot** (archaic) kind of wrist shot

shoving infraction in early hockey

shoving match pushing and jostling between players

Show, The major league (i.e., the NHL)

show well perform well

showboater 1. player who celebrates a goal with a flourish beyond merely raising his arms 2. any needlessly flashy or showy player

showcase 1. display player's talent for the purpose of trading him 2. game which allows a player to show off his talent (e.g., an all-star game)

showdown confrontation between teams or players

Showdown intermission feature on *Hockey Night in Canada* in 1970s which brought the best players of the day together to compete in a series of tests of skill

showing performance

shuffle 1. trade 2. shake up a team's lineup by scratching some players and inserting new players 3. **~ lines** change constitution of forward units 4. **~ personnel** trade, move, demote, or otherwise alter lineup 5. **~ the deck** alter team's lineup

shunt send (a player) to the minors

shut 1. **~down** a. stifle the opposition b. keep an opposing player off the scoresheet c. stop trying to score and focus instead on defence 2. **~ out** prevent opposition from scoring even once during a game 3. **~ the door** play tight defence

shutout 1. game in which the goalie does not allow a single goal 2. **~ sequence** length of time, recorded in minutes and seconds, during which a

particular team or goalie has not allowed a goal

shy 1. player who avoids physical play 2. **~ away from** avoid physical play

sick bay 1. infirmary 2. **in ~** on the injured reserve list

side 1. team 2. long edges of rink 3. **~ of the net** area of net behind end red line

sideboards boards in offensive end between blueline and end red line

sidelined unable to play; injured

sidestep avoid a check

sieve epithet for a weak goalie

sights set on 1. looking forward to 2. trying to catch 3. aspiring to

sign 1. of a player: apply one's signature to a contract 2. of a team: convince a player to commit to a contract 3. placard of support from a home fan

signal 1. hand or arm motion by referee to indicate nature of a penalty 2. **~ a change** indicate a new direction for a team (via a trade, coaching change, or other event)

signal

silent auction sale of team memorabilia, in which bids are written down, to raise money for charity; usu. staged during games

silver 1. ~ **beaker** Stanley Cup 2. ~ **chalice** Stanley Cup 3. ~ **medal** award for finishing in second place in international competition 4. ~ **mug** Stanley Cup

Silver Puck Award (1970s) award given to team that won the season series between the St. Louis Blues and Kansas City Scouts (both Missouri-based)

Silver Seven alternative nickname for Ottawa Senators during their reign as Stanley Cup champions (1902-06)

Silver Stick youth tournament, featuring Canadian and U.S. teams, founded in Ottawa in 1958 as a means of promoting international goodwill through hockey, the prize for each age group being a silver-plated hockey stick

silverware trophies

simon-pure amateur player whose status has not been defiled by receiving money to play (contrast with *shamateur*)

sin bin penalty box

Singapore IIHF member nation since 1996

single one ticket ("who's looking for a single?")

single-handed effort great rush by one player

single-referee system method of officiating in which only one referee patrols the ice

singles metal blades that attach to boots with screws or rivets

singleton one goal (by a team or player in a game)

sink 1. lead to defeat 2. score

sinker dipping shot

sinking defenceman defenceman who moves into the slot on offence to create a scoring chance

siren device sounded to indicate the end of a period or game

sit 1. bench (a player—"the Leafs will sit Smedsmo tonight") 2. be benched or scratched 3. ~ **back** play defence 4. ~ **on a lead** focus on defence to preserve a lead, making no attempt to score 5. ~ **out** be scratched from lineup 6. **puck ~s down** of a bouncing puck: finally stay flat on the ice

six team ("the Victoria six are in action tonight")

six-man hockey hockey played with six men a side as opposed to seven

sixth attacker extra skater employed by a team that has pulled its goalie (also "sixth skater")

sixty-minute skater (archaic) player in sufficient condition to play all out for the whole game

size 1. collective physical dimensions—height and weight—of a team ("they have more size this year than last") 2. ~ **up** assess

sizzler hard shot

sizzler

sizzling 1. of a shot: hard 2. angry

S.J. Sharkie mascot of the San Jose Sharks

skate 1. footwear used to glide along the ice 2. to glide along the ice 3. game of hockey ("the next skate is this Thursday") 4. **go for a ~** shirk one's backchecking duties 5. ~ **around**

move around an opponent through a combination of speed and good puck-handling 6. ~ **away** use speed to move towards the opposition goal faster than the opponents 7. ~ **by himself** of an injured player: practice alone during one's rehab 8. **~-by-skate** (U.S.) early radio term for play-by-play 9. ~ **circles around** vastly outplay ("they skated circles around us tonight") 10. ~ **guard** plastic protectors that slide over the ends of blades, enabling wearer to walk on surfaces other than ice without dulling them 11. ~ **holder** any equipment that keeps skates in place, usu. at the side of equipment bag 12. ~ **in on goal** move towards opposition net 13. **morning** ~ light warmup, usu. the day of a game, held before noon 14. **pre-game** ~ warmup about 45 minutes prior to the opening faceoff 15. ~ **his man off the puck** use speed and tenacity to take the puck from the puck carrier 16. ~ **save** use of a skate by the goalie to stop the puck 17. ~ **sharpener** machine used to maintain sharpness of skate blades 18. ~ **towards** close in on an opponent

skater 1. defenceman or forward ("teams can dress two goalies and 18 skaters") 2. someone skilled as such

skating 1. a. movement on ice while wearing skates b. ability to skate ("he needs to work on his skating") 2. ~ **drills** exercises intended specifically to improve skating ability 3. ~ **game** style of hockey that emphasizes speed and skill ahead of physical play 4. ~ **lane** clear path between skater and opposition end 5. ~ **on sawdust** skating on bad ice

skatist (archaic) hockey player

sked schedule

skein string of games ("they have an eight-game road skein coming up")

skid losing streak

skill 1. ability to play the game at a high level 2. ~ **player** player with a high level of ability 3. ~ **set** combination of various elements needed to play at a high level (speed, stickhandling, skating, etc.)

skills competition series of contests to determine the best players at various aspects of the game (skating, passing, shooting, etc.)

skim 1. (1870s) rush the puck 2. near miss 3. head towards

skipper coach; leader

skirmish fight

skirt white plastic protector at the base of the net that protects the mesh from being cut

Skyreach Centre former name (1978-2003) of Edmonton Oilers' home arena (renamed Rexall Place)

slam 1. hit hard 2. hard shot 3. ~ **it home** score

slap fine a player ("he's been slapped with a $500 fine for his actions")

slapper slapshot

slapshot 1. hard shot for which a player uses a full windup 2. ~ **artist** early reference to a player who possessed a good slapshot

slapshot

Slap Shot 1. mascot of Washington Capitals 2. hockey magazine 3. mascot of New Jersey Devils prior to 1993 4. mascot of Philadelphia Flyers in 1978-79

Slap Shot Hollywood movie starring Paul Newman that parodies violence and hockey of 1970s

slash 1. hit an opponent with the stick 2. ~ **from behind** hit an opponent with the stick as he skates up ice (common foul in old days)

slashing infraction for illegal use of stick on an opponent, punishable by a two-minute penalty

slated scheduled ("he's slated to return to action next week")

slaughter lopsided game

sleepless nights nocturnal phenomena experienced by coaches during a losing streak or players during a goal-less drought

slew foot pull a player's foot out from under him with one's own foot, usu. from behind, causing him to fall (very dangerous)

slide 1. skate along ice 2. slip along ice after falling while skating 3. losing streak ("they're on a three-game slide heading into tonight's game") 4. ~ **across to make a save** of a goalie: move from one side of the net to the other to make a save 5. ~ **it in** take a quick shot from in close that goes

slide

into the net 6. ~ **a pass** make a pass along the ice, usu. close to the opposition goal 7. ~ **the puck under him** beat goalie with a low shot

sliding pass pass along the ice (as opposed to a lifting or saucer pass)

slip 1. mistake 2. lose ground 3. ~ **by** deke 4. ~ **it in** score 5. ~ **the puck between players** make a quick, short pass through a group of players 6. ~ **the puck in** score from in close along the ice 7. ~ **through the defence** deke or skate past the defence unhindered 8. ~ **up** a. move up to b. make a mistake

slogging tough going

sloppy undisciplined or ineffectual

slot area directly in front of goal

Slovakia IIHF member nation since 1993

Slovenia IIHF member nation since 1992

slow 1. plodding, lacking in speed 2. ~ **down** a. decelerate b. deliberately try to stifle speed and offensive output of an opponent 3. ~-**footed** of a player: lacking in skating speed 4. ~ **glycolysis** also aerobic glycosis; breakdown of carbohydrates not associated with production of lactic acid 5. ~ **going** of a game: dull 6. ~ **ice** ice of poor quality 7. ~ **start** early part of game or season in which team is less effective than expected 8. ~ **to get up** injured (of a player) 9. ~ **to react** ineffective at anticipating opponent's move 10. ~ **whistle** continued play for several seconds after one or more players assumed play would be blown dead

slug 1. hit 2. player of limited skill

slugfest game with many fights

sluggish 1. of a game: dull 2. of a team or player: uninspired

slump prolonged streak of poor play resulting in accumulated losses, lack of scoring, or quality play

slush ice of poor quality

smack 1. hit an opponent 2. ~ **the puck** take a shot

small 1. pejorative for a player who is neither tall nor powerfully built 2. ~- **market team** team which plays in a city unable to generate income necessary for team to compete successfully with other NHL teams 3. ~ **victory** pyrrhic victory offering little consolation in big picture ("they outshot their opponents 35-14, but that's small victory in a game they lost 3-1")

smarts 1. keen hockey sense 2. is painful ("he took that shot in the ankle—that smarts")

smashing shot hard shot

smelling salts ammonia-based crystals formerly used to revive players who have been winded or knocked unconscious

Smith, Kate singer whose rendition of "God Bless America" proved a good-luck charm for the Philadelphia Flyers in the 1970s

Smiths Falls Stanley Cup challengers in March 1906

Smitty common nickname for players named Smith

smoke 1. hit an opponent hard 2. shoot the puck hard

smoking drive hard shot

Smoky City (archaic) nickname for Pittsburgh

smooth-skating gifted with top skating ability

smother 1. defeat soundly 2. cover up the puck 3. check closely 4. ~ **a loose puck** control puck by holding it until whistle stops play 5. ~ **the puck** hold puck until whistle stops play

smothering defence extremely effective defence

Smythe, Conn, Sports Celebrity Dinner see *Conn Smythe Sports Celebrity Dinner*

smother

Smythe, Conn, Trophy see *Conn Smythe Trophy*

Smythe Division one of four NHL divisions, 1974-93

Smythemen Toronto Maple Leafs during the years when Conn Smythe was in charge ("the Smythemen come to Detroit this Sunday night")

snap 1. go berserk 2. end a bad streak of some sort 3. ~ **it home** score 4. ~ **out of it** play well after a stretch of poor play 5. ~ **out of a slump** end a streak of poor play 6. ~ **pass** hard, quick pass 7. ~ **the puck** shoot quickly 8. ~ **shot** quick shot that requires neither the full windup of a slapshot nor the sliding motion of a wrist shot

snare of a goalie: make a great glove save

snatch win (a game)

sneak in 1. ~ **behind the defence** skate or handle the puck cleverly to get by the defence and move in on the goalie for a good scoring chance 2. ~ **on goal** handle puck cleverly and create close-in scoring chance 3. ~ **over blueline** make a clever move to get the puck inside the offensive end

sniff 1. taste; experience ("this is his first sniff of the playoffs in six years") 2.

consideration; notice ("despite his scoring ability, Watson didn't get a sniff from the NHL come draft day")

snipe score

sniper goal scorer

sniping good scoring

Sniper Cap fitted baseball-style cap embroidered with NHL team logo (renamed Shootout Cap)

snow 1. frozen precipitation which must be shovelled off an outdoor rink 2. shavings that accumulate on ice surface, esp. when players stop suddenly 3. ~ **shower** spray of snow created by a player who skates quickly towards a goalie and then stops equally quickly

snowed under overwhelmed

snowplow hook a man, usu. between the bluelines

can be exceeded without penalty under certain circumstances (compare to *hard cap*) 3. ~ **goal** goal surrendered because of defensive lapse or inattentive play by goalie 4. ~ **hands** excellent scoring skills 5. ~ **ice** slushy ice that inhibits skilful play 6. ~-**ice team** team that plays well on slushy ice, usu. because it lacks skilled players 7. ~ **pass** pass made accurately but with little velocity 8. ~ **play** play marked by little bodychecking 9. ~ **touch** easy team to defeat

softie player lacking in desire, esp. to play physically

soldier team player who lacks star quality but is essential to team chemistry and success

sole possession of a team: usu. of first place in any standings

snowplow

snuff out stop an offensive thrust

Society for International Hockey Research organization founded in Kingston, Ontario, in 1990, dedicated to the study of hockey's history

socks long, knit leg coverings which go on over shin pads

soft 1. of a player: lacking grit and toughness 2. ~ **cap** salary cap that

solid play play marked by efficiency and skill, though unspectacular

solo dash end-to-end rush by one player

solo rush var. of *solo dash*

soloist (archaic) player skilled in the art of solo dashes

solve 1. beat a goalie 2. defeat a team (usu. in the negative—"the Aeros

have been unable to solve goalie Kim
Martin all season")

something special very talented player

Soo 1. nickname for Sault Ste. Marie,
Ontario, or Sault Ste. Marie, Michigan
2. **American** ~ Sault Ste. Marie,
Michigan, team in International
Hockey League, 1904-07 3. **Canadian**
~ Sault Ste. Marie, Ontario, team in
International Hockey League, 1904-
07 4. ~ **Greyhounds** nickname for
Sault Ste. Marie Greyhounds, team in
Ontario Hockey League

sophomore jinx dramatic decline in
performance for a second-year player
after an excellent rookie season

sorrel-topped (archaic) red-headed

sort out recap ("the referee is over by
the penalty box sorting out the penalties from that brawl")

sortie 1. trip 2. rush up ice

South Africa IIHF member nation
since 1937

souvenir 1. injury 2. collectible 3. merchandise purchased at arena 4. any
puck that sails over the glass and into
the crowd 5. ~ **program** publication
containing player profiles, game
lineups, and stories on the team and
league, sold at arena esp. on night of
a game

spadework physical play in corners

Spain IIHF member nation since 1923

Spalding, A.G., & Bros. official outfit-
ters of many Canadian teams in the
19th century

Spalding puck official NHL puck
which replaced the Art Ross puck in
1940

span period of time ("the team has won
five games in a row, and in that span
Dickson has scored eight goals")

spar fight

spare 1. substitute 2. ~ **forward** in
"Original Six" era, a team's tenth for-

ward, most often used to kill penalties
3. ~ **goalkeepe**r a. backup goalie b.
practice goalie c. third goalie (on the
team's roster but not dressed) 4. ~
part a. seldom-used player b. player
with little value; a throw-in to a trade

spare goalkeeper

sparingly infrequently (usu. describes
way a fourth-line forward, seventh
defenceman, or backup goalie is used)

spark 1. ignite; set in motion ("Stastny's
hat trick sparked the Nordiques' rally
in the third period") 2. impetus
("Soetaert's save was the spark they
really needed") 3. **provide** ~ energize
one's team with a big hit or timely
goal

sparkle play extremely well

sparkplug player who inspires or ener-
gizes his team

sparse crowd poorly-attended game

Spartacat Ottawa Senators' mascot

spasm (archaic, mainly in women's
hockey) period of play

spear jab an opponent violently in the
stomach with the blade of one's stick

spearhead ignite, usu. an attack or rally

spearing serious infraction for jabbing
an opponent in the stomach with
one's stick, punishable by five-minute

major and automatic game misconduct, and possible suspension

Special 1. brand of hockey stick produced
by Doolittles of St. Marys, Ontario 2.
model of Wally stick produced by
Ingersoll Hockey Stick Company 3.
~ **Professional** model of Monarch
hockey stick produced in New
Hamburg, Ontario

special 1. talented 2. ~ **attention** close
checking 3. ~ **teams** power-play and
penalty-killing units 4. ~ **trophies**
NHL individual awards

specialist player who is particularly
adept at one facet of the game ("he's
their faceoff specialist")

spectacle outstanding game

spectator 1. fan 2. injured player

Spectrum home arena of Philadelphia
Flyers, 1967-1996

speculation 1. betting 2. rumours and
gossip about trades

speculator scalper

speed 1. velocity; ability to skate swiftly
2. ~ **ball** small, stuffed ball suspended to a point above the head,
and which snaps back rapidly when
punched, used by players to improve
hand-eye coordination 3. ~ **merchant** player who skates very quickly
4. ~ **skates** skates whose blades are
longer than their boots—used specifically for speed skating

speed skates

speedster var. of *speed merchant*

spell 1. period of time 2. relieve; substitute for 3. ~ **defeat** of an event in
a game: directly attributable to a loss
4. ~ **the end** of an event: tied directly
to a loss or departure of a player from
a team

spell off (archaic) provide relief,
substitute

Spengler Cup annual invitational tournament held in Davos, Switzerland,
from December 25-31, primarily
contested by club teams

spice 1. physical play 2. **add** ~ contribute
physical play to a team ("he adds a
little spice out there")

spill 1. trip or fall 2. **heavy** ~ hard fall,
usu. resulting in injury

spin twirl on skates to avoid being
checked or as a result of being checked

spinarama 180- or 360-degree spin to
avoid a check while maintaining control of the puck (also Savardian
spinarama, after Serge Savard; coined
by Danny Gallivan)

spine-tingling exciting

spirited 1. exciting 2. rough 3. ~ **affair**
exciting game 4. ~ **attack** enthusiastic, relentless offensive pressure 5. ~
game var. of *exciting affair* 6. ~ **play**
exciting play

spit expel saliva, mucous, or water from
mouth

spitting act of expelling saliva (sometimes during fight or other confrontation with opponent—extremely
unsportsmanlike and subject to suspension)

spleen vital organ situated on left side
of abdomen, which filters blood and
destroys old red blood cells

splendid 1. of high quality 2. ~ **condition**
game shape 3. ~ **form** var. of
splendid condition 4. ~ **hockey** game
with high level of skill 5. ~ **play** highly-

entertaining action 6. ~ **season** impressive performance over the course of a year ("he's having a splendid season so far")

splendiferous outstanding (of a play—used by Danny Gallivan)

splice joining of shaft to blade in manufacture of a hockey stick

split 1. exchange of wins in back-to-back games of a playoff series in one city ("with the split they head home with home-ice advantage") 2. ~ **the defence** successfully skate between the two opposing defencemen while maintaining possession of the puck to go in alone on the goalie 3. ~ **the duties** divide playing time between team's two goalies 4. ~ **a line** of a coach: break up a forward unit

splits acrobatic move by a goalie who extends his legs in opposite directions to make a save, usu. to cover part of one side of the net after making a save at the other

win to clinch the series or championship 2. ~ **a shutout** score a late goal to prevent the opposition goalie from recording a shutout

spoiler late in the regular season, a team eliminated from the playoffs that defeats playoff-aspiring teams, making it difficult, if not impossible, for them to qualify

Spokane Chiefs Memorial Cup champions in 1991

Spokane Flyers Allan Cup champions in 1976 and 1980

Spokane Jets Allan Cup champions in 1970 and 1972

sponsor 1. advertiser 2. small business that provides financial support for a local youth team

sport 1. wear ("the Habs are sporting their vintage sweaters tonight") 2. display, as a bruise, black eye, or stitches

Sportsmen's Battery 30th Light Anti-Aircraft Battery, a unit of the Canadian army in World War II,

splits

spoil 1. ~ **the celebration** win a playoff game that the opponent needed to

made up largely of hockey players and others associated with sports

Sportsmen's Patriotic Association level of amateur hockey in Toronto area which thrived in the 1930s

spot 1. **roster** ~ place in the lineup 2. ~ **the puck** see where the puck is 3. ~ **the team a goal** give up an early goal

spot duty infrequent use in a game

sprain twist a joint or hyperextend ligaments

sprawling 1. ~ **goalie** goalie whose style it is to fall, twist, and stretch to make saves 2. ~ **save** of a goalie: stop a puck by splaying his body in desperation

spray 1. pepper goalie with many shots 2. stop quickly, sending a cascade of snow into a player's face

spread eagle sprawl with all four limbs out-stretched

spring 1. time for playoffs ("they're not going to be playing this spring") 2. ~ **free** send teammate on a breakaway with a pass that puts him in the clear 3. ~ **skates** (late 19th C.) metal skate blades that attached to boots with a special locking device activated by a small lever

Springfield Civic Center home arena of Hartford Whalers for part of 1979-80, the team's first year in the NHL; also home to WHA New England Whalers for part of 1977-78 and all of 1978-79

spurt 1. sudden outburst 2. **scoring** ~ a number of goals scored in quick succession

spurting (archaic) rushing

squabble disagreement, usu. internally between player and team management or player and coach

squad team

squander waste, usu. a lead or a great scoring chance

square 1. tie the score ("the goal squares the game at one-all") 2. ~ **off** fight 3. ~ **to the play** positioned so that one faces the play directly 4. ~ **to the shooter** of a goalie: positioned so that he faces the puck carrier directly

squat crouch close to the ice without quite touching it

squeeze 1. ~ **him off the puck** check opponent into the boards, forcing him to relinquish the puck and end up out of the play 2. ~ **one's pads** puck-stopping technique whereby the goalie puts his pads together so that no puck can squirt through 3. ~ **the stick** a. literally, grip the stick too tightly b. be nervous; try too hard, usu. of a scorer

squirt 1. kids' hockey 2. ~ **over the line** of a puck: barely cross the goal line after being slowed down by the goalie as he tries to make the save

stab 1. glove save 2. ~ **at the puck** try to poke the puck free or propel it forward

stack pads of a goalie: drop to one's side and place one pad on top of the other

stage 1. play ("these two teams will stage a re-match this Saturday") 2. ~ **a comeback** rally to tie or win 3. ~ **a rush** take the puck and move up ice with it

stalemate tie score ("they played to a 3-3 stalemate")

stall 1. end winning streak ("their winning ways stalled after six games") 2. hold puck behind net 3. ~ **for time** use means (often devious) to delay the next faceoff, such as going to the bench for a new stick or ripping loose tape off a stick (also "stall in the faceoff circle")

stalwart 1. veteran 2. ~ **on defence** reliable defenceman

stamina endurance

stamp 1. distinctive mark on a hockey stick to identify a manufacturer or player 2. place names on the Stanley Cup using tools

Stampede Corral former home arena of Calgary Flames (1980-83) and WHA Calgary Cowboys (1975-77)

stance position of a goalie as he is ready to face a shooter

stand 1. ~ **his ground** of a player: maintain position even though he knows he will be hit by an oncoming player 2. ~ **him up** of a defenceman: stop backing up at a certain point, so as to check the rushing puck carrier before he gets too close to the goal 3. ~ **on his head** of a goalie: perform well under heavy pressure 4. ~ **square** directly face an opponent (proper positioning for centremen on faceoffs) 5. ~ **up** rallying cry when improved play is sought 6. ~ **up at blueline** var. of *stand him up* 7. ~ **up his man** var. of *stand him up* 8. ~**s up** of an early goal: prove to be the winning goal

standby goalie backup goalie

standby official extra on-ice official who watches the game but is prepared to work the game in case of injury (usu. only for playoffs or international events)

standees fans in the standing-room only section of an arena

standing 1. ~ **ovation** applause delivered by fans who rise to their feet 2. ~ **room** area where fans must stand to watch the game 3. ~ **start** beginning to skate from a stationary position 4. ~ **still** out of position and not reacting to the flow of the game

standings ranking of teams according to results of their games

standoff tie

standout star player

stands 1. seats in an arena 2. measures in height ("he stands six feet two")

standup goalie goalie whose technique entails remaining on his skates as much as possible (contrast with butterfly goalie, who drops to his knees often)

Stanley C. Panther mascot of the Florida Panthers

Stanley Cup 1. trophy donated to Canada by governor general Lord Stanley in 1893 for the amateur hockey championship of Canada 2. symbol of hockey supremacy as NHL champions 3. ~ **banner** flag raised to the rafters of a champions' home arena 4. ~ **celebration** party held after winning Stanley Cup, in dressing room right after victory and at times all summer 5. ~ **challenge** (archaic) prior to 1910, application by a team to play the Stanley Cup holders in a series 6. ~ **champions** winners of the Stanley Cup 7. ~ **finals** last stage of the playoffs in

Stanley Cup

which champion is determined 8. ~ **journal** feature on Hockey Hall of Fame website detailing the travels of the Cup over the summer with victorious players 9. ~ **parade** civic procession in the champions' home city in the days immediately following victory 10. ~ **playoffs** all rounds of post-season play in the NHL, leading towards the crowning of a champion 11. ~ **record** accomplishment which sets a standard in the history of Stanley Cup play, usu. statistical in nature 12. ~**pers** champions 13. ~ **ring** jewellery awarded by the Cup-winning team to its players and top employees to honour their championship 14. ~ **series** var. of *Stanley Cup finals* 15. ~ **trustees** two Canadian men (originally appointed by Lord Stanley) who adjudicated Cup competitions and challenges (up to 1910) and now oversee the care of the trophy

Stanley Park large public park in Vancouver, named after Lord Stanley

stanza period

staph infection the formation of abscesses just beneath the skin's surface

staple 1. hit hard 2. ~ **him into boards** hit an opponent hard along boards 3. ~ **him to the bench** of a coach: deny ice time to a player who is dressed for a game ("coach Burns has stapled him to the bench for this entire period after that bad giveaway")

Staples Center home arena of Los Angeles Kings

star 1. top player 2. play well ("he stars for the team every night")

Starr skates skates made by Starr Manufacturing Company of Dartmouth, Nova Scotia, which attached directly to a boot by use of a lever

Stars 1. nickname of Dallas team in NHL 2. short for (Minnesota) North Stars

"Star-Spangled Banner" U.S. national anthem, played before every NHL game involving a U.S.-based team

start 1. beginning of game 2. appear on ice for opening faceoff ("he'll start on right wing again") 2. ~ **and stop** practice drill in which players learn to start quickly and stop as quickly 3. ~ **back** backcheck 4. ~ **out** break out (of own end) 5. ~ **something** provoke a fight

starting 1. initial appearance in a game ("he'll be starting again on right wing") 2. ~ **goaltenders** goalies who begin the game for their respective teams 3. ~ **lineup** list of the 12 players who are on the ice for the opening faceoff 4. ~ **time** scheduled hour when game will commence

Starting Lineup series of action figures sold in 1990s

starts games played, usu. for a goalie ("he's winless in his last five starts")

statistician team or league employee who keeps numeric records of events of games (goals, assists, etc.)

statistics numeric representation of events of a game or games

station establish position

stationary bike exercise equipment that simulates riding of a bicycle, usu. employed after a game to reduce lactic acids

stats short for *statistics*

status 1. player's situation regarding his eligibility to play, related to factors such as health ("injury status"), availability to be drafted ("draft status"), or ownership of rights ("contractual status" or "free-agent status")

stay-at-home defenceman defenceman who is more adept at play inside his own blueline than rushing the puck or contributing to the team's offense

stay with a man shadow and check an opponent wherever he goes

steady 1. reliable 2. ~ **improvement** gradual and consistent increase in quality of play 3. ⁓ **play** unspectacular but very reliable play

steadying influence calm personality, usu. of a veteran, which lends stability to a team

steal 1. acquire the puck by stealth 2. one-sided trade

steam speed ("he's heading up ice with a full head of steam")

steer 1. direct or redirect a pass 2. ⁓ **the puck aside** of a goalie: make a save 3. ⁓ **clear of trouble** avoid a fight or a hard check 4. ⁓ **a man away** check opponent in such a way that he is forced to move away from the goal, rather than toward it

steer

stellar first-rate; excellent

step 1. **first** ⁓ initial move in making the NHL or rejoining team after injury ("he took the first step toward a full recovery this morning by skating for a few minutes on his own") 2. ⁓ **in** interfere 3. ⁓ **in over the blueline** move puck into offensive end 4. ⁓ **into the lineup** replace a player who is injured or playing badly 5. ⁓ **into one's man** check an opponent hard 6. ⁓ **into the rush** of a defenceman: skate with the three forwards deep into opposition end 7. ⁓ **into the shot** take a full windup before shooting 8.

⁓ **into a tough situation** enter game or join team under less-than-ideal circumstances 9. ⁓ **it up** increase tempo, energy, or effort 10. ⁓ **onto the ice** move from corridor or bench to ice surface 11. ⁓ **through** deke (an opponent) 12. ⁓ **up** a. elevate one's play b. move forward to get involved in play

stereopticon device used to update out-of-town game scores around 1900

Stevens Hotel Chicago hotel used by visiting teams during "Original Six" days

stew be angry, confused, or worried without expressing these feelings ("Williams will have to sit in the penalty box and stew for the next two minutes")

stick 1. piece of carved wood used to handle, pass, and shoot the puck 2. jab or poke a player illegally with the blade of the stick 3. stay with a team 4. **hot** ⁓ of a player: score at a high rate in recent games 5. ⁓ **boy** (archaic) young child who stands by the stick rack during games and gives players new sticks in the event theirs breaks during play 6. ⁓ **check** clever use of stick to take the puck from an opponent 7. ⁓ **fight** vicious battle between players who use their sticks to hit each other 8. ⁓ **measurement** measurement of the curve of a stick blade, performed by referee to determine whether stick is legal 9. ⁓⁓ **measuring gauge** instrument which helps referee determine the legality of a stick blade 10. ⁓ **out a pad** of a goalie: make a save using his leg 11. ⁓ **save** of a goalie: use the stick to stop the puck 12. ⁓ **side** side of the net that corresponds to hand in which goalie holds his stick (opposite of glove side) 13. ⁓⁓**-spraying room**

designated area at IIHF sanctioned events where sticks not made by official sponsors are spray-painted a neutral colour so that the brands are not visible   14. ~ **swinging** vicious assault on an opponent, using of the stick   15. **~-swinging duel** var. of *stick fight*   16. ~ **with** persevere   17. ~ **work** vicious use of sticks, usu. for slashing and high sticking

stickhandle deft control the puck with the stick

stickhandle

stickhandler player who performs the stickhandling

stickmen team ("the Toronto stickmen hope to win again this Wednesday")

stiff check hard hit

stiff resistance commitment to defence

Stinger mascot of the Columbus Blue Jackets

stingy 1. ~ **defence** team play on defence that does not allow many scoring chances   2. ~ **on rebounds** goalie who is particularly adept at controlling the puck after making a save

stint time (usu. brief) spent with a team or in a league ("he had a 15-game stint in the minors last month")

stir things up provoke a fight

stitches sutures used to close a cut

stitched up 1. of a player: having received stitches   2. of a wound: having been closed using sutures

stock skates (circa mid-1800s) skates that consisted of a blade affixed firmly to a block of wood which in turn fastened to the bottom of a boot

stockings var. of *socks*

stockings

Stompin' Tom Tom Connors, Canadian singer/songwriter famous for "The Hockey Song" (a.k.a. "The Good Old Hockey Game")

stone 1. make a great save ("Vernon stoned Linden from in close")   2. turn in an excellent goaltending performance ("Blue stoned the Jets the last time these two teams played")   3. short for *carborundum stone* used to sharpen skates   3. ~ **hands** lack of scoring touch

stonewall prevent opposition from scoring

stockyard tactics stickwork (slashing, high-sticking)

Stony Plain Eagles Allan Cup champions in 1999

stop 1. of a goalie: save   2. road game ("the Leafs' next stop is in Montreal for a game tomorrow night")   3. come to a standstill 4. **come to a** ⁓ stop skating 5. ⁓ **in play** break in the action, triggered by an official's whistle 6. ⁓ **a man** check a player off the puck 7. ⁓ **sign** patch worn on the back of kids' sweaters as a reminder that hitting from behind is dangerous and illegal 8. ⁓ **skating** a. of a team: lose energy b. of a player: come to a standstill 9. ⁓ **a team** defeat a team or prevent it from doing something it usually does well 10. ⁓ **time** method of timing a game in which clock stops when whistle blows play dead (as opposed to running time)

stoppage break in play ("he'll talk to his goalie during this stoppage to try to calm him down")

stops and starts practice drill at power-skating school in which players skate hard and stop when they hear a whistle, and start up again when they hear another whistle

stopwatch device used in early days to time games and more recently at the penalty bench as a backup in case the scoreclock fails

Stor Grabb (Swedish, "Great Men") list of Sweden's greatest players as compiled by the Swedish Ice Hockey Association

storm off ice leave the playing surface angrily

Storm Squad name of Carolina Hurricanes' cheerleaders

stout admirable ("he played a stout game tonight despite being injured")

stovepipe Cup description of Stanley Cup between late 1920s and 1948, when annual addition of bands left it with an elongated, tubelike midsection

straight 1. honest 2. ⁓ **arm** check an opponent by extending an arm around the head area and keeping it extended fully as he skates into it 3. ⁓ **blade** stick blade with no curvature 4. ⁓ **time** var. of *running time*

strain hyperextension of a muscle or ligament

strangers visitors

strap 1. fastening device on pads or helmet designed to keep them securely in place 2. ⁓ **on the pads** play goal ("I'll be strapping on the pads tonight")

strapping big and strong

stray 1. of a goalie: wander from the net 2. ⁓ **puck** puck that flies into the stands

streak any sequence of games that has a consistent result

streaky player or team that plays well for a stretch of games, then poorly for a stretch

street hockey var. of *road hockey*

street hockey

strength and conditioning co-ordinator member of team's training staff

strenuous (archaic) hard-fought

stress fracture hairline fracture of a bone

stretch 1. limber up muscles in preparation for play 2. ~ **pass** long, usu. two-line, pass that forces the defence to move back or try to set up a breakaway

stretching exercises calisthenics intended to loosen the muscles in preparation for play

stride 1. a step, on skates 2. distance covered in one step on skates 3. **long ~s** impressive distance covered with one stride 4. **short ~s** relatively little distance covered with one stride 5. **~s** a. sequence of steps on skates b. making headway

string 1. succession of games or wins 2. ~ **together** assemble a series of wins

strip take puck from opponent

strike 1. hit an opponent or official 2. refuse to play 3. score 4. ~ **early** score early goal

striped shirts 1. on-ice officials 2. uniforms worn by on-ice officials

strobes lights that hang from the rafters which allow still photographers to take high-quality action pictures

struggle 1. slang for a game 2. compete vigorously 3. difficulty; challenge ("it's been a struggle all year to score goals")

stubborn relentless (as a team's defence)

stuff 1. nonsense ("that's the sort of stuff you generally don't see at this level") 2. **rough ~** physical play 3. ~ **it in** shove puck into net from close range

stunt ploy

stupid penalty penalty called as a result of laziness or lack of discipline on penalized player's part

stylish showy; impressive

stymie prevent

sub short for substitute

sub-goaler backup goalie

subpar below expectations (e.g., "subpar performance")

subject to immediate recall player who is demoted but can be recalled at any time

submarine low, dirty hit intended to injure the knees

subscriber season-ticket holder

subscription regular mailing of program, kids' club material, or other team affiliated information

substance-abuse program program administered jointly between league and players' association, enabling players with addiction problems to seek treatment

substitute 1. relieve 2. player who comes on in relief for a teammate 3. ~ **goalkeeper** goalie who is inserted into the game to take over for the starting goalie

substitution process of inserting a new player into the game

succeed follow ("Sundin succeeds Gilmour as captain of the Leafs")

suck it up endure injury or other hardship without complaint or decline in playing ability

sucker punch hit delivered from behind, leaving opponent unable to defend himself

sucking wind of an out-of-shape player: trying to keep pace at a high level; gasping for breath

Sudbury Tigers Allan Cup champions in 1937

Sudbury Wolves Memorial Cup champions in 1932

sudden death 1. overtime period in which the next goal scored is the decisive one (also "sudden-death overtime")

suffer 1. ~ **an injury** be injured 2. ~ **a loss** lose a game

suicide 1. ~ **box** dangerous area between players' benches where photojournalist often works with helmet on his head 2. ~ **pass** pass from one teammate to another that leaves the receiver vulnerable to a big hit upon taking the pass

suite enclosed space in an arena with a view of the ice and furnished with luxurious amenities

sulk of a player: be moody or resentful, usu. with coach over lack of playing time

summary statistical breakdown of a game's events (goals, penalties, etc.)

Summit Series eight-game showdown between Canada and Soviet Union in September 1972

summon call up from minors or junior

superior more skilled than average; more skilled than opponent ("they received superior goaltending tonight")

Superleague top pro hockey league in United Kingdom, 1996-2003 (replaced by British Elite League)

Super Series series of exhibition games during the season between NHL teams and Soviet club teams, most often Central Red Army, scheduled periodically between 1975 and 1991

superstition belief that a ritual (usu. quirky) performed regularly will ward off bad luck or invite good luck

supplemental draft special draft instituted by the NHL from 1986 to 1994 allowing member teams to claim U.S. college players who were not eligible for the Entry Draft

supplementary discipline punishment (fines or suspensions) imposed by the league over and above what was meted out by the referee during the game the incident occurred

supply 1. provide (leadership, offence, stability, etc.) 2. score ("Chartrand supplied the winning goal early in the third")

support 1. assist a teammate in any way 2. cheer one's team on 3. **puck** ~ come to a teammate's aid in trying to gain possession of the puck, either by cycling, forechecking, or joining a rush

supporters fans

supporting cast less-heralded teammates of the star players

sure goal scoring chance that, despite the odds, does not result in a goal, whether because of an incredible save by the goalie or a horrible shot by the player with the puck

surplus excess ("they have a surplus of defencemen on the roster right now")

surge rally; mount an attack

surprise 1. perform over and above expectations 2. ~ **starter** backup goalie who starts a game when the number-one goalie is expected to play 3. ~ **win** a victory against a superior opponent ("given their injuries, this was certainly a surprise win on the road")

survivor player who manages to stay with a team or stay in the league despite all odds

suspend temporarily ban from playing, usu. because of an on-ice act of violence

suspenders straps worn over the shoulders and attached to pants to keep them in place

suspension period during which a player is banned from playing, usu. because of an on-ice act of violence

sustain 1. incur 2. ~ **an injury** var. of *suffer an injury* 3. ~ **a loss** var. of *suffer a loss*

Sutter any player who exhibits the traits of one of the six Sutter brothers who played in the NHL, notably a combination of determination, heart, and skill

sutures threads used to sew a wound closed

swamp 1. beat badly 2. apply great pressure on a shift

swap trade

swarm var. of *swamp*

swashbuckling players using their sticks to hit each other

swat 1. hit 2. ~ **an opponent** not particularly heavy hit 3. ~ **at loose puck** try to hit puck out of midair

sweater 1. top portion of uniform, bearing the name or logo of the team on the front and player's number and name on the back 2. ~ **number** numeric designation on the back of sweater, ranging from 0 to 99

sweater number

sweatering pull an opponent's sweater over his head during a fight to render him ineffective

Sweden IIHF member nation since 1920

Sweden Cup tournament between top national teams, held in Sweden only in 1980 and 1984

Sweden Hockey Games annual tournament between top national teams, held in Sweden each February

sweep 1. defeat opponent in any series by winning all games and losing none 2. ~ **away** var. of *sweep* 3. ~ **check** method of checking an opponent off the puck by swinging one's own stick along the ice at an unexpected moment and knocking the puck free 4. ~ **pass** pass made by dragging the stick along the ice behind the puck and following through to the puck all the while not lifting the stick 5. ~ **shot** (archaic) wrist shot

sweeper ice cleaner or resurfacer

sweet on keen ("the Canadiens are sweet on Vachon")

swell (archaic, used in women's hockey) nice, great

Swift Current Broncos Memorial Cup champions in 1989

swing of a defenceman: move up to the wing to play ("he's going to swing up to forward when the team goes on the power play")

swinging attack all-out attack involving all five players

swipe try to hit loose puck out of the way more than gain control of it

swipe

switch ends defend opposite end of rink to start successive periods

Switzerland IIHF member nation since 1908

swoop down on close in on goal

system strategy that requires adherence by players to a mandate set forth by the coach, usu. requiring strong commitment to defence

Tt

T abbreviation for tie, usu. in the standings

TD Banknorth Garden name (since 2005) of Boston Bruins' home arena (formerly FleetCenter)

THA official IIHF abbreviation for Thailand

THL Toronto Hockey League; original name for *Greater Toronto Hockey League*

TPE official IIHF abbreviation for Chinese Taipei (Taiwan)

TUR official IIHF abbreviation for Turkey

TV lights special banks of lights in arena that provide sufficient illumination for game to be broadcast properly on TV

TV timeout break in a game, lasting 70-120 seconds, to allow TV stations to broadcast commercials, called at the first whistle after the 6-, 10-, and 14-minute marks of each period

tabletop hockey hockey game played on a replica of an ice surface designed to fit on top of a table, featuring two teams of cutout or moulded-plastic "players" controlled with rods and a small, black plastic puck (also "table hockey" or "rod hockey")

tack on 1. add a goal 2. add a penalty

Tackaberry type of skate boot designed by George Tackaberry, manufactured for many years by CCM

tackle 1. pull down 2. play ("the Saints tackle the Raiders tonight")

tactician coach

tactics 1. strategy 2. dirty play

Taft, Sammy hatter on Spadina Avenue in Toronto in the 1950s who made it a habit to give a fedora to any player who recorded a hat trick in a game at Maple Leaf Gardens

tag 1. hit hard 2. ~ **a shot** (archaic) make a save

tag up 1. come back outside opponent's blueline to prevent an offside call 2. ~ **rule** rule that stipulates that players must clear the opposition end if they have entered it before the puck in order to avoid an offside call

tagged goal certain goal

tail-enders last-place team in the standings

tailspin losing streak or consistent bad play in the later stages of a game

taint of professionalism "contaminating" influence of accepting money to play (in violation of amateur ideal)

take 1. defeat in a fight ("I can take him") 2. select a player in a draft 3. win a game 4. ~ **the body** check an opponent instead of trying to strip him of the puck 5. ~ **care of himself** be capable of hitting and fighting so as to protect one's space on ice 6. ~ **a chance** a. gamble on a play (e.g., pinch at the blueline) b. gamble on a draft or trade ("we think it was worth taking a chance on him") 7. ~ **chances** play less conservatively when trailing in late stages of a game 8. ~ **charge** a. of a player: demonstrate leadership b. of a coach: show he's the boss c. of a referee: call many penalties to ensure play doesn't get out of hand 9. ~ **control** a. dominate a game b. take charge 10. ~ **exception to** retaliate, verbally or physically, to a hit 11. ~ **a high stick** be on the receiving end of a stick to the head or face 12. ~ **him!** entreaty by teammates to check a particular opponent 13. ~ **him to the ice** foul an opponent such that he falls to the ice 14. ~ **a hit** be on the receiving end of a check 15. ~ **it to them** play aggressively, either through physical play or overpowering offence 16. ~ **a man** guard an opponent or check him 17. ~ **the man** var. of *take the body* 18. ~ **a man down** trip, hook, or use other means to cause an opponent to fall, punishable by a two-minute penalty 19. ~ **a number** note the sweater number of an opponent who has committed a foul or dirty play so as to exact revenge on a later shift or in another game 20. ~ **on** play ("the Generals takes on the Rangers tomorrow night") 21. ~ **one for the team** absorb a hit, whether clean or dirty, without complaint or retaliation in situation when it would be disadvantageous to do so—e.g., late in a close game or in the playoffs 22. ~ **out** eliminate; check 23. ~ **over** a. dominate a game or season b. replace 24. ~ **part in** play or practise 25. ~ **a pass** receive the puck from a teammate 26. ~ **a penalty** incur punishment for an infraction 27. ~ **the play to** var. of *take it to them* 28. ~ **the puck** a. strip an opponent of the puck b. receive a pass 29. ~ **the puck to the net** skate hard with the puck to the goal with no intention of passing 30. ~ **the reins** assume coaching duties 31. ~ **a run** a. charge a player with intent to hit or injure him b. rally, usu. for a playoff berth 32. ~ **a shot** a. shoot the puck towards the goal b. var. of *take a hit* 33. ~ **shots** direct a quick series of pucks on a goalie to prepare him for a game 34. ~ **the starch out of** a. hit hard b. end opponent's rally with a goal 35. ~ **to the ice** play a game

talent 1. skill 2. player of skill ("he's a real talent")

talker player who distracts opponents with banter or trash talk

talk hockey talk about the game

talks negotiations

tally 1. goal 2. score 3. ~-**master** goal scorer

tame of a game: marked by little physical play

Tampa Bay Ice Palace former name (1996-2002) of Tampa Bay Lightning's home arena (renamed St. Petersburg Times Forum)

Tampa Bay Lightning NHL member team since 1992

tampering negotiating with a player or executive who is already under contract to another team

tandem 1. defence pair 2. a team's goalies (starter and backup)

tangle 1. fight 2. ~ **of players** pile-up 3. ~**d up with** fighting for position or for loose puck

tangle

tap 1. slash 2. initiate a fight by gently slashing opponent's shin pads

taper gussets triangular piece of material in the seam of sweater (underarm) or glove (fingers) for extra strength and flexibility

tape-to-tape of a pass: connecting perfectly with a teammate's stick

tap-in easy goal

tape 1. fabric coated on one side with adhesive, applied to stick blade to aid in controlling puck and to butt end to improve grip and prevent injury (mandatory) 2. clear adhesive used by players for shin pads and top of skates to keep these in place 3. video recording made to study games

tape measure narrow strip of metal or fabric, marked with units of measurement, used by referees to determine legality of equipment

target 1. intended receiver of a pass 2. slang for goalie 3. net ("that shot goes wide of the target") 4. player who is made the object of consistent physical contact or harassment 5. ~ **of boos** player singled out by the crowd for negative attention 6. ~ **on ice** player who is the object of consistent physical abuse by opposition 6. ~ **practice** shooting on goalie

target practice

tarsals seven bones in the ankle joint

taste 1. brief experience ("he got a taste of the NHL late last year") 2. ~ **victory** close to winning, but not yet won 3. ~ **defeat** lose

tattoo hit hard

Taylor, Cyclone, Trophy see *Cyclone Taylor Trophy*

T-blade type of skate blade with replaceable runners

"Team" term coined by coach Harry Sinden during Summit Series 1972 referring to a collection of players representing a country in international play (e.g., Team Canada)

team 1. group of players who regularly play together and often represent a city or business 2. ~ **bonus** extra money received by every member of a team after reaching a certain level of success or winning a championship 3. ~ **bus** mode of transportation, at the highest level usu. used to get from arena to airport or hotel, at lower levels from game to game and city to city 4. ~ **captain** player who wears the "C" on his sweater and leads the team 5. ~ **chemistry** unquantifiable ability of

team captain

a team to play better as a group than the sum of their individual talents would suggest, because of players' ability to support each other 6. ~ **dentist** doctor who specializes in oral health, who is employed primarily or exclusively by a team 7. ~ **doctor** medical professional employed by a team, who is present at games in case of emergency and who otherwise oversees the general health of the players 8. ~ **leader** player whose opinions and work habits are respected and emulated by teammates 9. ~ **meeting** gathering of only players for the purpose of overcoming problems such as poor play 10. ~ **official** front-office employee or executive who acts as a spokesperson for team, usu. in a public-relations capacity 11. ~ **photographer** photographer employed (usu. exclusively) to take pictures of players, games, and team functions 12. ~ **play** players' ability or willingness to work toward common objectives rather than individual goals 13. ~ **player** unselfish player who puts the needs of the team ahead of his own personal benefit 14. ~ **portrait** group photograph of the team, on ice with benches (usu. during training camp) or after a championship victory (end of season) 15. ~ **president** top executive of a team, usu. with input into trades and other decisions affecting club's performance 16. ~ **rules** code of conduct unique to a particular team (involving matters such as curfews, appearance, deportment, etc.) 17. ~ **speed** overall ability of a team to skate quickly in units, accentuating this ability over size and physical strength 18. ~ **spokesman** player who takes it upon himself to publicly discuss team issues

Team Europe one of two teams that played in the NHL All-Star Game for five years, 1998-2002 (the other being North America)

Team Special brand of Wally stick produced by the Ingersoll Hockey Stick Company

tearaway type of sweater that can literally be torn off player's body (as in a fight—now illegal)

technical timeout IIHF term for *TV timeout*

Teddy Bear Toss common event at junior games to collect toys for charity

tee it up player who has plenty of time to wind up and take as hard a shot as possible

tee time starting time of a golf game, usu. pejorative for team about to be eliminated from playoffs

tee time

teleconference discussion or meeting that makes use of telephone or computer connections so that people in various locations can take part; used to make announcements, interview players, etc.

telegraph unwittingly indicate one's intention, usu. of a pass

Telephone City (archaic) Brantford, Ontario

telestrator electronic device that allows user to superimpose drawings over a televised image, usu. used by a colour commentator or analyst to diagram explanations and observations

television timeout see *TV timeout*

Telus Cup Canadian national midget hockey tournament (formerly Air Canada Cup)

tempers 1. emotions, esp. anger or rage, which are in full force during the regular season but kept in check during the playoffs 2. ⁓ **are flaring** players getting frustrated, resulting in pushing and shoving, fighting, or other dirty play

tempo pace of the game, dictated by the frequency of whistles

tend 1. take care of ("he has to tend to that injury before returning to action") 2. ⁓ **goal** play goal

'tender goaltender

tendonitis inflammation of a tendon caused by overuse or sudden trauma

tendon any tissue that connects muscle to bone

tentative hesitant (describes play that often leads to a turnover, mistake, or goal)

tenths fractions of second, displayed on scoreclock during final minute of every period

10-year man (archaic) player who has been in the league a decade

terminate end, usu. in reference to a contract ("the Habs have terminated Lalonde's contract")

Tennis Series nickname given to 1932 Stanley Cup finals because Toronto defeated the New York Rangers in three games by scores of 6-4, 6-2, 6-4

term 1. season 2. duration of contract

terms details of a contract, usu. including base salary and important bonus clauses ("Smyth and the Oilers have agreed to terms on a four-year contract")

terrific 1. ⁓ **battle** hard fight for puck in a game, or to win a playoff series 2. ⁓ **pace** frenetic action 3. ⁓ **shot** shot that is hard, accurate or both

territory 1. portion of the ice that is fought for, often in front of the goal 2. zone ("the puck goes deep into Ottawa territory")

testimonial game (archaic) game played to raise funds for a charity or

for a sick or recently deceased member of the hockey community

test 1. game 2. shoot at a goalie ("Rivers tested him with a shot from the top of the circle")

Thailand IIHF member nation since 1989

their own backyard opponent's home arena, usu. in relation to a big road win ("we came in here and beat them right in their own backyard")

thin of a team: not rich with talent—contrast with **deep (2)** ("with all the injuries, they're thin on talent right now")

third 1. ⁓ **defenceman** goalie who handles the puck very well 2. ⁓ **goalie** a. extra goalie listed on team roster for international competitions 3. ⁓ **jersey** special sweater worn by most NHL teams, whose design and logo vary from the standard home or road versions 4. ⁓ **line** forward unit generally composed of players who are better checkers than scorers, yet are capable of scoring on occasion 5. ⁓ **man high** positioning in which third member of a forward line plays near the blueline (or even farther back) as the opposition tries to move the puck out of its own end 6. ⁓ **man in** a. player who gets involved in a fight between two others—punishable by a game misconduct penalty b. aggressive forechecking in which all members of a forward line chase the puck carrier 7. ⁓ **period** final 20 minutes of regulation time 8. ⁓ **star** third-best player of the game, as selected usu. by a member of local media 9. ⁓ **sweater** var. of **third jersey**

30-goal scorer player who has scored or is capable of scoring 30 goals in a season

30-second timeout break in play

lasting 30 seconds, one of which may be requested by each team during the course of a game

Thrash Atlanta Thrashers' mascot

Thrashers nickname of modern Atlanta team in NHL, 1999-present (opposed to Atlanta Flames, 1972-80)

thread 1. ~ **the needle** make a successful pass to teammate through a maze of players, skates, or other possible obstructions 2. ~ **a pass** var. of *thread the needle*

thread a pass

threat player capable of scoring at any time

threaten 1. ~ **to score** be in position to put the puck in the net 2. ~ **to walk out** be prepared to stop playing in order to get a renegotiated contract

three call to the puck carrier by a teammate to let him know there are three men on the rush

"Three Blind Mice" 1. (archaic) pejorative term for on-ice officials (when one referee and two linesmen officiated games) 2. tune played by organist to comment derisively on the work of the on-ice officials, usu. the referee

three-goalie system approximately equal rotation of three goalies, only two of whom may dress for any given game, over the course of a season

three-man combination (archaic) passing play involving three players, usu. the forward line

three-minute penalty minor penalty in NHL, prior to 1921

Three Nations tournament periodic tournament in women's hockey featuring the national teams of three countries (sometimes Four Nations tournament)

three-on-one rush in which three attacking players carry the puck into opposition end with only one skater (and the goalie) back to defend

three-on-one

three-piece goal stick goal stick made of three pieces of wood

three-point game game that is decided in either overtime or shootout in which the losing team gets one point in the standings and the winner two points

Three-Star selection tradition started in Toronto to honour the three best players of a game, originally to promote Imperial Oil's Three Star brand of gasoline

three-way deal trade in which players are exchanged among three teams

throat protector clear plastic guard attached to the base of the goalie mask to prevent the puck from hitting the throat

throng crowd

throttle defeat soundly, in a fight or game

through 1. break free and in on goal 2. finished (i.e., one's career) 3. ~ **centre** skate or pass up middle of ice 4. ~ **the**

middle var. of *through centre* 5. ~ **traffic** past or in between several players, usu. a shot

throw 1. ~ **a check** hit an opponent, body to body 2. ~ **everything at them** stage an all-out attack 3. ~ **him out of the circle** of a linesman: eject player from faceoff circle 4. ~ **him out of the game** of a referee: eject a player; issue game misconduct 5. ~ **it up the middle** make a pass through centre of ice 6. ~ **one's body in front of a shot** block a shot 7. ~ **a stick** illegal act, punishable by a penalty shot 8. ~ **one's weight around** play physically 9. ~ **a pass** shoot puck to teammate 10. ~ **puck upstairs** shoot high on goalie 11. ~ **punches** fight

thrust rush

thug player of limited skill who fights as a way of keeping his place on a team

thumb call a penalty ("Friday thumbed Keon for tripping on the play")

thumbnail sketch brief newspaper features of players

thump win by a lop-sided margin

thunder knock to the ice

thundering check particularly heavy hit

Thundering Herd nickname for Fort William Forts, Allan Cup champions in 1927

Thunder Bay Twins Allan Cup champions in 1975, 1984, 1985, 1988, and 1989

Thunder Bug mascot of the Tampa Bay Lightning

ThunderDome home arena of Tampa Bay Lightning, 1993-96

thwart prevent a good scoring chance

tibia shin bone

tic-tac-toe quick, three-way passing play

ticket 1. pass that allows bearer to gain admission into a game 2. ~ **booth** box office 3. ~ **holders** fans 4. ~ **office** (archaic) box office, often at a location away from the arena 5. ~ **prices** cost of admission 6. ~ **stub** portion of ticket retained by bearer upon entering arena

Tiki-talk nickname for impenetrable syntax of star Esa Tikkanen, whose mixture of English and Finnish produced comical results

tie 1. games in which both teams score the same number of goals; draw 2. ~-**downs** style of sweater in which Velcro fasteners, inside the sweater at the back, keep it on the players' body during a fight 3. ~-**down strap** var. of *fight strap* 4. ~ **game** game in which both teams score equal number of goals; draw 5. ~ **the can to him** fire (usu. a coach)

tie-break (also **tie-breaker**) 1. method of determining the winner of a game tied after regulation time or overtime 2. method of ranking teams with same number of points in standings

tie-up 1. ~ **the game** produce goal to equalize score 2. ~ **a man** mark an opponent closely and prevent him from getting into scoring position

tied down hampered, usu. pinned to the ice in a fight with a superior opponent

Tier I 1. in Canada, major junior hockey (i.e., under the umbrella of the CHL) 2. top level of AAA play in U.S.

Tier II level of hockey usually known as Provincial Junior A

tight-checking of a game: marked by few scoring chances and an emphasis on defensive play

tighten (their) grip 1. take significant lead in league standings 2. take control of playoff series

tighten up 1. put renewed emphasis on defence 2. of ice: dry fully

tilt game

time 1. point (measured in minutes and seconds) when a goal is scored or penalty incurred 2. period between one event and the next ("it has been a long time, nearly 30 minutes, between goals in this game") 3. prompt shouted to puck carrier to remind him that he is not being pressured and can take an extra moment to make a pass or play (short for "you've got time") 4. ~ **remaining** number of minutes and seconds left in a game, period, or penalty 5. ~ **servers** players in penalty box

timekeepers 1. off-ice officials who sit between the two penalty boxes and run the scoreclock and keep track of goals and penalties 2. ~' **bench** area where timekeepers sit during the game

timeout 1. see *30-second timeout* 2. break in proceedings during the Entry Draft, during which a team may request to negotiate a trade or discuss strategy regarding its next selection

timer 1. timekeeper 2. timing device (i.e., game clock)

Tim Hortons chain of coffee-and-donut shops founded by longtime Leafs' defenceman, ubiquitous across Canada and sponsors of kids' hockey across the country

Tim Horton Trophy annual trophy awarded to best Leafs' defenceman, but presented only once, to Larry Murphy, in 1996

Timbits

Timbits house-league hockey program sponsored by Tim Hortons; players scrimmage during intermission of NHL games in six Canadian cities, as well as AHL and junior games

timing 1. hand-eye co-ordination 2. co-ordination between players so that they are in correct place at appropriate time

tingling exciting, usu. to describe spectacular save

tinker alter lineup, usu. in experimental fashion that suggests coach is having trouble getting satisfactory results

tip 1. redirect (the puck) 2. very end of stick blade 3. words of advice, usu. from veteran to youngster 4. ~ **the beam** weigh ("he tips the beam at 180") 5. ~ **the scales** weigh 6. ~ **the Toledos** var. of *tip the scales* (after the Toledo brand of scale)

tip-in goal scored by deflecting a teammate's shot

tired 1. of a player: lacking energy 2. of a team: exhausted ("the Flames played in Los Angeles last night, got here at 3a.m., and are a tired hockey team right now")

tireless worker player who never stops trying, never gives up

Titan brand of hockey stick

title holders champions

toe 1. tip of stick blade 2. ~ **drag** one-on-one deke in which puck carrier pulls puck back, away from the defender, and, as defender lunges forward (out of position), pushes puck forward again, close to his body, usu. able to continue unhindered 3. ~ **save** save made by goalie with top part (toe) of skate

toil work, often in obscurity ("he's been toiling in the minors for more than a decade")

Tokyo Arena arena which hosted two

NHL regular-season games between Mighty Ducks of Anaheim and Vancouver Canucks on October 3 and 4, 1997, the first time NHL regular-season games were played outside North America

tongue part of skate that protects top of foot and which provides padding between foot and laces

tongue-lashing harsh words of criticism within dressing room, usu. administered by team captain or coach

Tonight on Ice Tampa Bay Lightning's game-night program

too many men 1. short for **too many men on the ice** 2. ~ **on the ice** infraction called when a team is caught with more skaters on the ice than it is entitled to, punishable by a two-minute bench minor penalty

too small negative assessment rendered by scouts or general managers of an aspiring NHLer who, while skilled, is not perceived as being tall or strong enough to play in the league

tools skills

toot whistle

toothpick 1. broken stick 2. small stick 3. road hockey stick with thin blade worn down by play on asphalt

top 1. most important or skilled (e.g., the top league, the top defenceman) 2. defeat ("the Jets topped the Nordiques 4-3") 3. ~ **billing** status as most important attraction or feature of team 4. ~ **corner** one of two corners of the goal over the goalie's shoulders 5. ~ **gun** elite scorer 6. ~ **hole** (archaic) first-rate 7. ~ **line** best forward unit 8. ~~**notch** most skilled 9. ~ **of the circle** part of one of the four faceoff circles farthest from the goal 10. ~ **of the crease** area just outside the goal crease 11. ~ **of the net** a. var. of **top corner** b. B-shaped area of mesh on which goalies place water bottles and where, if the puck lands, play is whistled dead 12. ~ **prospect** young player with excellent skills who promises to be a star in NHL one day 13. ~~**ranked** of the highest calibre 14. ~ **rung** first place 15. ~ **shelf** upper part of the net 16. ~ **speed** maximum velocity, usu. skating

toot

Top Prospects Game annual game organized by CHL showcasing the best 40 undrafted junior players in one game

topple defeat

Topps prominent hockey card manufacturers

tops the best ("the power play is tops in the league right now")

toque headgear worn for outdoor play

torn knee ligaments common knee injury requiring a long layoff or surgery

Toronto Arenas NHL member team 1917-19 (became Toronto St. Patricks); Stanley Cup champions in 1918

Toronto Canoe Club Memorial Cup champions in 1920

Toronto Dentals Allan Cup champions in 1917

Toronto Granites Olympic gold medallists in 1924 and Allan Cup champions in 1922 and 1923

Toronto Maple Leafs NHL member team since 1927 (formerly Toronto St. Pats)

Toronto Marlboros 1. Allan Cup champions in 1950   2. Memorial Cup champions in 1929, 1955, 1956, 1964, 1967, 1973, and 1975

Toronto Nationals Allan Cup champions in 1932

Torontos (archaic) any Toronto team

Toronto St. Michael's Majors see *St. Michael's Majors*

Toronto St. Patricks Toronto team in NHL, 1919-27 (renamed Maple Leafs)

Toronto Trolley Leaguers Stanley Cup challengers in March 1908

Toronto Wellingtons Stanley Cup challengers in January 1902

torpedo potent offensive formation which takes advantage of two-line passing, introduced in Sweden in early 21st century

Torpedo type of skate made of wood and metal in U.S. circa 1895

toss 1. ~ **a hit** bodycheck an opponent 2. ~ **him from a game** issue game misconduct   3. ~ **one's weight around** play especially physically

total domination hyperbole for superior play

total goals (archaic) playoff series, usu. of two games, in which the team with the higher aggregate score was declared the winner

Totem Trophy introduced in 1936, intended as an annual trophy to represent hockey supremacy on the Pacific Coast, but awarded only once, to the Toronto Maple Leafs after they beat Chicago 13-9 in a three-game, total-goals series during a post-playoff barnstorming tour

touch 1. take brief possession of puck 2. ~ **icing** see *icing (6)* 3. ~ **off** a. trigger a brawl b. begin a comeback 4. ~ **pass** short pass marked by finesse and guile more than strength

tough 1. physically strong or intimidating 2. ~ **customer** player who is physically strong, usu. a good fighter 3. ~ **grind** reference to length of NHL schedule 4. ~ **guy** goon; fighter 5. ~ **loss** disappointing or shocking defeat, perhaps on overtime or last-minute goal, or despite vastly superior play 6. ~ **sledding** difficult time 7. ~ **to handle** player who is difficult to move off the puck or move out of the slot area

toughness of a team: capacity for physical play, determination, or hard work

tour 1. NHL career 2. tenure with a team ("this is Perreault's third tour with the Leafs")

tour de chapeau Fr., hat trick

toy with of a skilled player: make a defender look helpless by virtue of masterful stickhandling

tour de chapeau

trade 1. swap of players between two or more teams 2. ~ **bait** player who is being offered to many teams by the general manager for a possible trade 3. ~ **chances** play a game marked by end-to-end action in which both teams have an abundance of good scoring opportunities 4. ~ **deadline** fixed date, late in the season, after which teams are not permitted to trade players 5. ~ **demands** strong requests by a player to be sent to another team 6. ~ **freeze** period during which players may not be traded (e.g., between Christmas and New Year's) 7. ~ **insults** argue with one or more opponents 8. ~ **punches** fight 9. ~ **rumours** speculation, usu. in the media, over which players will be traded to which teams 10. ~ **winds** var. of *trade rumours*

trademark 1. licensed logos of a team or league which may not be freely reproduced without consent 2. ~ **move** signature move

trading block on the ~ of a player: available for trade

trading card type of card with a photo of a player, usu. in action, with biographical and statistical data on the reverse, which is collected and traded

traffic 1. congestion anywhere on the ice (i.e., many players in a small area)

2. ~ **in front** crowding in the crease and goal area 3. **in** ~ make a play while in a tight space 4. **through** ~ of a pass: made in congested area

trail be behind in the score ("Montreal trails 3-1 after two periods")

trailer last player on the offensive rush to cross the blueline, often left unguarded and often the player in best position to receive a pass (also "trailing man")

Trail Smoke Eaters Allan Cup champions in 1938 and 1962 and World Championship gold medallists in 1961

trainer member of team's staff responsible for general health and welfare of players

training 1. exercise or fitness regimen 2. ~ **camp** pre-season period when players convene to get into shape, learn to play with new teammates, try out for the team, or otherwise prepare for the upcoming season

transaction roster move (trade, sale, release, signing, demotion, or promotion of a player)

transition 1. change or period of adjustment from one team to another, one league to another, one generation of players to the next 2. ~ **game** changeover from offence to defence, or vice versa

trap 1. catch out of position 2. defensive scheme designed to prevent goals rather than create scoring chances (e.g., the neutral zone trap) 3. **so-called** ~ euphemism for that style of hockey ("they play the so-called trap with their own little variation") 4. ~ **the puck** of a goalie: catch or freeze the puck on the ice

trapped 1. caught out of position 2. ~ **offside** caught inside offensive blueline while teammate outside blueline has the puck

trapper goalie's catching glove

trash talk vulgar, offensive language aimed at distracting or upsetting an opponent

travel 1. go on road to play in opponent's arena 2. ~ **day** day off, free of a game or practice, to allow team to get to city of road game

Tre Kronor (Swedish) name of Sweden's men's national hockey team

treat to watch highly-skilled player

treatment care administered by the trainer or team doctor to an injured player

trenches corners, esp. during playoffs, when struggles for the puck become more intense

trial 1. experiment, usu. involving a player at a new position 2. tryout ("Armstrong is with the big team for a three-game trial")

triangle 1. defensive formation employed in its own end when a team is playing two men down 2. ~ **offence** see *cycling*

tributes accolades and compliments for a player, often upon his retirement

triceps muscle at the back of the arm that permits extension of the arm at the elbow

trick 1. outsmart 2. **turn the** ~ (archaic) a. score a goal b. record a hat trick 3. ~ **shooter** player adept at curving his shot or generally flummoxing goalies with his shot

trickle 1. ~ **wide** of a puck: roll just wide of the goal, usu. after being partially stopped by the goalie or deflected in front 2. ~ **in** of a puck: just roll over the goal line and never reach the back of the net 3. ~ **over the goal line** var. of *trickle in*

tricky player with superior stickhandling skills

Tricolore Italian national team

Tricouleur alternative nickname for the Montreal Canadiens

trigger 1. start, usu. a scoring spree 2. ~ **a comeback** goal or event that starts a rally

trigger man top scorer

trim 1. beat badly 2. make cuts from lineup or team roster

trio forward line

trip 1. defeat ("Toronto tripped up New York, 4-3") 2. place stick in the path of an opponent's feet or legs, causing him to fall to the ice, punishable by a two-minute penalty 3. **make a** ~ **to the penalty box** incur a penalty 4. **road** ~ lengthy series of games away from home arena

triple minor three minor penalties to one player on the same play (rare)

tripping see *trip (2)*

triumph victory

Trolley League nickname given to Ontario Professional Hockey League, Canada's first fully pro league, which began in 1908 and featured four teams in southern Ontario that travelled to games by electric railway (trolleys)

troops players

trophy any award for individual or team achievement

trophy

trouble 1. dangerous scoring situation 2. player looking for a fight

troublemaker player who goes out of his way to instigate a fight

trounce defeat handily

trousers (archaic) officials' pants

truck vehicle parked under arena or in nearby parking lot, containing mobile production facility to broadcast game

true form play to full potential ("he's finally playing to true form this season")

Truro Bearcats Allan Cup champions in 1998

Trushinki bylaw nickname given to former Bylaw 12:6 of NHL rulebook forbidding any player with less than 3/60 vision in one eye to play in the

trustee one of two individuals charged with overseeing competition for and presentation of the Stanley Cup

try shot ("it was a nice try, but the goalie made the save")

tryout audition (usu. by an amateur or minor pro player) for a permanent spot on a team through training camp or game situations

T-start stance assumed when beginning to skate from a stationary position, characterized by skates being placed perpendicular to one another

tube skates blades embedded in a tubular metal support which are attached with screws and rivets to boots

tug hook

tumble 1. fall to ice 2. drop in standings

tumble

league; named for Frank Trushinki of the Kitchener Greenshirts, who played senior hockey, lost most of his vision in one eye, but returned, only to suffer an equally serious injury to his good eye, thus leaving him virtually blind

turban (archaic) head bandage

Turkey IIHF member nation since 1991

turn 1. use skates to alter direction 2. ~ **around** a. look in the opposite direction to which one was originally looking b. change fortunes from bad to good 3. ~ **aside** of a goalie: make a save   4. ~ **away**   a. player who decides at the last moment not to block a shot   b. var. of *turn aside*   5. ~ **back** defeat, repel attack   6. ~ **in play** change in momentum from one team to the other   7. ~ **inside-out** deke a man thoroughly   8. ~ **of events** occurrence that favours one team in particular   9. ~ **the tables** reverse one's fortunes   10. ~ **the trick** a. (archaic) score a goal   b. record hat trick (score three goals)

Turner Cup trophy awarded to IHL champions, 1946-2001

turnout 1. number of players attending tryout or training camp   2. number of fans attending game or other team function

turnover loss of possession of the puck

turning point moment in a game that decides its outcome

turtle instigate a fight through dirty or illegal tactics but then cover oneself and refuse to defend oneself

tussle 1. game   2. fight

tutor 1. junior or minor pro coach   2. teach

Tuuk skate blade introduced in the 1970s, consisting of plastic holder and steel runner instead of all-steel blade, making it safer and lighter

20-goal scorer player who scores, or is capable of scoring, 20 goals in any given season

20-year man player who has played in the NHL for 20 years or more

twice-a-day regimen of intense practices, usu. in training camp or for special tryouts (also "two-a-day")

twig stick

twine goal net

two 1. short for two minutes (i.e., a minor penalty)   2. call to a player with the puck to let him know there are two men on the rush

228th Battalion member team of National Hockey Association in 1916-17, playing out of Toronto and featuring players who were enlisted in the armed forces during the First World War

two-game, total-goals series type of playoff series common before 1936, in which the team that scored the higher number of aggregate goals after two games was declared winner

two-goalie system use of two goalies in an approximately equal number of games over the course of the season, rather than a number-one goalie who handles the bulk of the chores

two-line pass forward pass that crosses one of the bluelines and the centre red line (formerly considered offside; most pro leagues now allow this pass)

two-hander vicious slash whose perpetrator uses both hands on his stick to deliver the blow

two lines short for two-line pass, resulting in offside (rule amended in recent years—"that pass goes over two lines, so the faceoff will be deep in the offending team's end")

two-man combination pair of players who are especially effective playing together

two men short short-handed situation in which one team has three skaters on the ice and two in the penalty box while its opponent has all five skaters on ice

two-on-oh rare situation in which the puck carrier and a teammate rush in on the goalie, with no other defensive players in their path

two-on-one rush in which the puck carrier and a teammate rush in on the goalie, while only one member of the defending team is in their path

two out of three best-of-three series

two-pad stack goalie save which entails

the goaltender droping to his side and putting his pads parallel to the ice, one on top of the other, to block a shot

two points number of points in the standings awarded to the victorious team

two-referee system modern system whereby games are officiated by two referees (one keeping abreast of play, the other following players behind the puck)

two-three-two (2-3-2) playoff format in 1990s in which the higher-seeded team would host games 1, 2, 6, and 7, while the lower-ranked team would host games 3, 4, and 5, thus reducing amount of travel the standard setup (2-2-1-1-1) entailed

two-way 1. ~ **contract** contract under which a player receives one salary if he plays in the NHL and a much lower one if he is sent to the minors 2. ~ **play** player's ability to play both offence and defence, to score and to defend 3. ~ **player** player particularly skilled at both scoring and defence

tyke level of hockey for players age 4-6

Uu

UFA *unrestricted free agent*

UHL *United Hockey League*

UKR official IIHF abbreviation for Ukraine

USA official IIHF abbreviation for United States of America

USA Hockey governing body for hockey in the United States of America

USAir Arena name of Washington Capitals' home arena (formerly Capital Center), 1993-95

USHL *United States Hockey League*

ugly 1. unpleasant or inelegant ("they won ugly tonight") 2. ~ **goal** goal scored without much skill (off a skate or leg, deflection off a defenceman, etc.) 3. ~ **incident** violent or unsportsmanlike event on ice

Ukraine IIHF member nation since 1992

ulna bone on the forearm that runs from the elbow to the wrist along the pinky-finger side of the hand

ulnar nerve nerve in the elbow

ultrasound transmission of sound waves through soft tissue to create an image or to relax the area and hasten its rehabilitation

umpire (archaic) judge of play

unaided unassisted (usu. a goal)

unanswered goal goal scored by one team after which the opponent does not score in a particular period or game

unbalanced schedule schedule in which a team does not play all other teams in the league an equal number of times, usu. to emphasize games within divisions or conferences

unbeaten streak stretch of consecutive games which a team ties or wins

unbeatable playing particularly well

uncanny mysterious; exceptional skill ("he has the uncanny ability to be in the right place at the right time")

unceremonious without respect, as the firing of a coach

unconditional release termination of a player's contract by a team, with neither party under any further obligation toward the other

unconscious 1. loss of consciousness 2. playing so incredibly well as to appear not to be in control of one's actions ("Rheaume was unconscious in net last night")

uncork shoot the puck hard

uncover find, usu. a top prospect

uncovered in the open, waiting for a pass

undefeated 1. having avoided losing over a particular stretch of games 2. ~ **streak** var. of *unbeaten streak*

Under-17 tournament or team featuring players younger than 17 (i.e., midget age) usu. as of December 31 of the year of the event

Under-18 World Championship tournament sanctioned by IIHF featuring players under 18 years of age as of December 31 of the year of the event

Under-20 World Championship tournament sanctioned by IIHF featuring players under 20 years of age as of December 31 of the year of the event (also World Junior Championship)

under the gun under pressure

under way in progress—usu. used by play-by-play announcer early in a period ("we're just under way here in the first game of the Stanley Cup finals")

underclothes garments worn under the equipment to keep a player warm, usu. long johns or shirt or one-piece outfit

underclothes

underdog team that is not expected to win a particular game or series

undermanned competing with fewer players in uniform than the rules permit, usu. because of injury or illness

underrated player who is better than most scouts or fans give him credit for

understaffed var. of **undermanned**

underwear var. of **underclothes**

undisclosed injury injury whose nature is not publicized by team, either because severity is yet to be determined or because team does not want opponents to find out (esp. common during playoffs)

undisclosed sum amount of money usu. involved in trading or signing a player to a contract

undrafted player who has not been chosen in the NHL Entry Draft and whose rights, therefore, do not belong to any specific team

undress deke a player beautifully and thoroughly

undress

unexpired penalty penalty which still has time remaining

unfit for (normal) play 1. of ice: in unplayable condition 2. of a player: ill or suffering from some malady that prevents him from playing in a game

uniforms sweaters, pants, and socks (i.e., outer garments) worn by members of a team to identify themselves as such

unimpressive of a player or team's performance: failing to meet expectations; lacking quality or skill

unit 1. forward line 2. defensive pairing 3. **play as a ~** of a specific group of players on the ice: play together effectively

United Center Chicago Blackhawks' home arena, 1994-present

United Hockey League low minor pro league, 1998-present (previously the Colonial Hockey League)

United States of America IIHF member nation since 1920

United States Hockey League 1. minor pro league centred in Midwest, 1945-51 2. U.S. junior league, 1979-present 3. U.S. semi-pro league, 1961-79

University Cup national championship trophy for Canadian university play

University of Manitoba Allan Cup champions in 1928 and Memorial Cup champions in 1923

University of Toronto Blues Allan Cup champions in 1921

University of Toronto Grads Allan Cup champions in 1927 and Olympic gold medallists in 1928

University of Toronto Schools Memorial Cup champions in 1919

unleash 1. release a shot 2. shoot hard

unmolested untouched or unchecked ("he walked in on the goalie unmolested")

unnecessary roughness Rule 83 in the 1950s, later replaced, calling for a two-minute minor penalty

unplayable 1. of the puck: in such a position that the referee has no choice but to whistle play dead 2. of an ice surface: in poor condition, perhaps so much so that it would be dangerous for a game to proceed

unpredictable inconsistent

unrestricted free agent player who is without a contract and free to sign with any team of his choosing, while his former team is not entitled to any compensation

unsigned without a contract

unsportsmanlike 1. ungentlemanly 2. ⁓ **conduct** rough or dirty play not covered by other minor penalties such as high sticking or elbowing, punishable by a two-minute penalty

Unsung Hero Award common award among U.S.-based teams to honour a player whose contributions to the team are generally underrated

untouched unmarked; unchecked

untouchable star player deemed by a general manager as one whom he will not trade

unwritten rule part of an implicit code among players that is not spelled out in the rulebook

up 1. ahead in the score ("Ottawa is up by two goals in the final minute of play") 2. ⁓ **against** a. shadowing b. facing ("the Senators are up against the Flames tonight") 3. ⁓ **front** on a forward line 4. ⁓ **ice** toward the offensive end 5. ⁓ **the middle** through the area of ice farthest away from the boards—the centre lane of the ice, end to end, as it were

up and down the wing of a winger: playing well positionally, but without much ability to improvise

update newsworthy information regarding player injury, out-of-town score, or other development

upend check, trip, or otherwise knock an opponent off the puck

uphill battle struggle against the odds, as a team must do after falling behind in a game or series if victory is to be accomplished

upper berth top bunk of two in a sleeper car during years when players travelled by rail between cities

upper berth

upper-body injury deliberately vague description of injury to top half of the body, to ensure that opponents don't try to aggravate that injury further

upper-body strength physical strength in the top half of the body

upper hand advantage of some sort, usu. on the scoreboard, in terms of momentum or on the power play

upside potential ("his skating isn't the best, but his upside is worth the investment")

upstairs 1. high shot 2. **go** ~ call for video review of a disputed goal

urine sample as part of drug-testing process, that which must be supplied by one player randomly selected from each competing team during international games and tournaments

use 1. of a player: utilize ("they use him exclusively as a penalty killer") 2. ~ **sparingly** of a coach: use a player only occasionally during a game, series, or season 3. ~ **the body** engage in physical play marked by heavy checking 4. ~ **your head** instruction or mantra to think before doing, to be smart rather than rash

useful of a player: not a star, but a valuable contributor nonetheless

usher 1. employee of arena who helps patrons find their seats 2. ~ **in** begin, as in a new era ("the arrival of Crosby has ushered in a new era of hockey in Pittsburgh")

usherette female usher

usherette

utility player undistinguished yet versatile player who can capably fill a variety of roles on a team

utility role duties performed by a utility player ("they've given Belak a utility role but he seems happy just to be on the team")

V v

V for victory; symbol worn by the Detroit Red Wings on their sweaters during Second World War

vs. abbreviation for *versus*

vacancy place in lineup

vacant net net unguarded by goalie

vacate 1. leave a particular area of the ice 2. ~ **the net** of a goalie: leave the net, usu. either to play the puck or to go to the bench for an extra attacker 3 ~ **the zone** cross a blueline ("he had to vacate the zone to prevent the offside")

Valeri Kharlamov Trophy award presented by Russian newspaper *Sovetsky Sport* to the best Russian player in the NHL

valuable 1. important to a team 2. ~ **trade** trade that improves the quality of the team

Vancouver Canucks NHL member team since 1970

Vancouver Canucks Hockey Magazine Vancouver Canucks' game-night program

Vancouver Millionaires Stanley Cup champions in 1915

Varsity model of Hilborn hockey stick produced by Salyerds of Preston, Ontario

Varsity Arena home rink of the University of Toronto Blues since 1926

Vaughn equipment maker specializing in goalie equipment

vaunted highly regarded

Velcro fastening apparatus used primarily to keep shin pads, elbow pads, and shoulder pads in place, and goalie glove on hand

Velcro inserts var. of *tie-downs*

velvet hands attributes possessed by a player with superior scoring ability

venture from net of a goalie: roam around outside the crease

verbal exchange heated argument; trash talking

verdict score or result

Vernon Canadians Allan Cup champions in 1956

versatile capable of doing many things effectively, such as playing more than one position or playing different styles

versus against ("it's Rimouski versus Shawinigan tonight")

veteran 1. player who has been in the league for several seasons 2. ~ **leadership** example set by an experienced player to inspire teammates and teach younger players

Vezina Trophy NHL goaltending award; presented 1927-81 to goalies playing at least 25 games for team that allowed fewest goals, and since 1982 to goalie judged best in the league by a poll of NHL general managers (initial criteria for Vezina adopted by William M. Jennings Trophy in 1982)

vicinity proximity; general area ("the pass was nowhere in the vicinity of Lemieux")

vice anything that stands in the way of training (drinking, smoking, bad eating habits)

vice president executive who is second in rank only to the president

vice president of operations executive responsible for issues pertaining to the running of a team or arena

Vics short for Victorias, either Montreal or Winnipeg (teams that competed for the Stanley Cup shortly before and after 1900)

victim 1. player who is outsmarted ("Johansson was the victim of a patented Middleton fake") 2. player who is hit hard ("he was the victim of a Scott Stevens hit at the blueline") 3. player who is attacked viciously

victimize 1. fake an opponent badly ("Phaneuf victimized Johansson at the blueline") 2. score on a goalie ("Bossy victimized Garrett in the first period")

Victoria Cougars Stanley Cup challengers in March 1914

Victoriaville brand of hockey stick

Victoriaville Tigers Allan Cup champions in 1968

victory win

victory-bound on the threshold of a win in a game or series

video 1. recording of a game or play 2. ~ **coach** coach whose job it is to analyze a team's tendencies—whether his own team's or an opponent's—to better prepare for future games 3. ~ **goal judge** official who reviews videotape of a goal and renders judgement on its legality, in cases where the referee is in doubt 4. ~ **replay** the use of videotape to examine a play, usu. a contested goal 5. ~ **review** process by which videotape is studied by a video goal judge 6. ~ **supervisor** official who has final say in video review decision

vigorous 1. energetic, usu. checking 2. ~ **workout** tough practice or game

Viking Cup biannual tournament since 1981 hosted by Augustana University College in Camrose, Alberta, featuring national teams from around the world

villain perpetrator of act of violence

vim energy

violation infraction; foul

violence use of excessive force—i.e., beyond the generally accepted limits of physical play

vision ability of player to see all the players on ice to make better passes, intercept pucks, and play a superior game ("he has great vision")

visiting coach coach of the visiting team

visiting team team that has traveled to arena from another city, region, or part of town to play a game (opposed to home team)

visitor visiting team, as designated on the scoreboard (also "visitors")

visor plastic shield attached to the front of a helmet to help prevent facial injuries

visor

visualization method of preparation whereby a player tries to form a mental image of what is likely to happen during a game to be played in a few hours' time, the idea being that the more he rehearses in his mind's eye, the better are the chances they will occur during play

voluntary retired list (archaic) list of NHL players who have decided not to play in the NHL any longer

voluntary retirement (archaic) decision by an NHL player to stop playing which, once rendered, made him ineligible to play anytime, anywhere for the next year

voluntary suspended list (archaic) list of NHL players whose clubs were punishing them and who were not allowed to play anywhere until their names were removed

voting any method of balloting pertaining to the naming of all-star teams or awarding of trophies

vulcanized rubber rubber hardened by combining with sulphur and heating, from which pucks are made

W 1. slang for win 2. abbreviation for win in the standings

WC *World Championship*

WCHA *Western Collegiate Hockey Association*

WCHL *Western Canada Hockey League*

WHA *World Hockey Association*

WHL *Western Hockey League*

WJC *World Junior Championship*

W-L-T won-lost-tied, used in standings for team or goalies' records

WM Weltmeisterschaft, German for World Championship and most common abbreviation for that annual tournament

WPHL *Western Professional Hockey League*

Wachovia Center Philadelphia Flyers' home arena (formerly First Union Center)

Wade's World private suite at Ottawa's Scotiabank Place, paid for by Senators' defenceman Wade Redden, which hosts sick and terminally ill children from Children's Hospital of Eastern Ontario

wager place a bet

waiting in the wings 1. state of near-readiness experienced by a player who is recovering from injury or a prospect whose development is proceeding rapidly 2. holding pattern experienced by same sort of players, but for whom a roster spot has not yet opened

Waiver Draft (outdated) draft (formerly known as Intra-League Draft) in which teams' unwanted players were made available to other teams; abandoned by NHL under collective bargaining agreement of 2005

waivers system by which a team that does not want a player or wishes to send him to the minors must first offer him to all other teams in the league

wakeup call event that shakes a team or player out of complacency

Wales Conference short for Prince of Wales Conference

walk 1. ~ **in** skate in on goal unmolested 2. ~ **in alone** var. of *walk in* 3. ~ **in on goal** var. of *walk in* 4. ~ **in unmolested** var. of *walk in* 5. ~ **into the shot** get a full windup to shoot the puck as hard as possible 6. ~ **it off** recover quickly from minor injury, usu. to the lower body after blocking a shot, by walking in the runway behind the players' bench 7. ~**-on** player who attends training camp without a contract and little chance of making the team 8. ~ **out** a. skate in front of the net from behind net b. leave a team suddenly, usu. in a contract dispute 9. ~ **out in front** var. of *walk out* 10. ~ **right in** var. of *walk in*, extra emphasis

walk in alone

wall 1. boards 2. shoot puck around boards ("he walled the puck the other way")

wall rats standing-room fans at Joe Louis Arena in Detroit

wallop 1. hit hard 2. beat badly

Wally brand of hockey stick made by the Ingersoll Hockey Stick Company in Dresden, Ontario

Walter Woods Red Flash brand of hockey stick

waltz 1. fight 2. ~ **in alone** move in on goal unmolested

wand 1. stick 2. ~ **waving** brazen use of stick

wander roam

wandering goalie goalie who strays from his crease to play puck, usu. to negative effect

war 1. tough game or series; used most often in reference to 1972 Summit Series 2. ~ **chest** a. extra money held in reserve for players acquired in mid-season (used frequently by Pat Quinn as Toronto coach) b. fund built up by owners and/or players' union and players in case of labour disruption 3. ~ **tax** levy against players' salaries during the war years

War of 1812 nickname given to the Toronto-Montreal game of December 9, 1953, when a bench-clearing brawl erupted at 18:12 of the third period and referee Frank Udvari handed out 18 misconducts and two majors (evenly distributed), leaving each team with a goalie, three skaters, and no players on the bench for the final 1:48 of play

ward off prevent, usu. a shot, an offensive thrust, or bad luck

warm body acquisition, usu. of moderate value or skill, who can play right away (as opposed to draft choice or prospect); usu. acquired by a team under pressure to make a trade

warming shack (archaic, western Canadian) enclosed space near an outdoor rink where one might escape cold

warmup exercises (performed on ice or in dressing room) to prepare for a game

warning caution issued by a referee

warp curve of a stick blade

warrior tough, durable player who can log a great deal of ice time or is willing to absorb a great deal of punishment

Warroad Lakers Allan Cup champions in 1994, 1995, and 1996

wartime hockey hockey played during the Second World War

Washington Capitals NHL member team, 1974-present

washout 1. cancellation or nullification of a goal, icing, or offside 2. shutout

wassail (archaic) Stanley Cup celebrations, particularly drinking champagne from the Cup

waste hit an opponent hard

wasted 1. ~ **opportunity** great chance which goes for naught 2. ~ **effort** great play that has no positive result 3. ~ **chance** var. of *wasted effort*

watch check one's man closely

water bottle plastic bottle kept on bench for players and atop the nets for goalies

water bottle

wave 1. of a player: try to bat the puck out of mid-air 2. of a goalie: try unsuccessfully to make a glove save 3. ~ **off** a. penalize b. cancel or nullify icing or other call 4. ~ **off a goal** disallow a goal 5. ~ **out** of an official: eject a player from the faceoff circle

weak side 1. side on which a goalie has the least success stopping puck 2. side of the rink opposite to where play occurs

weakness deficiency which an opponent can exploit tactically to gain an advantage

weapons 1. skills 2. sticks

wear a letter serve as team captain or alternate/assistant captain, and thus have a "C" or "A" embroidered on one's sweater

wear the "C" serve as team captain

weather the storm survive a surge by the opposition without surrendering a goal (also "weather the attack")

weave attack European style of play from 1970s in which the three forwards skated in circles rather than straight lines to advance the puck to the goal

weaving 1. fancy skating 2. circular style of skating

webbing effect effect created by illegally modifying a goalie's sweater where sleeves meet torso, thus enabling him to block more of the net

weekend pair back-to-back games on Saturday and Sunday

weight room area of dressing room equipped so that players may develop their muscles

weight-training lifting weights

welcome addition new player who improves a team's quality immediately

well 1. ~**-balanced** team with a variety of skills (i.e., three lines that can score, good penalty killing and power play, solid goaltending) 2. ~**-directed**
accurate shot 3. ~**-earned** deserved (as a victory, extra ice time, or a few days off after a long stretch of frequent games) 4. ~**-timed** a. executed in a timely fashion (as a shot on goal) b. of a goal or victory: of particular importance 5. ~**-travelled** having been traded several times or played for several teams 6. ~ **wide** of a shot: intended for the net but missing it by a significant margin

West Coast part of North America immediately adjacent to Pacific Ocean, usu. in reference to a road trip by a team from the East Coast

West Coast Hockey League minor pro league, 1995-2003, which then merged with ECHL

Western Canada Hockey League 1. major pro league, 1921-25, comprising teams in Alberta and Saskatchewan (and, after PCHA folded, British Columbia) 2. minor pro league, 1932-33, which continued as Northwest Hockey League in 1933-34 3. major junior hockey league, 1967-78 (renamed Western Hockey League)

Western Canada Junior Hockey League major junior hockey league, 1967-68, renamed Western Canada Hockey League

Western Collegiate Hockey Association NCAA Division I conference with teams primarily in Midwestern U.S.

Western Conference one of two conferences in the NHL, 1993-present

Western Hockey League 1. major pro league, 1925-26 (formerly WCHL), which was the last non-NHL league whose teams competed for the Stanley Cup 2. minor pro league, 1952-74 3. major junior hockey league (formerly WCHL), 1978-present, with teams throughout western Canada and northwestern U.S.

Western Professional Hockey League defunct minor pro league, 1996-2001, which purchased Central Hockey League and continued under that name

Westerners (archaic) term that usu. referred to PCHA teams

West Toronto Nationals Memorial Cup champions in 1936

Western rules rules of early hockey which continued to allow for seven players a side after Eastern leagues had changed to six-a-side hockey

Western swing road trip through western U.S. or Canada

whack 1. hit 2. ~ **at a loose puck** try to bat a loose puck using the stick 3. ~ **it in** score from close range 4. ~ **an opponent** hit an opponent with stick

whale of a game great game for team or player; one that is fun to watch

Whalers nickname of Hartford's NHL team, 1979-97, and New England team in WHA, 1972-79

wheel 1. skate fast 2. **bad** ~ sore knee or leg 3. ~ **around** a. skate past, usu. a forward around opposition defence b. turn quickly 4. ~**s** possessed of great speed ("he has great wheels")

whip 1. defeat soundly 2. shoot quickly 3. make hard pass 4. put team through a hard practice

whipping boy scapegoat, so designated usu. by a coach or fans of a team ("Mahovlich was Imlach's whipping boy for years")

whirling dervish small, speedy player with tricky moves who is difficult to check

whirlwind fast-paced series of events, as many games in a short period of time

whish 1. shoot quickly 2. skate quickly past

whistle 1. wind instrument used by referee to signal when play should stop

and start 2. ~ **a hard shot** take a hard shot 3. ~ **it home** score 4. ~ **it wide** shoot hard but off target 5. ~ **the play dead** blow whistle to stop play 6. ~**-tooter** on-ice official 7. **late** ~ whistle blown a moment or two after play has seemingly already stopped 8. **slow** ~ var. of *late whistle*

Whitby Dunlops Allan Cup champions in 1957 and 1959

Whitehorse Huskies Allan Cup champions in 1993

white 1. ~ **ice** area immediately outside goalie's crease that is not blue 2. ~ **player** clean player 3. ~ **skates** hockey skates painted white (worn briefly in NHL by California Golden Seals) 4. ~ **tape** tape for sticks, shin pads, etc., that is white as opposed to the more popular black tape 5. ~ **tip** protective piece of plastic attached to the back end of the tube skate

whiteout playoff tradition in Winnipeg (and later Phoenix) that saw nearly all fans in arena wear white shirts

whitewash shut out ("Sawchuk white-washed the Bruins 2-0 last night")

whiz 1. shoot hard 2. wizard

wholesale changes 1. large-scale alterations of a team's roster 2. replacement of all five skaters on ice during a stop in play

whomp defeat badly

whoop cheer, celebrate (also "whoop it up")

wicked of a shot: hard or dangerous

wicket name for hockey used in 1830s, primarily in Nova Scotia

wickets 1. pads 2. name of goal area in early game ("they defended their wickets with all effort") 3. goalie's legs ("that shot went in through the wickets")

wide 1. ~ **margin** large advantage, in the final score or score of a game in progress ("they're ahead by a wide margin") 2. ~ **of the goal** missing the net by a good many feet 3. ~ **of the mark** var. of *wide of the goal* 4. ~ **of the net** var. of *wide of the goal* 5. ~ **open** a. of a style of hockey: fast-paced, offensive-minded   b. of a player: in the clear 6. ~-**open net** net that is largely (or completely) unguarded because goalie is out of position 7. **go** ~ skate around a man to the outside of him 8. **shoot** ~ miss the net with a shot

Wild nickname of Minnesota's NHL team, 2000-present

Wildcat Senior model of EL-WIG hockey stick produced in Durham, Ontario

wild scramble

wild 1. ~ **brawl** bench-clearing brawl 2. ~ **game** game full of great scoring chances, big hits, and end-to-end action 3. ~ **player** player who has a tendency to lose control of his emotions and behave violently on ice 4. ~ **scramble** frenetic fight for the puck in front of the goal 5. ~ **stab** that which was taken by Paul Henderson in scoring game- and series-winning goal in Game 8 of 1972 Summit Series, as described by Foster Hewitt

Wild Wing Anaheim Ducks' mascot

will-call window part of the ticket office where tickets purchased in advance or set aside for special guests are held, to be picked up prior to the game

William M. Jennings Trophy NHL award given annually to the goalies who play at least 25 games for the team that allows the fewest goals over the course of a season

Willingdon Cup established in 1930, a team trophy given to the Ottawa Senators player who records the most assists in a given season

Wilson kind of hockey stick

wilt fade; lose, esp. late in a game

win 1. prevail over an opponent   2. ~ **column** part of the standings listing how many games each team has won in a given series or season 3. ~ **from** (British) defeat 4. ~ **the draw** gain possession of puck at the faceoff 5. ~ **ugly** defeat opponent without displaying superior skill

wind 1. great speed   2. breath, esp. when lost after a fall or hard hit ("Dye just had the wind knocked out of him")

wind up 1. prepare to unleash a shot 2. prepare to make a lengthy rush with the puck

wind up

windburn sensation of stinging, red cheeks, experienced by a defenceman after an opponent has skated by him with great speed and unmatched skill

winded temporarily short of breath after a sudden and strong hit

window derogatory for visor

windshield derogatory for visor

Windsor Arena see *Border Cities Arena*

Windsor Bulldogs Allan Cup champions in 1963

Windsor Hotel hotel in Montreal where the NHA was founded in 1909 and the NHL was founded in 1917

Windy City nickname for Chicago

wing 1. short for left wing or right wing 2. arm or shoulder 3. ~ **forward** (19th C.) one of the two forwards other than the centreman

Winged Wheel symbol of Montreal AAA, later used by Detroit Red Wings

winger 1. forward who lines up at left or right wing 2. hard shot ("he let go a winger the last period")

Winger, The Atlanta Thrashers' game-night program

wingman winger

wings 1. the two forward positions other than centre 2. metaphoric place where a promising player awaits chance to break in with team

Wings short for (Detroit) Red Wings

winless 1. without a win, usu. in reference to a series of games in which the team has managed only to lose or tie 2. ~ **skein** var. of *winless streak* 3. ~ **streak** series of consecutive games in which a team has failed to win

winning percentage ratio of points a team has earned to the total possible points available

Winning Spirit Vancouver Canucks' game-night program

winningest most successful at winning

Winnipeg Arena home arena of Winnipeg Jets in WHA, 1972-79 and NHL, 1979-95

Winnipeg Braves Memorial Cup champions in 1959

Winnipeg Elmwoods Millionaires Memorial Cup champions in 1931

Winnipeg Falcons 1. Olympic gold medallists and Allan Cup champions in 1920 2. Memorial Cup champions in 1921

Winnipeg Hockey Club Allan Cup champions in 1913 and 1931 (also called the Winnipegs)

Winnipeg Maple Leafs Stanley Cup challengers in March 1908

Winnipeg Maroons Allan Cup champions in 1964

Winnipeg Monarchs 1. Allan Cup champions in 1915 2. Memorial Cup champions in 1935, 1937, and 1946

Winnipeg Jets WHA member team, 1972-79 and NHL member team, 1979-95 (moved to Phoenix, renamed Coyotes)

Winnipeg Rangers Memorial Cup champions in 1941 and 1943

Winnipeg shot wrist shot patented by players from Winnipeg in 1893

Winnipeg 61st Battalion Allan Cup champions in 1916

Winnipeg Victorias 1. Stanley Cup champions in 1896, 1901, and 1902 2. Allan Cup champions in 1911 and 1912

winter a season ("this is his sixth winter with the team")

winter ballet hockey

wiped defeated badly

wire shoot the puck hard

with authority confidently (of a shot or a hit)

"With Pick and Shovel" column on hockey written by Lou Marsh in 1930s

within striking distance of a goal: close enough that a tie or win might be possible ("Koivu's goal puts Finland within striking distance of Sweden")

witness watch; see ("a record crowd witnessed the action at the arena last night")

witnesses fans

wives' lounge private area within the arena set aside for players' wives and girlfriends

wizardry expert puck-handling or skating ability

woes troubles

women's hockey version of hockey played by women with its own set of rules (as opposed to men's hockey)

Women's Nationals national tournament to determine championship of women's senior hockey in Canada

wonder skilled player

wonky injured, esp. weak or shaky ("he's had wonky knees for years now")

won-lost record numeric summary of a team's wins and losses

wood 1. ~ **puck** (late 19th C.) puck made of wood 2. ~ **skates** (archaic) skates with wooden blades 3. ~ **stick** stick made of wood 4. **good** ~ solid contact between stick and puck, resulting in a hard shot

woodchopper hacker

Woody Dumart hockey sticks brand of sticks named after the NHL star of the 1930s-1950s

Wooden Sticks golf course in Uxbridge, Ontario, owned in part by NHL players Joe Nieuwendyk, Gary Roberts, and Steve Rice

woozy dizzy

work 1. performance ("his work was outstanding tonight") 2. ~ **harder** make extra effort to succeed 3. ~ **in on goal** stickhandle or skate through opposition in a determined manner

4. ~ **stoppage** term, favoured by NHL commissioner Gary Bettman and former NHLPA executive director Bob Goodenow, for a strike or lockout 5. ~ **the power play** control the puck in the offensive end with the man advantage 6. ~ **the puck along the boards** cycle or maintain control of the puck along the boards 7. ~ **the puck down low** cycle the puck deep in the opposition end 8. ~ **their way out of their own end** move puck out of the defensive end effectively

workhorse player, usu. defenceman, who can play a great deal without losing his effectiveness

workload amount of playing time, usu. for goalies ("he's handled a heavy workload the past month, but he'll get the night off tonight")

workout practice

World Championship annual tournament sanctioned by the IIHF to determine the hockey championship of the world

World Cup of Hockey periodic international tournament, organized by NHL and successor in name to the Canada Cup, featuring mostly pro players from top hockey countries

World Hockey Association rival major pro league to NHL, 1972-79

World Hockey Challenge tournament for under-17s which replaced the Quebec *Esso Cup* in 1992

World Junior Championship annual tournament sanctioned by IIHF for players under 20 years of age

World Pond Hockey Championships since 2000, annual outdoor tournament played on Roulston Lake in Plaster Rock, New Brunswick

World's Series (archaic) Stanley Cup playoffs (from days when NHA/NHL champions competed with western champions)

World War III name given by the game's official scorer to the World Junior Championship game of January 4, 1987, played between Canada and the Soviet Union in Piestany, Czechoslovakia, which was halted after a bench-clearing brawl

World Women's Championships annual tournament sanctioned by IIHF to determine the best national women's team in the world

wrangle disagreement

wrap up the win do something that assures a team of victory, usu. score an insurance goal

wraparound shot on goal that originates from behind the net, when a player swoops the puck in front to try to surprise the goalie

wrestling match physical confrontation between two players who don't fight but who tussle until they are separated

wriggle 1. stickhandle 2. ~ **through** deke

Wrigley sponsor of Canadian national midget hockey tournament, 1974-78 (renamed Air Canada Cup)

wrist 1. joint connecting hand to arm 2. shoot the puck 3. ~ **cuff** bottom part of the goalie glove which protects the wrist and which connects to the palm and glove itself 4. ~ **guard** plastic protection for the wrist 5. ~ **shot** shot whose power is generated mostly through the wrists

wrister var. of *wrist shot*

written report documentation submitted by an on-ice official after a game that has featured a violent or controversial play

wrong wing var. of *off wing*

wraparound

Xx

X-ray machine photographic equipment that is able to create images of bones

X's and O's basic symbols used to represent players when a coach diagrams plays on a blackboard

X's and O's

Yy

YUG official IIHF abbreviation for Yugoslavia

yack complain, generally to officials or opposing players

yank pull the goalie

Yannigans (usu. pl., archaic) rookies

yap 1. talk incessantly to opposing players to try to distract them 2. complain to an official about a call

yapper player who yaps

yappy prone to yapping

yard slang for one hundred dollars

yawning 1. ~ **cage** wide-open net 2. ~ **net** var. of *yawning cage*

year usu. in reference to a specific season ("he's having a good year")

yellow lacking courage

yellow poplar kind of wood used to make of hockey sticks, particularly for the shaft

yeoman's service outstanding performance, esp. when dealing with a heavier workload than usual ("he's doing yeoman's service for us tonight")

yeoman's work var. of *yeoman's service*

yep! quick call to a teammate to confirm that one is open for a pass (as opposed to "no," meaning one is not open to receive a pass)

yield allow, usu. goals

young 1. inexperienced 2. youthful 3. ~ **team** a. team that is lacking in experience or has many youthful players on its roster b. exciting team

Young Canada Night annual game during the Conn Smythe era at Maple Leaf Gardens, usually the last home game for the Leafs before Christmas, when children got into a game for free when accompanied by a parent; one lucky boy got to call play-by-play with Foster Hewitt for a short time during the game

Young Guns game var. of *Young Stars game*

young nats slang for young nationals, any junior-level team representing Canada

Young Stars Game game held during NHL All-Star Game break which features players under 25 still on their first NHL contracts, playing three, ten-minute periods of 4-on-4 with running time

youngster inexperienced player

Youppi Montreal Canadiens' mascot since 2005-06; formerly the mascot of the Montreal Expos before that team relocated to Washington in the spring of 2005

youth 1. young player 2. ~ **hockey** amateur hockey for young people below junior age (also "minor hockey") 3. ~ **movement** efforts by a team to replace older players with younger ones 4. ~ **plan** var. of *youth movement*

Youth model of McVean's hockey stick produced in Dresden, Ontario

"you've got mail" facetious expression by players to officials who may have made a mistake on a call, implying that the league's head of officiating will notify the official by e-mail the next day

yo-yo player who is frequently shuttled between a major league team and its farm team

Yoyogi Arena arena in Nagano, Japan, which hosted men's and women's hockey at the 1998 Olympic Winter Games

yuckers lesser players on a team who never play, only practice (i.e., Black Aces)

Yugoslavia IIHF member nation from 1939 until 2003 (succeeded by Serbia and Montenegro, and, in 2006, Serbia)

Zz

ZZ nickname of Zarley Zalapski (NHL, 1987-2000), the only player in NHL history whose first and last names both began with the letter Z

Zamboni 1. ice-resurfacing machine (after Frank Zamboni) 2. ~ **driver** operator of a Zamboni

Zambonied v., to resurface the ice ("we can go on as soon as the ice has been Zambonied")

zebra slang for official (after black-and-white striped sweaters)

zig-zag 1. method of skating, feinting, and darting to avoid being checked 2. ~ **rush** player who utilizes zig-zag moves to make his way up ice

zing rattle, usu. the puck off a goal post

zinger hard shot

zip 1. energy 2. American slang for no score ("they won two-zip") 3. ~ **in** skate quickly toward opposition goal 4. ~ **a shot** shoot hard

zipper scar or stitches

zone one of three sections of the ice, delineated by lines (offensive zone, defensive zone, neutral zone)

zoom skate quickly

Zamboni

Acknowledgements

Although this is a book that was created mostly by me on scraps of paper, napkins, and other small surfaces, several friends and colleagues need still be mentioned for providing assistance of one sort or another. First and foremost, a special thanks to publisher Jordan Fenn, who accepted my proposal about 30 seconds after seeing it. He understood what it was about, and supported me on the project from that day to this. Secondly, Lloyd Davis needs a special mention (as well as, most likely, an Aspirin!). He edited the manuscript (sometimes one-handed), taking my thousands of entries and pell-mell definitions and creating a unified whole—no mean task, indeed. Thirdly, to fantastic designer Kathryn Zante, who took a simple (and lengthy) Word file and transformed it into an appealing book—line by line, word by word, letter by letter! Also, to the talented Wayne Downey for the appropriate illustrations.

Others had a smaller hand in polishing definitions or offering suggestions, namely: Szymon Szemberg, Frank Selke, Paul Patskou, Bill Fitsell, Len Kotylo, Darren Boyko, John Kreiser, Carl Lavigne, John Halligan, George Fosty, Brian Logie, and Craig Campbell. To everyone at the Hockey Hall of Fame, where I spent so much time poring through old newspaper clippings and journals, looking for long-forgotten words and phrases from the game's early days: Danielle Siciliano, Miragh Addis, Phil Pritchard, Izak Westgate, Steve Ozimec, Dave Stubbs, Peter Jagla, and Anthony Fusco.

Lastly, to those nearest and dearest to me who put up with my long hours and eat with me when I'm hungry: new home-owers Liz and Ian, Zack and Emily, me mum, and long-term companion (okay, okay—wife—there, I said it) and future suture-inventor Mary Jane Nguyen.

About the Illustrator

Wayne Downey, a graduate from the Ontario College of Art, is a graphic artist/illustrator who also enjoys teaching cartooning classes for young students and drawing/painting classes for adults. Wayne resides in Tottenham, Ontario with his wife and three children.